Drinking Around the World

Terry W. Lyons

Drinking Around the World
Copyright ©2013 by Terry W. Lyons
ISBN: 978-0-9885902-8-1
Library of Congress: 2013923032

La Maison Publishing, Inc.
www.lamaisonpublishing.com
ISBN: 978-0-9885902-8-1

Table of Contents

ACKNOWLEDGEMENTS

Friends with close ties to the countries discussed in this book reviewed each of the chapters for accuracy. I owe a special "thank you" to John Burke, Jack and Hope Cortissoz, Marieke Dam, Catherine Gama, Peter and Joan Notaro, John and Megs Phipps, Agnita Ricks, Eve Siegert and Sonny and Angela Stewart.

Don Casey, David Lyons, John O'Neill, and Neil Stalter reviewed the entire manuscript and offered many helpful suggestions.

As with my first book: " Bar Hopping Thru America" I could not have made it through the editing and publishing steps without the professional advice of Gene Hull, author of many books, including the recent *The Sun God Is A Ham* book of poetry. Once again, thank you Gene.

I really appreciate the patience and professional guidance of Janet Sierzant, author and President of La Maison Publishing, Inc.

And to my wife, Babs, who encouraged me from the beginning and helped with everything from the research to the typing, thank you very much.

INTRODUCTION

*C*onsumption of alcohol in some form has taken place in every country and corner of this planet for thousands of years. It is amazing that every civilization has independently discovered the process of brewing beers, fermenting berries, and distilling grains. What is so interesting is that each region or country has its own culture concerning the use of alcohol.

The cultural variations include the type of alcohol consumed (wine, vodka, whiskey, gin, etc.), where it is drunk (pubs, cafés, homes, clubs), when it is drunk (after work, on the way to work, only at parties, celebrations, special events), and why only certain types of alcohol are used for various ethnic, religious and national occasions.

For example, in Western cultures champagne is synonymous with celebration. If champagne were served as an ordinary drink, someone would invariably ask, "What are we celebrating?" In the U.S., wine is considered an appropriate beverage for meals or celebration, while beer is more likely used for informal relaxation-oriented occasions, sports events or cookouts.

Imported beverages usually have a higher status than local brew. For example, in Poland wine has high-status, while native beers and vodka are considered ordinary.

Some drinks are symbols of national identity; Guinness beer for the Irish, tequila for Mexicans, whiskey for Scots. In addition, in some countries certain drinks are considered masculine while other sweeter, weaker beverages are for women.

A whole country's culture can be assessed from drinking patterns. France, for example, is a wine drinking nation, while the British are a beer-drinking country. We will examine how these differences affect behavior and attitudes toward drinking in general.

You may have "a drink" anywhere, but "drinking" is a social act subject to all sorts of customs and rules. Almost all countries and cultures have specific, designated environments for social drinking. It was discovered that even the native tribes of Zaire in Africa had a small clearing in the forest dedicated to the consumption of palm wine. Each culture seems to develop its own unique drinking-place.

The southern European countries of Italy, Spain and France tend to favor highly visible drinking places; sidewalk cafés, bistros with large windows (open in the summer), patios and courtyards.

Meanwhile in northern Europe (Britain, Ireland, Scandinavia) and North America, drinking-places are likely to be enclosed with small or frosted windows, interior partitions and solid walls. Some of this difference might be explained by climate considerations; but the primary reason for the open drinking-space versus the closed space is a result of the cultural differences regarding alcohol. Southern European countries accept alcohol as a natural element of everyday life; it is included in common behaviors, just as sleeping or eating. However, in northern Europe and North America where there is a more ambiguous and uneasy relationship with alcohol, we find the drinking-space to be more hidden, more secretive, not open and accepted as part of the general landscape.

Thus, we have the traditional Irish pub with its "snug" in the corner and partitions everywhere. The snug was the small-enclosed room in the corner of an Irish pub where women were allowed to drink, since they were not allowed in the bar until the 1960s. The beer was passed through a small window in the snug by the bartender. Most of the time he had no idea who was drinking it.

Regardless of the variations in the type of bar, there are also characteristics that are common to all drinking-spaces. The public bar performs a "time-out" function where the customer can transition from one environment or stage to another. This is the reason for stopping by the bar and having a drink on the way home from work, or in the case of the Italians and Spanish, having a drink on the way to work.

The bar, wherever it is located, has always served as a facilitator of social bonding. Status and social rank are replaced by an openness and social access in the bar atmosphere. The whole layout of the bar is designed to promote social interaction: décor, the toasting, the music, the games, the seating - and the drinking.

Each country and each region has its own traditions involving what to drink and when and where to drink it - and on certain occasions, how much to drink. Across all cultures, a common denominator for celebrating or performing a ceremony is the presence of alcohol.

Major life-cycle events, such as a birth, coming-of-age, graduation, marriage, and, yes, even death, are marked by rituals that include drinking alcohol. In fact, in many countries alcohol is the central element of the occasion. In Poland the christening is celebrated at a local tavern with a few drinks to "wet the baby's head." Mexican-Americans celebrate with liquor supplied by the baby's godfather.

In many countries, including America, each stage of a wedding is celebrated with alcohol – the engagement, the bachelor party, the "bachelorette" party, the bride's shower, and finally the wedding. The drinking at each of these "stages" is part of the ritual - beer at the bachelor party, wine for the girls, and, of course, champagne for the wedding folks.

In many cultures, the rite of passage extends to almost any important life-changing event. There might be a promotion, a new house, or retirement; all these require drinking as part of the celebration

In America, and many other countries, specific drinking patterns are a key ingredient of any holiday celebration. It is eggnog or Tom and Jerry's for Christmas, champagne to toast the New Year, and more beer is sold on July 4th than any other day of the year. The Mardi Gras pre-Lenten Carnival merely requires lots of drinking.

Across world cultures, the purpose of having a drink is not always the same. The stop at the tavern on the way home from work, or the waiting cocktail as you arrive home, are part of the ritual of transition from work to play. In Spain and France, it is common to have a drink on the way to work, and perhaps one at lunchtime to "re-fuel." In Peru, alcohol is consumed before any work requiring physical effort: such as roofing, painting, or construction.

For all these rituals, celebrations, and traditions around the world, why is alcohol the essential element? Why should alcohol, rather than any other substance, be the universal symbol of the festivity? The ritual of the Mass of the Roman Catholic Church requires wine for the offertory; but for many people a beer is required after mowing the yard on a hot summer afternoon.

In addition to alcohol being included in every major ritual around the world, the type of alcohol used for these celebrations has a meaning of its own. The type of drink served defines the nature of the event.

In all cultures across all countries, drinking is a social act, and one of alcohol's primary characteristics is the facilitation of social bonding. It lowers barriers, eases social

4

tensions, promotes relaxation, and tends to enhance the positive aspects of a celebration. The various rituals of pouring, toasting, sharing, and round-buying, all serve to promote conviviality.

> *"Well ya see Norm, it's like this. A herd of buffalo can only move as fast as the slowest buffalo. So when the herd is hunted, it is the slowest and weakest one at the back that is killed first. This natural selection is good for the herd as a whole, because the general speed and health of the whole group keeps improving by the regular killing of the weakest members."*
>
> *"The human brain works that way too. It only operates as fast as the slowest brain cells. Excessive intake of alcohol, as we know, kills brain cells. But naturally, it attacks the slowest and weakest brain cells first. So, regular consumption of beer eliminates the weaker brain cells, making the brain a faster and more efficient machine. That's why you always feel smarter after a few beers."* – Cliff Clavin from *Cheers*.

A LITTLE BIT OF
HISTORY

*A*lcohol and the custom of drinking alcohol have been around a long time – at least 12,000 years. The discovery of late Stone Age beer jugs has established the fact that intentionally fermented beverages existed as early as 10,000 BC.

Fermentation is the chemical process that produces ethanol, the type of alcohol that is drinkable versus wood alcohol or methanol, which can cause death or blindness if consumed by humans. Fermentation takes place naturally when practically any organic substance decomposes. Therefore, acceptable alcoholic drinks can be made from potatoes, apples, peaches, berries, grapes, wheat, corn, coconuts, honey, etc.

It is not known whether the first alcoholic drink was Mead made from fermented honey, beer from potatoes, or wine from berries. The earliest evidence of alcohol in China are wine jars from Jiahu, which date from about 7000 BC, making China the first known place in the world to develop alcoholic beverages. This early drink was made by fermenting rice, honey and fruit. A Chinese imperial edict around 1116 BC makes it clear that the use of alcohol in moderation was prescribed by Heaven.

In the 13th century, Marco Polo set out on his Asian travels and wandered from Arabia to Vietnam for 24 years. Polo documents the use of alcohol throughout Asia, including the areas occupied by Muslims whose religion forbids the use of alcohol. Apparently there are many ways around this ban, as is usually the case, including calling it medicine.

Beer was the major beverage among the Babylonians, and as early as 2700 BC, they worshiped a wine goddess and other wine deities. Babylonians regularly used both beer and wine as offerings to their gods. Around 1750 BC, the famous code of Hammurabi devoted attention to alcohol. The code included no penalties for drunkenness; the concern was for fair commerce in alcohol. Penalties were severe. Diluting the alcohol with water, or cheating on the exchange of corn for beer, could result in being thrown into the water to drown; a common punishment at the time.

The brewing of alcoholic beverages dates from the very beginning of ancient civilization in Egypt. The Egyptian God Osiris was believed to have invented beer, a beverage that was considered a necessity of life, it was brewed in the home every day.

The ancient Egyptians made at least 17 types of beer, and 24 varieties of wine. Alcoholic beverages were used for pleasure, nutrition, medicine, ritual, remuneration, and funeral purposes. The latter involved storing the beverages in tombs of the deceased for use in the after-life. The tombs of the Pharaohs contain wine cellars filled with jars of wine. The pyramid builders of ancient Egypt (3100 BC) were each allotted 1½ gallons of beer per day. And they did a pretty good job!

Popular Egyptian festivals were always celebrated with drinking wine. Egyptians even imported wine from other areas, known today as Iran and Turkey. These wines were rated and labeled for intended use, i.e., festival wine, wine for paying taxes, and wine for "offerings."

Historians believe the world's oldest known recipe is for beer, and beer was probably a staple before bread. A common greeting in ancient Egypt was "bread and beer."

By 2000 BC the Egyptians were soaking barley in water until it made a paste, which they baked, soaked in water again, and left in a warm place to ferment. Then they squeezed the beer out of the paste and drank. Taverns flourished in ancient Egypt and writings include many warnings about drunkenness.

The art of winemaking reached the Olympic Peninsula around 2000 BC, and the first popular alcoholic beverage in Greece was Mead, a fermented beverage made from honey and water. As wine became popular, it assumed the functions so commonly found around the world: religious rituals, hospitality, daily meals, and medicinal purposes. Hippocrates identified numerous medicinal properties of wine.

Among Greeks, the Macedonians viewed intemperance as a sign of masculinity, and were famous for their drunkenness. Their king, Alexander the Great (356-323 BC), developed a reputation for inebriation.

The Greek philosophers had some wonderful comments on wine and drinking. Aristotle considered grapes inedible and of use only for wine. Socrates commented that "Wine does of a truth, moisten the soul and lull our grief to sleep." Heraclitus (540 BC), "It is better to hide ignorance; but hard to do when we relax over wine." Dionysna, Greek God, is best known as a personification of the vine and of the exhilaration produced by the fermented juice of the grape. On the other hand, some Greek philosophers, including Plato (429-347 BC), were very critical of drunkenness.

The Roman god of wine was Bacchus. The Roman Empire began in 753 BC, and the Romans practiced great moderation in drinking for almost 600 years. By the second and first centuries BC, the traditional Roman values of temperance, frugality, and simplicity were replaced by heavy drinking, degeneracy, and corruption.

In the last century BC, the Roman poet Horace wrote in praise of alcohol: "think of the wonders uncorked by wine. It opens secrets, gives heart to our hopes, pushes the cowardly into battle, lifts the load from anxious minds, and evokes talents. Thanks to the bottle's prompting no one is lost for words; no one who is cramped by poverty fails to find release." Today, 2000 years later, there can be no quarrel with this description of the benefits of alcohol.

When Julius Caesar took over Britain in 55 BC, he complained about the absence of grapes and wine. The only drink was Mead, which he compared to rainwater and honey. The Romans tried to correct this problem; but since they could not grow grapes they had to settle for apple wine and hard cider.

In defense of Mead, the term "honeymoon" comes from the custom of the bride's father giving the happy couple a month's supply of Mead to cement the union.

Signs for "public houses" go back 2000 years to Pompeii and Herculaneum, when a board showing two slaves carrying a wineskin noted the shop of a wine merchant. In ancient Pompeii you can see the remains of wine shops, massive stone bars, and benches for the customers.

Wine leaves symbolized Bacchus, the God of wine, and were displayed outside drinking establishments called tabernae, from which the term tavern is derived. Checkers was a common tavern game and the Romans brought it to England, where it became extremely popular.

With the dawn of Christianity and its gradual

displacement of the previously dominant religions, the drinking attitudes and behaviors of Europe began to be influenced by the New Testament. Both the Old and New Testaments are clear and consistent in their condemnation of drunkenness.

There are many references in the Bible to the use of wine by Jesus and St. Paul considered wine to be a gift of God, and therefore inherently good. Christianity and the planting of vineyards and production of wine spread simultaneously across Europe. "*Let the vine be the first fruit you plant, others can wait their turn.*" Alcaens, 600 BC. The word "wine" appears in the Bible 161 times; "vineyards" are mentioned 72 times.

As social and political unrest increased when the Roman Empire began to collapse in the fifth century, concern grew among rabbis that Judaism and its culture were in danger. This prompted more detailed Talmudic rules concerning the use of wine. These included the amount of wine that could be drunk on the Sabbath, the way in which wine was to be drunk, the legal status of wine in any way connected with idolatry, and the extent of personal responsibility for behavior while intoxicated.

With the collapse of the Roman Empire and the decline of urban life, monasteries became the repositories of the brewing and winemaking techniques that had been developed. The monks carefully guarded their knowledge and produced virtually all beer and wine of good quality until the 12th century.

The monasteries had the resources, security, and stability, in an often turbulent time in history, to improve the quality of their vines and their wine-making skills. In addition to making wine necessary to celebrate Mass, the monasteries produced large quantities to support the maintenance and expansion of the monastic movement.

The most important development regarding alcohol in the Middle Ages was distillation. Knowledge of the distillation process had existed since the ancient Greeks; but it was not until the 12th century that the distillation of alcohol entered the scene.

Knowledge of the process spread slowly among monks, alchemists, and physicians who were interested in alcohol as a cure for ailments. At the time, alcohol was called "aqua vitae" or "water of life." The Scandinavian aquavit spirit gets its name from the Latin phrase "aqua vitae."

As the end of the Middle Ages approached (1500 A.D.), the popularity of beer spread to England, France and Scotland. Beer brewers were recognized officially as a guild and the alteration of wine or beer became punishable by death in Scotland. Also, at this time, the consumption of distilled spirits as a beverage, not just for medicinal purposes, began to take place. It has been said of distilled alcohol that "the 16th century created it, the 17th century consolidated it, and the 18th popularized it."

One beverage that made its debut during the 17th century was sparkling champagne. Dom Pérignon, wine-master in a French abbey around 1668, developed strong bottles and an efficient cork to contain the effervescence, along with a technique for blending the contents. It took another 100 years before champagne became popular.

The original grain spirit, whiskey, appears to have been first distilled in Ireland, and by the 16th century, it was widely consumed in parts of Scotland.

Distilled alcohol was originally used mainly for medicinal purposes, and the use of gin as a social drink grew very slowly. The alcohol was generally flavored with juniper berries. The beverage was known as "jenever," the Dutch word for juniper. The French changed the name to "genièvre" and then the English shortened it to "gin." The English government actually promoted gin production to utilize surplus grain and to raise revenue through tariffs and taxes. The result was a flood of cheap alcohol on the market, and by 1735, the so-called "Gin Epidemic" was in full bloom. By 1742 this nation of 6.5 million people drank over 18 million gallons of gin. And this was consumed by the small minority of the population living in London and other major cities. People in the countryside drank mostly beer, ale and cider.

It was estimated that enough gin was consumed in London for every man, woman and small child to put away a quart a week, on top of their beer.

From the peak of 18 gallons in 1743, gin production dropped to 2 million gallons by 1758. This rapid decline was the result of a number of factors. These included the production of higher quality beer at a lower price, rising corn prices, higher taxes, raising the cost of gin, increasing criticism of drunkenness, and industrialization with emphasis on a sober and efficient labor force.

While drunkenness was still an accepted part of life in the 18th-century, the 19th century brought a change in attitude toward alcohol. Drunkenness came to be defined as a threat to industrial efficiency and growth. For the first time organized groups began promoting the moderate use of alcohol or temperance. Ultimately, as we progressed toward the 20th century, these groups became abolitionists and pressed for the total prohibition of the production and distribution of beverage alcohol. Unfortunately, as we witnessed in the 1930s in America, prohibition does not solve social problems, but created additional problems, compounding the situation.

Beer arrived in America when the Pilgrims landed at Plymouth Rock in 1620. The European custom of avoiding water as a beverage continued to be observed in this country, and the colonists set out making beer in the home. Eventually they discovered hard cider, fermented from the bountiful apple orchards of New England. As this country grew and developed, beer makers from Germany arrived and beer improved.

At the same time, Irish and Scotch immigrants began to settle in America and they brought skills for the distillation of grain into whiskey. Rum came on the scene around 1650. Rum is made by fermenting and distilling the industrial waste by-product of sugar refining - molasses. The European sugar cane plantation owners' encouraged rum production since it was an unexpected windfall. The English navy was responsible for spreading this new beverage around world. By 1657, a rum distillery was operating in Boston, and a few years later rum production became New England's most prosperous industry. Rum remained the colony's favorite drink until the early 1800s when whiskey arrived with the Scotch and Irish immigrants. Whiskey was ideally suited to this country with its abundant grain and pure water.

Eventually, with improvements in brewing, coupled with refrigeration and cheaper bottles and cans, beer became the most popular drink and remains number one today with wine in second place. The current craft beer and brew-pub expansion has given a significant boost to beer when it appeared it would be overtaken by wine.

Throughout history, alcoholic beverages have played an important role in the development of mankind. Initially, it was considered a basic element needed for survival and self-preservation. Beer, wine and mead were not only safe to drink, they provided an important source of nutrients and calories.

The importance of alcohol is demonstrated by the fact that it has frequently been used as a medium of exchange. In medieval England ale was frequently used to pay rent, tolls, or debts.

From the very beginning, alcohol has been a part of religious ceremonies, and this continues today in Christian and Jewish services.

The medicinal and therapeutic properties of alcohol were recognized by the ancient Greeks and included in the writings of Hippocrates. Many of these were overblown and incorrect, but quite a few have stood the test of time. Science has now proven red wine could be beneficial in preventing heart problems.

Lastly, let us not overlook the role alcohol has served in enhancing the enjoyment and quality of life. It can serve as a social lubricant, enhance the flavor of food, provide entertainment, and facilitate relaxation.

While alcohol has always been abused by some, as most things are, it has clearly been beneficial to most.

So we must admit that it is not just the fact that alcohol has been around longer than any other beverage except water, it is the chemical properties of alcohol that have the potential to alter conscious behavior, that makes it the choice world-wide, across all cultures, for marking or celebrating life's major moments.

In addition to each region, country or culture having its own unique customs of which alcoholic beverage to drink, where to drink it (pubs, cafes, nightclubs, bars) and when to drink (before work, at work, after work); we also have a wide range of rules and regulations governing the consumption of alcohol. For example, the legal drinking age in America is 21, the highest in the world; Germany, Poland and Greece set the age at 16. In most countries, including France, Russia and Ireland, the drinking age is 18.

Even within countries, laws affecting alcohol vary widely. In many U.S. states, driving with a blood alcohol level over .08% is a criminal offense, resulting in loss of license, and in many cases, mandatory jail time. Other states consider DWI far less serious. Sweden has zero tolerance for drinking and driving, one drink and you are over the limit. Rules involving drinking in public vary widely by country.

This book describes the uniqueness of drinking practices in over 20 countries around the world. It explores the history of alcohol in each country, and how the current drinking customs became established. Finally, an up-to-date description of alcohol consumption is provided for each country (where they drink, what they drink, rules and regulations, festivals and customs).

AUSTRALIA

"You can't be a real Country unless you have a beer and an airline - it helps if you have some kind of football team, or some nuclear weapons, but at the very least you need a beer." – Frank Zappa

Australia has always been one of the world's great drinking nations. It is believed that during the "convict era," when rum was used as currency, the colony's inhabitants drank more alcohol per capita than at any other time in human history. The high rate of consumption is understandable considering the First Fleet brought enough food for two years and enough grog for four. And if you have ever been to one of the European museums and seen the ships, and the conditions aboard the ships, that transported the prisoners from England and Ireland to Australia, you would realize the survivors were a hardy and determined group.

Between 1788 and 1868, approximately 162,000 convicts (including 25,000 women) were "transported" to Australia. These consisted of petty thieves from the working-class towns in the Midlands and North of England, and Irish convicts charged with political crimes and social rebellions.

As the British began to colonize Australia, the Australian pub appeared as a direct descendent of the British and Irish public house. However, there were a number of distinctive features that set it apart from the classic pub. Similar to American Colonial days, and the settling of the West in the United States, the Australian pub served multiple functions. Simultaneously acting as an inn, post office, restaurant, and general store; but most importantly, it was the meeting or gathering place. In appearance it was a combination of an Irish pub and a Colonial tavern. In most cases, especially as the gold fields took over, the pub was the first structure in the area, and the town grew up around it.

Pubs proliferated in the 19th century, especially during the gold rush that began in the 1850s. The typical Australian pub of this time was quite different from the cozy, family-friendly cottage atmosphere of the original British public house. The Aussie pub was a good deal larger; many were three stories high, usually including several very spacious bar areas, as well as large overnight accommodations on the upper floors.

Accommodations were a vital facet of Australian pub operation (just as it was for the U.S. Colonial tavern) and Australian pubs are usually registered for business under the formal name "hotel." In fact, the more upscale ones may place the name "hotel" before the pub name, i.e., **Hotel Birchip**, etc.

The "public accommodation" was the major source of lodging for tourists, commercial travelers and business people until late in the 20th century. Many pubs rented rooms to long-term tenants who lived and ate at the pub, sometimes for decades, much like a boarding house. The tradition of public accommodations, although it has declined considerably, continues today with pubs joining together in a cooperative that operates under the name "pub stays."

Major regional and country pubs, dating from the 19th and early 20th century, are often imposing structures and lavishly decorated inside and out. Because of Australia's hot summers, wide awnings and verandas were common around pub exteriors. The balconies and verandas were often fitted with elaborate iron lace facings and cast-iron columns. The interiors of these pubs featured very high ceilings (12 feet or more). Embossed tin paneling was widely used when it became available in the late 19th century.

The main bar typically featured large and very impressive serving areas intricately carved with finished wood or stone designs. There were brass rails, ceramic or brass pump handles, tiles, plenty of mirrors, etched glass panels and many other types of decorations.

Even relatively modest pubs featured impressive bars carved from native Australian red cedar, and often embellished with decorative ceramic tiles and marble or brass fittings.

Following the consolidation of the brewing industry in the early 20th century, many new pubs were built and the older pubs were either extensively renovated or demolished and replaced with new structures. It is possible to define a number of distinctive features that describe the Australian urban pub of the mid-20th century. The typical pub of the 1950s was very functional, stripped-down; but with the popular Art Deco style, and usually two or three stories high, with terrazzo floors. There were normally several inter-connected bar rooms clustered around a central bar, and many of the suburban pubs had an enclosed outdoor area known as a" beer-garden." The beer-garden was able to accommodate families with children and offered food and drinks. Children still are not allowed in any other area of the pub in Australia. As with the 19th century pubs, the floors above the bar provided rooms for overnight or long-term rental.

One unique and especially notable decorative feature of Australian pubs in the 1920s and 1930s was the paint-on beer advertisement. These were often mounted on the exterior walls of pubs. The special ads were elaborate craft products created by teams of skilled commercial artists, many of whom worked for the breweries their entire working lives.

The creation of these beer ads was a specialized craft - they were entirely hand-painted in reverse on thick glass, and then wall-mounted in heavy brass frames, which were highly polished. Some exterior displays were made with translucent paint, so they could be illuminated from behind. They featured striking and often highly stylized designs, and compositions, painted in vibrant colors; and in many cases the text in some parts of the graphic were accentuated with real gold leaf.

These displays varied in size, but the larger examples were as much as nine square feet or more. They often depicted archetypical Aussie sporting scenes - swimming, surfing, sailing, horse racing, cricket or football - or social events such as picnics, dances, and parties.

Many deco-style pubs had sections of curved façade, because a large proportion of Australian pubs were built on street corners, and these spaces were often highlighted by the large curved frames of these colorfully painted beer ads. Because of their inherent fragility and location, many of these marvelous works either deteriorated beyond repair or were destroyed by accident or vandalism. Over the years, as advertising materials (and the pubs themselves) were progressively modernized during the late 20th century, almost all the hand-painted beer ads were removed, but their distinctive style has become a respected art object and the best surviving samples are now museum pieces or expensive collectors' items.

Another major difference between Australian pubs

and drinking establishments in other countries is that for most of their history Australian pubs were strictly segregated along gender and racial lines. The main bar of the typical Australian pub was the so-called "public bar"; however, this title was an ironic misnomer, since until the 1970s only men were permitted to drink in public bars. Most pubs included a "ladies lounge," but in many pubs ladies were only admitted to the lounge bar when accompanied by a male, and it was common not to allow women to buy drinks for themselves.

This sexual segregation persisted into the 1970s and began to break down after women's rights activists started to publicly challenge the custom. One of the most celebrated incidents took place in January 1973, when a group of activists staged a protest in the public bar of the Hotel Manly in Sydney. They were refused service on the premise that the hotel had insufficient toilets for women. The ladies' response was to chain themselves to a railing that ran around the bar. The event gained wide media attention and caused the hotel industry much embarrassment. Within a few years the long-standing sexist custom had disappeared.

In a twist of fate, despite their long history of segregation, pubs provided an important source of income for many women. The following description is very similar to the "ale wives" in 17th century England, and the custom in Colonial America of granting tavern licenses to widows. The selfish reason for this was the town council, not wanting to support widows and their children, found it more prudent to grant a tavern license than to place the widow on the "poor roles."

Widowhood and wife desertion were much more common in 19th century Australia than today, and in the absence of any social safety net for single mothers, women had to explore every available option to provide for their families, especially in remote areas. Pub-keeping provided jobs, not only for widows and deserted wives, but also for many female ex-convicts.

It was comparatively lucrative work, so pub-keeping became a welcome and preferred option for many women. The evolution of the "classic" pub and the women's roles in the pub developed together in the mid-19th century, when the term "barmaid" first came into common usage.

Barmaids, like many other working women, had to fight against the traditional gender challenges of lower pay rates and social stigmatization. Unlike other classes of working women, such as domestic servants and shop staff, barmaids were often stigmatized and shunned. This discrimination was exasperated by the "morals" campaigns that were waged around Australia from the 1880s to the 1920s, when religiously-motivated temperance activists deliberately fostered a negative image of the barmaid as a "loose woman" who lured men into pubs to drink and squander their money.

The reality was often the exact opposite. Barmaids typically prided themselves on their ability to pour, chat, and keep a clean bar simultaneously – not to mention their ability to support themselves and their family – and they deeply resented this characterization by temperance societies, but the stereotype stuck. Even though many barmaids loved the job because it offered better pay and greater freedom than typical female occupations like household servants, barmaids remained the object of scorn by "proper" society.

Australia's beer-drinking culture is descended from the northern European tradition, which favors grain-derived alcoholic beverages like beer and spirits, as opposed to southern European countries like Italy and Greece, where wine is the popular drink. Australia has long had one of the highest per capita rates of beer consumption in the world. The wine industry did not appear on a major scale in Australia until the 1970s.

For the period between 1800 and 1950, alcohol production and consumption in Australia was dominated by beer and spirits. Perhaps because of the generally hot, dry climate, Australian beer drinkers came to favor chilled Pilsner style beers. Pilsners are pale lagers with a light body and a prominent hop character.

This trend toward Pilsner beer was aided by the consolidation of the brewing industry, and the development of hop growing, especially in Tasmania. Refrigeration was a big help in the expansion of the beer business, and Australia was one of the first countries to adopt this new invention on a wide scale, and pubs were always the first local businesses to use refrigeration.

Australian beer has always had slightly higher alcohol content than comparable British or American brews, typically between 4 and 6% alcohol. Many light beers are now available with alcohol content of 2% to 3%, notably Tasmanian Boags and Hahn.

Beer production in Australia began as small, private breweries supplying local pubs. The industry rapidly became both larger in scale and more centralized as brewers adopted mass-production techniques during the late 19th century, and new modes of transport came into operation.

By the 20th century, the major brewing firms had become very large, vertically integrated businesses. They owned the breweries and ran truck fleets and distribution networks, and the major brewers owned chains of pubs across the country. The premises were typically operated on a leasehold basis by licensed publicans, very similar to the British arrangement.

As they grew, the larger and more successful firms began to take over smaller breweries, although they often retained the older brand names and the loyal clientele of those brands. Tooheys continued to distribute "Tooth's KB lager" and "Resch's Pilsner" and "Dinner Ale" after they had bought and eventually closed Resch's and Tooth's breweries. By the mid-20th century, the brewing industry was dominated by a handful of large and powerful state-based companies; the Tooth's and Tooheys in Sydney, Carlton United in Melbourne, Castlemaine in Brisbane, West End, and Cooper's in Adelaide and Swan in Perth. These brands effectively became unofficial mascots for their respective states. For example, Victoria Bitter in Victoria, and XXXX (called Four X) in Queensland. On the international level, Foster's is the big export brand.

In the late 20th century these beer empires began to expand overseas; Carlton's Foster's group and Castlemaine Toohey's empires now control significant segments of the brewing and beverage industry in Australia, the UK, Europe, and many other regions.

Another special feature of the Australian drinking culture was known as the "six o'clock swill." From the advent of the eight-hour workday until the late 1970s, just like most other countries, the workday ended at five o'clock. Since all pubs closed by law at 6 PM, workers would head for the nearest pub and drink as much as possible before the 6 PM closing. The early closing was established by the government in an effort to improve public morals and get men home to their wives earlier in the evening – the morality police at work once again. In reality, this practice fostered an environment of alcohol-related problems that became very destructive and persisted for most of the 20th century. Only changes to the liquor laws allowing pubs to stay open until 10 PM corrected the problem.

Gaming and betting, although illegal, have always been a part of Australian pub culture. Off-track betting and legalized gambling with casinos are recent additions to the Australian gaming scene. Previously, pubs were the major venue for the collection of bets and the distribution of winnings.

One of the betting games closely associated with the Aussie pub is a coin game called, "two-up." "Two-up" is a traditional Australian gambling game involving a designated "spinner" throwing two coins in the air and betting whether the coins will both fall heads up, or both tails up, or with one head and one tail. This game is traditionally played on "Anzac Day" in pubs and clubs throughout Australia.

The game was brought to Australia by the English and Irish convicts and spread throughout the country. "Two up" was especially popular with Aussie soldiers during World War I. For many, many years the game was illegal, except on Anzac Day, April 25. This is a national day of remembrance in Australia and New Zealand. It began as a day to honor the members of the Australian and New Zealand Army Corps (Anzac) who fought at Gallipoli in Turkey during World War I. It now more proudly commemorates all those who died and served in military operations, similar to Veteran's Day, or Armistice Day, in the United States. Playing "two up" on Anzac Day in streets and pubs throughout the country has become a national institution.

An interesting note: following federation in 1900,

Australia's first Prime Minister was Edmund Barton, known as "Toby Tosspot" due to his fondness for drinking. Another Prime Minister, Bob Hawke, was also renowned for his drinking. He is immortalized in the Guinness book of records for downing 2½ pints of beer in 11 seconds. Bob Hawke is quoted as saying, "this feat was to endear me to some of my fellow Australians, more than anything else I ever achieved." He was also a Rhodes Scholar and Oxford graduate.

Alcohol continues to play an important role in the social fabric of Australian society and the "shout" is the mainstay of the Australian pub. The Australian term "shout" or "shouting" refers to the custom of buying rounds of drinks when part of a group; known as "treating" in the U.S. The ritual and the etiquette involved in this Australian tradition are interesting.

"No dragging the chain": It is a well-understood obligation that slow drinkers must keep up with faster members of the shout.

"Immediacy": Never accept a drink if you don't plan to participate in the shout.

"Reciprocal": Never accept a drink from the group and then just buy one for yourself when it's your turn.

"Consistency": Changing drinks during a shout is considered poor form.

"Free will": The order of the round is determined by each individual voluntarily declaring it is their shout (turn). Fellow members should not ever need to remind an individual of their obligation to the group.

"Abstaining": From time to time, an individual may wish to pass on a round. Ideally, they should wait till the completion of every group members' rounds before abstaining from future rounds. If absolutely necessary to pass during mid-round, they should request a non-alcoholic beverage.

"Gender neutral": Should a woman be given a drink that has been purchased in the course of buying a round, she's part of the round. All previous rules apply. And don't forget, a round can consist of as few as two people.

The shout offers the outsider the quickest and easiest way to be inducted into a social group and to be treated as an equal, regardless of economic, political, or national background.

Australia has come a long way since the first grape vines arrived with the First Fleet in 1788. These days there are dozens of recognized grape-growing regions, and over 550 major wine companies. Australia is the 10th largest wine producing country in the world.

The Australian National Wine Center is located in Adelaide, and is an architectural masterpiece. The displays concentrate on Australia's 60 wine regions, and there are interactive exhibits that allow you to blend your own virtual wine. There is a tasting gallery, a bar, and a restaurant overlooking the wine center's own vineyard.

The Australian wine industry is the fourth-largest exporter of wine around the world, shipping over 200 million liters per year to a large international market. There's also a large domestic market for Australian wines with the locals consuming over 550 million liters each year.

Due to differences in soil, climate, and topography, Australia is able to produce different wine varieties and styles. The predominant varieties are Shiraz, Cabernet, Sauvignon, Chardonnay, Merlot, Semillon, Pinot Noir, Riesling, and Sauvignon Blanc. The wine industry is a significant contributor to the Australian economy through production, employment, exports and tourism.

Early Australian wine-makers faced many difficulties, particularly due to the unfamiliar climate. By the late 20th century Australian wines were beginning to win high honors in the yearly French competitions.

Prior to 1980 Australian wine production consisted mainly of sweet and fortified wines. Since then, Australia has become a world leader in both quantity and quality of wines it produces.

The struggling world economy has not been good for the wine business for the past several years, and Australia has had its own additional problems. A run of bad luck, including two droughts and wildfires, has victimized the industry; but the biggest blow was self-inflicted. A few years ago Australian wines were the hottest items around, especially the Shirazes with the quirky names (Mad Hatter, Dead Arm, Ball Buster) and the eye-catching labels.

The problem is Australia has made itself synonymous in the minds of many wine aficionados with cut-rate, generic wines. Thanks to industrial production giants like Jacob's Creek and Rosemont, Australia has long been a prime source of mass-market Chardonnays and Shirazes. But the wine that caused the image decline was Yellowtail, whose colorful label featured the Australian wallaby. The packaging, combined with the decent quality and low price (under $10), proved to be a sales master stroke. In just three years Yellowtail became the most popular imported wine in the United States with sales of about 4 million cases annually. As recently as 2010, sales had doubled, and now account for almost half of Australian wine purchased in the U.S.

However, what was good for the Yellowtail, and the Sicilian immigrants that founded the company in 2001, was not so great for Australian wines as a whole. The brand spawned a legion of imitators with critter labels featuring penguins, crocodiles, and anything else native to Australia. Now the wine bargain bin has become crowded with low-cost producers from countries like Argentina, Chile and South Africa.

In the 1960s and 1970s, Liefraumilch, a cheap wine, became the symbol of German wine around the globe, and it took years to upgrade the image of German wine; now, Australia has embarked on a marketing campaign to restore its reputation as a source of premium products.

You can embark on your own personal journey to discover the quality and range of varieties of wine produced in over 550 Australian wineries; many, many of these wineries are top-shelf outfits and almost every one offers tours and tastings.

The legal drinking age in Australia is 18, and each Australian state has its own set of liquor licensing laws. Until the late 20th century, bottled and canned alcoholic drinks could only be sold at retail at the local pub, and the type and amount of alcohol that could be sold was also restricted.

The pub-based "bottle shop" is commonplace in Australian pubs. In contrast, in most American bars, it is illegal to sell packaged goods or alcohol, "to go." This is governed by state laws and there are, of course, exceptions.

Australia now has "sales only" retail outlet chains that sell packaged goods but do not serve alcohol. These places now account for most of the alcohol sold in the country. It is still not normal for alcohol to be sold at retail in grocery stores in Australia; however, it can be found in supermarkets in some states.

Hours vary from pub to pub, but most open daily from

around 10 AM or noon to 10 PM or midnight.

As in most countries these days, drunk driving is considered a serious offense and will mean a court appearance, as well as a fine. The maximum blood-alcohol level is .05%.

A unique Australian quirk is if you order a beer in a pub or bar, be aware that the standard glass size varies from state to state. In Sydney, you may order a schooner or a smaller midi, if in a more upscale spot you will be offered a pint or half-pint. In Melbourne or Brisbane, a midi is called a pot, while in Darwin it's called a handle, and in Hobart a ten. Smaller glasses are available, but depending on where you are, they may be called a pony, a seven, a butcher, a six, or a bobbie. Good luck! Just use your hands to describe the size you would like.

Originally, pilsners were beer-of-choice for Australians, and that gradually gave way to lagers. Now, just as everywhere else, the micro-brew fashion has taken over.

The following is not a list of the best bars because, as in every country, the bar scene changes frequently, and what was a great place last year is out of business this year. The pubs and bars described here are interesting, historical places that have stood the test of time, and represent a little bit of the Australian drinking culture.

KALGOORLIE:

Kalgoorlie is located in Western Australia on what used to be the richest square mile of gold-bearing earth ever discovered. It still produces around 2000 ounces per day out of the ground. The "Super Pit" is the world's biggest open-pit gold mine (2 miles long, a mile wide and 1200 feet deep). The Empire State building would disappear inside. Gold was discovered here in 1893.

The town (population 32,000) has the appearance of a Western movie set. The city retains much of its original gold-fueled architectural extravagance; such as wrought-iron lace verandas and balconies. You can have a beer in one of the many 19th century pubs that line the main street. **The York Hotel** is a splendid example of this wonderful 19th century Australian pub architecture.

MELBOURNE

A young lady in Melbourne has developed a clever and popular game involving a pack of 52 playing cards called "Bar Secrets of Melbourne." The cards have photos, directions, and maps of the hippest and most unusual bars and pubs in town. The cards are sold for $10 all over town in bookstores and newsstands. Locals randomly choose a few cards and spend the evening exploring dark alleyways, climbing stairs to lofts and descending down into basements, always facing something new and unique.

Young and Jackson is Melbourne's oldest and most famous pub. Climb the stairs to the bar to see the painting that has scandalized and titillated Melbourne for over 100 years. "Chloe," the larger-than-life nude painted by Jules Lefebvre in Paris in 1875, was brought to Melbourne in 1884, for the Great Exhibition. It has held a special place in the hearts of residents and customers ever since. This pub has been around since 1853, free tastings and tales of the hotel's history can be had at **Chloe's Bar** every Saturday. Located at the corner of Flinders and Swanston Streets.

SYDNEY

Hero of Waterloo Hotel, 81 Lower Fort Street. This sandstone landmark, built in 1845, was reportedly once used by "press gangs" who would trap customers, push them through a trap door and cart them out to sea to serve on the cargo ships.

Lord Nelson Hotel. Kent and Haggle Streets. Another sandstone landmark and a rival of the Hero of Waterloo for the title of Sydney's oldest pub. The place makes its own prize-winning beer and serves it English-style in pints and half-pints.

Marble Bar, Sydney Hilton Hotel. This place, because of the ornate architecture, is a tourist attraction in itself. It is full of oil paintings, marble columns, and a marble bar, dating from 1893.

If you are in SYDNEY in late February or early March, you will think the whole city has gone gay. The Sydney Gay and Lesbian Mardi Gras parade is one of Australia's major events. With dozens of floats, buff dancers, and thousands of spectators, this is a giant party. Similar gay events are held in other major cities; New York City, Toronto, San Francisco, but the holiday may be Halloween in the U.S., or Midsummer in Canada, or Corpus Christi Sunday in Sao Paulo, Brazil (end of May or early June). Incidentally, the Sao Paulo gay parade is considered the largest of this type in the world

BRISBANE

Has a wide variety of historic pubs and most are well-preserved:

Breakfast Creek Hotel, 2 Kingsford Smith Drive. Built in 1889, this enormous pub is a Brisbane institution. Listed in the national heritage register, a visit to the city isn't complete without a steak and beer "off the wood," at the Brekky Creek. There's also a lush tropical beer garden.

Regatta Hotel, 543 Coronation Drive. This heritage hotel with three stories of iron-lace balconies overlooks the

Brisbane River and dates from the 1880s.

Story Bridge Hotel, 200 Main Street, Kangaroo Point. This is the home of the annual Australian Day cockroach races, January 26, and many, many other unusual events. Built in 1886, the place sports a new beer garden and restaurant-bar that is literally built into the base of the bridge.

Normandy Hotel, Musgrove Road. Built in 1872 and features the giant Morton Bay fig tree in the beer garden.

Plough Inn, South Bank Parklands. Wonderful architecture and it has been operating since 1885.

Eatons Hill Hotel, 646 S. Pine Road. Claims to be the largest pub in the world. Opened in 2011, it has 9 bars and 100 beer taps. Capacity of 7,000.

BELGIUM

"A food lover's dream, but a beer lover's Heaven."

*B*eer is your entrée to authentic Belgian culture.
In Belgium "beer rules" and there are over 100 varieties from 180 separate breweries. Many visitors to Belgium come specifically for beer tours of the entire country. Every major city in Belgium has interesting beer related attractions - breweries, famous beer, cafes, and other historic beer related items.

Along with wine, monasteries began brewing beer in the 5th century following the collapse of the Roman Empire. The monasteries carefully guarded their wine and beer producing knowledge and held a virtual monopoly until the 12th century.

During the Middle Ages power shifted towards the guilds, and beer workers were recognized officially as a guild. Beer became a popular drink and the number of breweries increased dramatically. The end of the 18th century and the aftermath of the French Revolution caused the destruction of many monasteries and breweries and it took almost a century to recover.

By the end of the 19th century, Louis Pasteur had discovered pasteurization and other techniques to improve the overall quality of beer. By 1900, there were over 3000 breweries in Belgium. By 1914 World War I had begun and was followed by the economic crisis of the 1930s and World War II. At the end of the Second World War, there were 755 breweries left and now there are 178.

There's been a consolidation of breweries in Belgium, just as in the rest of the world. The largest Belgian conglomerate is now known as AB In-Bev, which owns Anheuser-Busch, Stella Artois and a host of other brands around the world.

Recently a counter-trend has developed and small breweries and craft beers are returning to the marketplace.

Since beer is so important to the drinking culture of Belgium, a description of the beer-making process is worthwhile. Beer-making, just as wine production, is a complex procedure with lots of nuances. The main ingredients are barley, or wheat for wheat beer, water, hops, and yeast. Other items may be added during the brewing process, such as herbs or fruit. The final product is influenced by the quality and quantity of each ingredient and how and when they are added to, and mixed with, the water.

The first step is to soak the barley in water to cause germination. At the right moment germination is stopped and the barley is roasted in the kiln, the roasted barley is next added to a giant kettle of hot water. The strength of the beer is determined by the length of time the barley is left to stew with the water. Next, the barley is removed and hops, or malt, are added. The hops, which come from a small flowering plant, make a beer taste bitter and act as a counterpoint to the sweetness of the malt.

Now, the resulting liquid, known as "wort," is ready for the fermentation step. Yeast is added, and depending on the type used, will stay on the top of the tank, or sink to the bottom. Top fermented beers have a much fruitier taste. During the fermentation about 40% of the wort turns into alcohol and carbonic acid. The unfermented remainder of the wort gives the beer a distinctive spicy taste. The carbonic acid is bonded in the beer under counter-pressure and gives the beer a distinctive spicy taste. When poured, this rises to the top and creates the head of foam. Finally, the yeast is filtered out, except for some wheat beers, and the beer will usually set for a few weeks before being bottled, canned or kegged.

Beers are divided into two main categories, lagers (Budweiser, Corona, Coors, Miller High Life) and ales (Guinness, Newcastle).

Lagers are bottom-fermented beers because the yeast sinks to the bottom of the vat. Lagers are fermented at lower temperatures than ales and they take longer to brew.

Ales are made with top-fermented yeast, which is faster than bottom-fermented lagers, resulting in a more full-bodied, sweeter taste. Because of the sweetness, a hardy amount of hops is often added to give a more balanced flavor.

Trappist beer has been called the "champagne of Belgium." Only seven of the 174 Trappist monasteries world-wide brew Trappist ale and six of the seven are in Belgium. The other one is in the Netherlands. The Trappist order takes its name from the Trappist Abbey in Normandy France. The Cistercian order operated this monastery and by 1664 the Abbot felt the Cistercians were becoming too liberal. The Abbot introduced strict new rules for the Abbey and the so-called "strict observance" was born.

"Strict observance" refers to the Trappist goal to follow closely Saint Benedict's rule and take the vows of stability, fidelity to monastic life, and obedience. Benedict also insisted on silence and it plays a role in the Trappist way of life. Contrary to popular belief, they do not take a vow of silence. However, Trappist monks will generally speak only when necessary, and idle talk is strongly discouraged. Meals are usually taken in contemplative silence and members listen to a special reading.

A fundamental tenant of the order is that they should be self-supporting. As a result, most monasteries produce goods that are sold to provide income. In addition to beer, the monasteries produce bread, cheese, other foodstuffs, and clothing.

The original Trappist Abbey in Normandy had its own brewery by 1685 and originally brewed beer to feed its members as a part of self-sufficiency.

The Trappist monasteries that now brew beer in Belgium were occupied in the late 18th century by monks fleeing the French Revolution. The first recorded sale of beer to the general public was on June 1, 1861.

The Trappists have received greater attention in recent years because of the writings of Thomas Merton, a member of the order. Worldwide, there are over 2000 Trappist monks and 1800 Trappistine nuns.

In 1997, the Trappist Abbeys founded the International Trappist Association (ITA) to prevent non-Trappist commercial companies from using the Trappist name on beer, cheese, wine, etc.

For a beer to be labeled Trappist beer it must meet the following criteria:

1. The beer must be brewed within the walls of a Trappist monastery.
2. The monks must play a role in its production.
3. The income received must be used to cover living

expenses of the monks and maintenance of the buildings and grounds. Remaining funds are donated to charity for social work.

4. The Trappist breweries are constantly monitored to assure irreproachable quality of their beers.

The term "Trappist beer" tells you that the beer is from one of the seven Trappist monasteries permitted to use the logo, but it does not describe the beer, since the beers have very little in common. However, all Trappist beers are top-fermented ales, and since they are not pasteurized, the yeast continues to produce alcohol while in the bottle. So, they're great to begin with, and get better over time.

The current Belgian Trappist producers are the following: Remy Rochefort ale is brewed at the Abbey de St. Remy, about 80 miles southwest of Brussels. This ale is plum-colored and full, with a creamy head. Alcohol by volume (ABV) is 8%. The recipe for the beer remains a mystery, and the water used comes from a well on the monastery property. Unfortunately, at this Abbey, tours are not available.

Two places to try the three dark Trappist ales produced here are located in the small town of ROCHEFORT.

The Limbourg Café dates from the beginning of the 20th century, and **The Luxembourg** has over 30 Belgian beers on their menu.

CHIMAY is 76 miles south of Brussels and home of the Notre Dame de Scourmont Abbey, brewer of Chimay beer and producer of a wonderful cheese selection. Chimay beer comes in red, white, and blue labels. The colors refer to the labels and the beer itself. Red Chimay is deep red and tastes soft and fruity, 7% alcohol. Blue Chimay is dark brown, full and richly flavored, 9% alcohol. White label is blonde in color, 8% alcohol. The Abbey is not open to the public, but you can visit the church and gardens.

The Abbey's beer and cheese can be tasted in the nearby **Auberge De Poteaupre,** located less than a half-mile from the Abbey. Of the seven Trappist beers, Chimay is the most readily available worldwide.

Westvleteren is considered by many to be the best beer in the world, and it is the annual first-place winner in scores of tasting competitions. Only a very limited quantity of this beer is produced each year and cars line up outside the Abbey doors in order to stock-up. The limit is one case per car, but due to the demand, people often drive away with much less. The monks only produce enough beer to support themselves and their good works, and it is not distributed around Belgium.

The St. Sixtus Abbey was founded in 1831, and the brewery began operation eight years later. Only 29 monks live here, and devote their lives to prayer, study, and manual labor. They produce three kinds of beer: Blonde (5.8%), Eight (8%), and Twelve (10.8%). The Blonde beer has a slightly bitter taste, and the Eight is sweeter and fruity, Twelve, known as the "Flemish Burgundy" because its excellence equals that of Burgundy wine, has a strong malt flavor, and is one of the most potent Belgium beers (10.2% alcohol).

The St. Sixtus Abbey is located in the town of WESTVLETERN, 86 miles west of Brussels, and there is a **café** located across the street from the Abbey. It has a large barroom serving all three types of Westvletern beer, and an exhibition displaying a view of monastery life and a history of the brewery.

WESTMALLE, 21 miles northeast of Antwerp and 50 miles northeast of Brussels, is home of the **Abbey of our Lady of the Sacred Heart**, brewer of Westmalle Trappist beer. This is a beautiful Abbey founded in 1794, and has been brewing beer since 1836. The Dubbel (7%) is red-brown, fruity, and spicy. It is the only Trappist beer available on tap, all others are bottled. Their Tripel beer is creamy and gold. Across the street from the Abbey is a large brasserie, **Café Trappist,** serving enormous plates of Trappist cheese to accompany your beer.

The Abbey d'Orval in Orval, 118 miles southwest of BRUSSELS, produces six Orval Trappist beers. These are the most unique of all the Trappist beers. They are dark orange in color and have a dry and bitter taste (6.2%). The water used comes from a spring on the grounds of the monastery.

Founded in 1070, the Abbey d'Orval flourished for 700 years before being destroyed by French troops in the aftermath of the French Revolution. The abbey was rebuilt in the 1920s and the brewery started operating in 1931. The brewery here turns out more than fourteen million bottles of beer annually.

The brewery and most of the monastery's buildings are closed to the public; but there is a small museum, gardens and church available for visitors. Orval beer and cheese are available at **Hostellerie d'Orval** and **L'Ange Gardien,** both located in the village of ORVAL.

ACHEL is a tiny village in the northeast corner of Belgium, about 70 miles north east of Brussels**. The Achelse Kluis Abbey** is the most recent Trappist monastery to produce beer. In 1999, the monks here began producing highly fermented beer, Achel Blonde Eight (8%), Achel Brune (8%), and Achel Extra (8%). Although extremely private, this monastery is a little more open to visitors than the other Trappist Abbeys. There are tours available for groups, and a guesthouse with meals for overnight guests. An adjacent building houses a bookstore, art gallery, gift shop and cafeteria for tasting the Trappist beers.

Following the Trappist Abbeys establishing the International Trappist Association, the Union of Belgian Brewers introduced the "Certified Belgian Abbey Beer" logo. This logo designates beers brewed under license to an existing or abandoned monastery.

The requirements for registration under the logo include the monastery having control over certain aspects of the commercial operation, and a proportion of the profits going to the abbey or its designated charities. As of 2011, there were 18 certified abbey beers in Belgium.

There are a few beers that are special to Belgium, and one is wheat beer. This type of beer originated in the Flemish part of Belgium in the Middle Ages. Traditionally, it is made with a mixture of wheat and barley. Before hops became widely available in Europe, beers were flavored with a mixture of herbs called "gruit." In later years, hops were added to the gruit, and that mixture continues to be used today in most Belgian and Dutch wheat beers. The traditional flavor of Belgian wheat beer is largely influenced by the addition of coriander and orange peel after fermentation.

Lambic is a wheat beer brewed in the Pajottenland region, southwest of Brussels, by spontaneous fermentation. Most modern beers are fermented by carefully cultivated strains of brewer's yeast; Lambic fermentation; however, is produced by exposure to the wild yeasts and bacteria that are native to the Senne Valley, in which Brussels lies. After fermentation, the beer undergoes a long aging period, ranging from 3 to 6 months (considered "young") to 2 to 3 years. Lambic is produced in an open vat, allowing the airborne wild yeasts to wander into the mixture to begin the fermentation process. This unusual process gives the beer its distinctive flavor: dry, sharp, with a sour aftertaste. Lambic is a draft beer that is seldom bottled; thus, it is usually available only in its production area near Brussels. After they have aged, Lambics are often sweetened with sugar and fruit. The most common fruits are sour cherry, raspberry, peach, and apple.

There are several other distinctively Belgian beers; but the bulk of production and consumption consists of pilsners; technically not a Belgian beer as it was invented by the Czechs, and dominated by the Germans. Pilsners account for 75% of the total beer production in Belgium; and Belgium exports 60% of its beer. A pilsner is a lager, bottom fermented, light, refreshing and hop-centered beer. These are not the beers for connoisseurs, but Belgium does have three top brands: Jupiler, Maes pils, and Stella Artois; the most well-known name.

A distinguishing feature of Belgian beer is that virtually every brand has its own special drinking glass imprinted with a logo or name.

One of the more common types is the tulip glass, the body is bulbous; but the top flares out to form a lip, which helps trap the aroma and retain the head.

The Trappist and abbey ales prefer large, stemmed, bowl-shaped glasses known as chalices or goblets. The chalice is thick-walled, while the goblet is more delicate and thin. The brand name is printed on the glass.

A vessel similar to a champagne flute is preferred for serving Belgian Lambics and fruit beers. The narrow shape helps maintain carbonation and displays the sparkling color and soft lacing of these beers.

In addition to all these glass varieties provided by the

brewers, many Belgian cafés serve beer in their own special "house" glassware.

Except for the Trappists, most Belgian breweries, large and small, are open to the public. This can be a wonderful experience at one of the smaller, older locations. The Association of Belgian Brewers has a website giving location, tour hours, etc. for most of the breweries: *www.beer paradise.be.*

LEUVEN, 16 miles southeast of Brussels, is considered the beer capital of Belgium, and is home to a university dating from 1425 and to Stella Artois, the premier institution of Belgian brewing. Beer has been made on this site since 1366. Master Brewer Sebastian Artois took over the operation in 1717, and the barley beer, Stella Artois, was launched in 1926. This is now a mammoth operation and tour reservations must be made well in advance of your visit.

The Cantillion Brewery in BRUSSELS is family-run, and has produced Lambic beers since 1900. On a tour here you will see everything from start to finish, including aging containers and bottling machines.

The Brewers House in Brussels is the 18th century headquarters of the Belgian Brewers Association. The basement houses a small museum that includes an excellent video presentation of the brewing process.

There is even a museum dedicated to hops, National Hops Museum, located in POPERINGE, in the northwest corner of Belgium.

Other wonderful brewery tours include **Palma Breweries** in STEENHUFFEL where there is the medieval Diepenoteyn Castle and a herd of Belgian draft horses. In TOURNAI, one of the oldest cities in Belgium, the **Brunehaut Brewery** continues to use recipes that date back to the first Crusade.

BEERSEL, 8 miles south of Brussels, is home to the Drie Fonteinen Brewery, a popular stop for devotees of real Lambic, Gueuze and Kriek beers. There is a nearby 15th century castle to visit as well.

While beer is certainly the most popular drink in Belgium, gin, known as jenever in Flanders and as genieuve in the South, is the hard liquor favorite. This strong drink is often served in glasses only a little larger than a thimble. It is a Belgian custom to fill the small glasses to the brim, so that only surface tension keeps it from overflowing. Faced with this situation, you are forced to lean over for the first sip, rather than trying to pick up the glass. Belgium has 70 distilleries producing over 270 varieties of jenever flavored with juniper, coriander, and other herbs and spices. One brand, Van Damme jenever, comes in a stone bottle.

The **National Jenever Museum** is located in HASSALT, 49 miles east of Brussels. The museum dates from 1803, and includes one of the country's oldest distilleries. Following the tour, you can sample jenever from over two dozen distilleries and compare ages, flavors, and alcohol content. You may want to book a local hotel room in advance.

Belgium is absolutely loaded with wonderful bars, cafés and other drinking spots. The following list will cover only a few of the more historical places in the major cities.

Brussels has a café serving alcoholic drinks on virtually every corner. A good place to begin sampling Belgian beers is **Bier Circus** (02-218-0034). This place has a large selection of brews from every section of the country. **A La Mort Subite** (02-513-1318) is named after a dice game established by bankers over one hundred years ago. The menu here includes over 600 brands of beer. By the way, the name translates to "sudden death." which is the name of one of the beers sold here.

Falstaff (02-511-8789) is a legendary 1904 Tavern with stunning décor and stained-glass scenes depicting Shakespeare's Falstaff tales.

La Fleur en Papier Doce (02-511-16- 59) is located in a 16th century house. This spot has been operating since 1846, and has always been a mecca for poets and writers. This is a delightful atmospheric old pub, much like a social club where you can enjoy drinking and good conversation.

Delirium Café boasts of having over 2000 brands of beer. This place made the Guinness book of records for having the most beer available. The sign over the door is adorned with a pink elephant. Located in the Quartier de I'llot Sacre in central Brussels.

Chez Morder Lambic (02/539-1419) is a grungy bar famous worldwide for its extensive beer list – 600 Belgian brews and a few hundred foreign ones.

Like most Western European cities, Brussels has a sizable number of Irish bars which are thriving and extremely popular with the younger crowd. All are easily recognizable with names like **James Joyce, Kitty O Shea,** the **De Valera's,** and **Fabian O'Farrell's.**

Het Elfde Gabod means "the 11th Commandment," and is decorated with around 400 religious statues. The building dates from the 16th century, and they serve a wide selection of beers.

ANTWERP, Belgium's second city has some very special and historic places to sample Belgian beer. There are 2500 taverns in Antwerp, one for every 200 inhabitants.

Den Engel (03/233-12-52) is a delightful old-style café dating from 1579. Located on the main square across from the fountain and below the cathedral's soaring spires, the place has wood paneling on two levels. The feature attraction is a round glass called a "bolleke" ("little ball") in which they serve Antwerp's very own yeasty, copper-colored De Koninck beer.

De Groote Witte Arend (03/233-50-33) is located in a 17th century former monastery, and you will be serenaded by classical music.

De Pelgrom is in the vaulted brick cellar of a 16th century tavern with long wooden benches and candlelight.

Bierhuis Kulminator (03/232-4538) pours 550 kinds of beer, including EKU-28, known as the strongest beer on earth.

DeVagant (03/233-15-38) offers an opportunity to take a break from the beer experience. This place deals exclusively in jenever – and has 200 varieties available. An upstairs restaurant specializes in jenever-based sauces, and the walls are covered with jenever memorabilia.

The city of GHENT offers pub crawls by reservation. One unusual spot is **Herberg de Dulle Griet** (09/234-24-55). If you order the 1.2 liter Kwak beer in the collector's stein and wooden stand, you will be asked to leave one shoe as deposit when you order.

Also in Ghent, **Thet Dreupelkot** (09/224-21-20) is the place for jenever. The café produces its own brand, in a variety of flavors including chocolate and vanilla.

Keep in mind, once again, that Belgium is a beer-lovers paradise with over 800 types of beer available and many of these have a high alcohol content, 8-10% alcohol by volume, versus the usual 5-6% ABV.

Kriek, a fruit-flavored beer, and Duval, a very strong blonde beer, are Belgian favorites. Wittekerke Rose from the Barik brewery in Bavikhove is a blend of regular Wittekerke wheatbeer and 10% raspberry fruit. A very popular beer in

Belgium. Almost all the popular Belgian beers are served in their own special glasses where the shape is geared to best showcase the beer's particular characteristics.

Licenses are not required for selling beer or wine in dining establishments. As a result, almost all restaurants, cafés, pubs, and even snack bars, offer beer and wine. Also, there is no minimum age for consumption of beer or wine. The minimum age for purchase or consumption of hard liquor is 18, and a license is required for the sale of liquor.

As the story goes, one of the Trappistine monasteries had a policy of only speaking two words, once a year, at each nun's annual meeting with the Abbess or Mother Superior. On the first anniversary of this particular nun's commitment to the order, she said to the Mother Superior, "shoes tight." A year later, on her second anniversary, she commented, "food bad." The third year, when she met with the Mother Superior, she announced, "I quit." The Mother Superior replied: "I'm not surprised, you've been bitching since you came here."

BRAZIL

"Here's to alcohol the rose colored glasses of life" – *F. Scott Fitzgerald*

Brazil is a huge country with a very diverse population, which has a large effect on the drinking culture. Geographically, Brazil is the fifth largest country in the world, and it is also the fifth most populous. Sao Paulo is the largest city in South America with over 17 million people, ranking as the third largest city in the world. This population is made up of Germans, Italians, Portuguese, Japanese, and Spaniards. More than half the population claims Italian descent. Sao Paulo is also home to the largest Japanese population outside Japan, and, as a result, sake is a big drink in Sao Paulo.

If you're going to enjoy a once in a lifetime drinking experience in Germany, you must go to Oktoberfest, and if you are going for another lifetime experience you need to attend "Carnaval" in Brazil. Carnaval is the pre-Lenten celebration that takes place for about a week every February or March depending upon when Easter is scheduled. This is summertime in Brazil, and the event is a super-sized New Orleans Mardi Gras and is held in every major city in Brazil: but the best ones are in Rio de Janeiro and Salvador.

Rio's event is billed as the biggest party in the world. Accurate or not, if it even comes close, it has to be good. The highlight is the Samba School Parade featuring tens of thousands of costumed dancers, thousands of percussionists and hundreds of floats. The city of Salvador's Carnival is honored in the Guinness Book of Records as the biggest street carnival in the world.

Combine this festival atmosphere with Brazil's national cocktail, and you have the ingredients for a good time. Caipirinha is made using Cachaca, sugar and lime juice, poured over ice, and served in an Old-Fashioned glass. This drink is everywhere in Brazil, but was little known outside the country until recently. It is now listed as an official cocktail of the International Bartenders Association. The word "caipirinha" is a version of "caipira," which refers to someone from the country-side, the equivalent of American "hillbilly." Sometimes the word caipirinha is used to describe any drink containing cachaca and fruit juice.

Cachaca is the number one distilled beverage in Brazil, and is often called pinga. This product is made from fermented sugarcane, but the process is slightly different from the one used to produce rum. Rum is made by distilling molasses, a by-product from sugar refineries that boil the cane to extract as much sugar crystal as possible. Cachaca is made from sugarcane juice that is fermented and is distilled; cachaca is produced prior to the crystallization of sugar, molasses is made after crystallization.

Cachaca, like rum, has two varieties, unaged (white or clear), and aged (dark or gold). White cachaca is usually bottled immediately after distillation, and tends to be cheaper and is used in mixed drinks like caipirinha. Dark cachaca is the premium variety and is aged in wooden barrels for up to three years. Some very high quality varieties are aged for up to 15 years. The flavor is influenced by the type of wood used to make the barrel. These premium types are meant to be drunk straight or on the rocks. The product is typically between 35% and 54% alcohol by volume. Brazil produces over 1.5 billion liters (390,000,000 gallons) of cachaca annually, and almost all of this is consumed domestically; less than 1% is exported.

The region around PARATY, 97 miles southwest of Rio de Janeiro, is a UNESCO World Heritage historic site and is very well-known for its cachaca. Several distilleries are located nearby and each year on the third weekend of August, the city celebrates the Festival da Pinga (alternate name for cachaca).

Beer, known as "Chopp" in Brazil, has a long history in this country. Amazon tribes have been making manioc and corn beers for over 2000 years. The most popular of these is a hearty, dark beer used during social and religious festivals. All types of celebrations are accompanied by beer in the Amazon. One tribe used to add the cremated remains of human bones to ensure that their ancestors would carry on in them. It gives new meaning to a toast for the departed, "here's to Johnny," and down the hatch. One beer to try is Xingu that is sold throughout Brazil.

The first breweries in Brazil date back to German immigration in the early 19th century. The brand Bohemia claims to be the first Brazilian beer with production beginning in 1853 near Rio de Janeiro. Two other important brands still in production, Anarctica and Brahma, were first produced in the 1880s.

Currently, Brazil is the world's fourth largest market for beer with over 88 million barrels produced in 2010, and an annual per capita consumption of 14 gallons. Pilsner beers are the most popular choice with a 98% market share. InBev, the world's largest brewer, a Belgian company, owns the biggest brands in Brazil; which include Antarctica, Brahma, and Skol. InBev also owns Stella Artois, Becks, and Budweiser (Anheuser Busch).

More and more microbreweries are starting up in Brazil every year. Better known ones include Baden-Baden (the first in Brazil) Wals, Colorado, and Dado Bier. Considering the total alcoholic beverage market in Brazil, beer is the most competitive area.

During the Carnaval period each February there is an explosion in consumption. In the four major days of the festival over 106,000,000 gallons of beer are consumed. This represents around 4% of the yearly production. In addition to bottled and canned beer, chope or chopp, a pale blonde Pilsner draft beer is extremely popular. Major producers of the draft beer, once again, are Antarctica and Brahma.

The first grapevines were brought to Brazil in 1532 by the Portuguese colonists, and the Jesuits established the vineyards and wineries to produce wine for the Catholic Mass. Nothing much happened until the Italian immigrants began to arrive in the late 1800s. Wine quality has improved as the government has established a system to certify wines by origin, and warrants the quality, similar to the arrangement used in European countries. Today, there are hundreds of wineries producing quality product in Brazil.

In Rio de Janeiro the closest thing to a London pub or a Paris café is known as a "botequin." These are the places where locals gather for those end-of-the-day drinks or late-night political or philosophical discussions. These places are not fancy, by any measure, but they are rich in character and local flavor. There are certainly many up-scale options scattered around the city; but the most interesting are the small, hole-in-the-wall, down-to-earth, watering holes where one can kick back with an ice cold beer, a snack, and catch up on all the latest local news and gossip.

The following are a couple bars that will get you acquainted with the botequin culture.

Bip Bip is an internationally acclaimed botequin; it has been featured on the Parisian daily Le Monde front page. The attraction here is the music and great samba. Located in Copacabana (821-2267-9696).

Bracacense has been voted the best botequin in Rio; the New York Times called it the best in Brazil. The excellent food and top-shelf beers are the attractions here. **Bar Garota de Ipanema.** Rio de Janeiro (021-2523-3787). This is the bar where songwriter Antonio Carlos Jobim and his pal, the lyricist, Vinicius de Moraes were sitting in their favorite spot when schoolgirl Heloisa Pinheire walked past and inspired them to write the 1962 classic "The Girl From Ipanema." Now, even the street is named after them, Rua Vinicius de Moraes.

Arco do teles. This is an area that looks like a movie set of old Rio, with colonial buildings and cobblestone streets, and is home to over a dozen bars and botequins. Just pick any one and you'll be in for some of the best music and people-watching in town.

Rabo de Peixe – SAO PAULO (001-3842-8666). This is a perfect example of a Brazilian pub. Situated on the corner, the patios spread out on three sides. A wonderful opportunity to sit outdoors with a chopps (draft beer), and watch the world go by.

A few rules apply to drinking alcoholic beverages in Brazil. First, the official legal drinking age is 18, but it is rarely enforced. Beer, wine and liquor can be purchased seven days a week at just about anywhere, including grocery stores and snack stands. Also, drinking is permitted outdoors in public places and in motor vehicles. The one hitch, which is strictly enforced, the legal alcohol limit for driving is 0.00, zero!

Happy hour in Brazil (pronounced and written in English) is a big deal. Unlike most countries, where the term refers to early-evening hours when drinks are discounted; in Brazil it simply means the time at the end of the workday when you head to a bar for a drink. Despite the absence of discounted drinks, the term and the custom are very popular in Brazil.

As in most developing countries, you must be very careful about the use of water and ice made from unpurified water. This is not a problem in the major cities, but can become a serious problem in less populated areas. Use bottled water, fruit washed in purified water, and ice made from purified water.

CHINA

"Who loves not wine, women, and song, remains a fool his whole life long. Martin Luther.

The Chinese have been drinking alcoholic beverages longer than anyone else on this planet. Fermenting grain (millet was the major grain used) into yellow wine is believed to have first taken place in China over 4000 years ago. Legend claims that Yidi, the wife of the first Dynasty's king, Yu (about 2100 BC), invented the method of fermenting grain into alcohol. God bless her!

The 20th century stopped progress in China for over 50 years. First, the Japanese invasion and occupation in the 1930s was a major catastrophe, followed by the Communist rule for over 50 years.

Now, however, progress is taking place at lightning speed. In the roaring 20s Shanghai was the place to be, the land of style and opportunity. Almost 100 years later, Shanghai is undergoing one of the fastest economic expansions the world has ever seen. The city has over 3000 skyscrapers, more than New York, and 2000 more are on their way. Greater Shanghai has a population over 21 million and the growth rate remains at a consistent 10% each year. The population has more than doubled in the past 15 years. This explosion of growth is occurring in all the major cities in China, including **Beijing**, the capital, **Hong Kong** and **Guangzhou**, known historically as Canton.

Traditionally, there was no bar scene in China and Chinese drinking was confined to using alcohol to accompany eating food in the home or at a restaurant. Along with everything else, this tradition is undergoing rapid change and bars and cafés are appearing in all the major cities.

Western alcoholic beverages are either fermented from fruit juices that already contain simple sugars (wine), or malted grains with sugar converted from starch using the grains own enzymes (beer). Chinese alcohol (jiu) and many other East Asian beverages are fermented from sugars converted from grain starch using enzymes from certain mold strains.

Three major alcoholic drinks are readily available and consumed in Chinese culture.

1. Huang jiu, literally "yellow liquor," is fermented from grain (rice, barley, millet, sorghum, or other grains) with alcohol content in the 10 to 25% range.

2. Bai jiu, literally "white liquor," is distilled from grains; sorghum, corn, and potatoes. Technically, these are vodkas and alcohol content is from 80 to 120 proof. This drink has a very harsh taste, and is difficult for Westerners to enjoy. The quality and price ranges over a wide spread, from dirt cheap paint thinner to decent, very expensive stuff. "How do you know when you have been in China too long? When you enjoy a nice glass of bai jiu."

3. Yao jiu is medicinal alcohol infused with everything from herbs to animal parts and used to treat ailments ranging from hypertension and rheumatic pains to depression and colds. There are specific Yao jius to treat the respective life-cycle problems of men and women.

Unlike Western culture these Chinese drinks are

warmed before being consumed. They are usually heated to about 100°F, not high enough to boil off any of the alcohol. The feeling behind this custom is that warming allows the aromas of the alcohol to be better appreciated by the drinker.

Beer was not known in China until about 100 years ago when the Germans set up a brewery in Quindao in 1903. This was followed by investments from Japan, Russia, England and France. Today, there are over 900 breweries in China, and China ranks second in the world in beer production, after the United States. Beer is the second most popular drink after bai jiu and gaining popularity rapidly. A bottle of Chinese beer, 500 ml, is larger than typical beer bottles, but the alcohol content is generally lower. China's most well-known brand is Tsingtao, available world-wide.

Wine made from grapes was produced in China as early as 200 BC. Wine was popular with the Imperial Court, and among the upper class, but production and distribution were always very limited.

Food shortages during various periods in Chinese history caused the government to prohibit both the production and consumption of wine and all other alcoholic beverages. So, wine as part of the alcohol mix in China remained insignificant until about 1980. At that time, the Chinese government became more open and began to welcome foreign investment as part of its economic reform. H. Remy Martin, large cognac producer, Allied-Lyons, British conglomerate, Seagram, Canadian producer, and many other European and American companies entered the Chinese market. The result was a series of joint ventures involved in the production of wine. Wine remains a minor, but growing, beverage in a market dominated by bai jiu and beer. China now offers custom tours for those especially interested in wine and gourmet food. Red wine is often consumed in formal settings, like business meetings, and the Chinese frequently add ice cubes or mix it with a soft drink like Sprite.

A Chinese phenomenon is the major role played by cognac in Hong Kong, not in the rest of China, but certainly in the former British Colony. Somewhere in the second half of the 20th century cognac emerged as the ultimate symbol of prestige, status and conspicuous consumption in Hong Kong society. In a way, this role can be traced to the part drinking has always played in Chinese culture.

Cognac is a brandy aged in oak barrels for a minimum of 30 months under the tight guidelines and quality control of the Bureau National Interprofessional du Cognac. The production of cognac is restricted to the area around Cognac in western France. The Asian market accounts for more than half of the annual world sales of cognac based on value.

Drinking alcohol has always had great ritual significance in Chinese culture and for thousands of years it has been considered a central component of every major ceremony that merits either celebration or memorialization. These events include births and deaths, farewells and reunions, holidays and festivals; if it's an "occasion" it merits a drink and it can express joy or sorrow. A Chinese saying: "A thousand cups of wine is not too much when good friends get together." Another saying: "Frequent drinking makes friends surrounding."

Whether drinking beer or bai jiu, toasting is usually a big part of drinking in China. When drinking wine or spirits, or beer at a table, both the host and the guests are expected to observe certain rules of etiquette and behavior.

The glass should be full at all times, else guests may think they are lacking due respect. Of course, the elders and superior persons present should always be served first. A toast represents esteem and it is important to participate; to refuse would be extremely impolite. When making a toast, everyone is required to stand and a few nice words are said followed by a clinking of glasses and a cheer "ganbei" (empty the glass). When touching glasses it is considered polite if you lower your glass below the other one because it implies modesty. Finishing the drink in a single swallow is also symbolic and preferred. You can see the problem this presents when, as stated earlier, it is important for the host to always keep the glasses full.

Traditionally, depending on the occasion, and the social ranking of the guests, there are specific rules regarding almost all elements of the drinking process. These include the size of the drinking vessel used, the seating positions of the guests, the order of serving drinks (who is first and who is last), the number of food dishes provided, and the quantity of drinks served to each guest. These complex rules are formalized in the "Book of Rights" and the Imperial Court employed "drink masters" to oversee the proper drink rituals at all state dinners. The Book of Rights is a record of Confucian teachings regarding proper behavior among individuals at specific events.

Over time, these formalized rules governing drinking in social occasions have become normal practices among the general population.

Some of the practices include the following customs:
Drinking is a social activity and should always include others. Drinking alone is frowned upon, as is drinking to get drunk. Drunkenness is looked upon with contempt and considered a disgrace.

Drinking is a blessing when consumed in moderation.

Social hierarchy governs drinking etiquette and the eldest should always drink first.

Snacks or meals should always accompany drinking.

In summary, in Chinese culture drinking alcohol is a cultural performance used to reinforce social solidarity. It is interesting that from the beginning these codes and rules made no mention of excluding anyone on the basis of status, gender, or even age. By the way, there is no minimum drinking age in China. Alcohol is sold everywhere: grocery stores, corner shops, in retail outlets. The custom of restricting the sale of alcohol to specialized, licensed outlets as practiced in North America and elsewhere, does not apply in China. However, Hong Kong continues to follow laws and customs governing alcohol based on the British system.

On a world-wide basis the Chinese are light consumers of alcohol and alcoholism is rare. Recent studies show Hong Kong's per capita consumption of alcohol at 5.8 gallons per year. This compares to 26.5 gallons per person per year in Germany, 18 gallons in the US, and 15 gallons in Japan.

Drinking games have always played an important role in Chinese entertainment. The Chinese term for these games is "Jiuling" and it dates back to the very early Zhou Dynasty when games were introduced to regulate people's drinking habits regarding proper courtesy and etiquette. There were even special designated officials to manage these aids for drinking. Jiuling evolved through Tang, Song, Ming and Qing Dynasties (over 1000 years), and eventually became quite precise and fashionable in its form and practice. Jiuling is now considered a unique part of Chinese culture.

Jiuling comes in a variety of forms depending upon the drinker's social status, literary status and other interests. The three main categories are general games, contest games, and literal games.

The general game category includes games that everyone can play; such as joke telling, riddles and flower passing. This category is usually used at banquets or other large functions.

In China contest games can include everything from dice and chess to archery and arrow throwing. The two most popular throughout China are "finger guessing" and "animal betting."

In finger guessing two people stretch out fingers from 2 to 20. Each shouts a number from 2 to 20 and the one that is equal to the number of extended fingers wins and the other must drink.

In animal betting, a game everyone in China can play, one player uses his chopstick to tap the other person's chopstick and shout out one of four terms: stick, cock, tiger, or insect. The rules are simple: stick beats tiger, tiger eats cock, cock pecks insect, insect bores stick. It is very similar to the Western game of scissors, rock, paper. Paper covers rock, rock breaks scissors, scissors cuts paper.

Literal games are played by the more educated classes who have knowledge of traditional Chinese culture. These games are a lot of fun, and can become quite sophisticated. They can include references to proverbs, fairy tales, poems, etc. They may even include improvisation and acting (similar to charades). Fast response is the key to winning.

Unfortunately, as in other countries, these games, which were used to preserve drinking etiquette, have gradually become the vehicle to force overdrinking and promote gambling.

The major cities of Beijing, Shanghai, Guangzhou (Canton)

and, of course, Hong Kong have social venues approaching what Westerners are familiar with in their own countries. Otherwise, the bar scene can be quite variable in China. The Chinese prefer to go to places like tea houses, and karaoke bars, rather than pubs or neighborhood bars. Their first choice for consuming alcoholic beverages is to drink at home or in a restaurant with dinner. However, as with everything else, this is beginning to change with the new openness and prosperity. Western-style pubs devoted to drinking are beginning to gain ground with the younger, local population, and, of course, with the increasing number of foreigners in China: visitors, businessmen, and employees.

Given China's drinking culture and an up and down 4000- year history of feast or famine, peace and war, including the recent 50 years of Communist domination; it is not surprising that it is not possible to compile a list of famous ancient pubs and bars. The only city with a semblance of this culture is Hong Kong.

HONG KONG became a British colony in 1842, when Britain acquired Hong Kong Island as a spoil of the first Opium War. In 1997, Hong Kong was handed back to China, and is classified as a Special Administrative Region (SAR) of China, and is permitted to have its own internal government and economic system for the next 50 years after China took control. The official language is English.

MACAU is just 40 miles west of Hong Kong across the Pearl River estuary. After being a Portuguese colony for 400 years, Macau was given back to China in 1999, and like Hong Kong, it is a Special Administrative Region for 50 years. This little place, 11 sq. mi. in total area, has become the gambling capital of Asia. While the Chinese are not known for their drinking prowess, they are preeminent when it comes to gambling. Macau is the only place in China where gambling is legal. Annual revenue, which is growing by leaps and bounds, even in a depressed economic climate, is more than five times the amount earned by Las Vegas strip casinos. Most all the hotels here have casinos and all the larger Las Vegas brands are represented: Wynn, MGM Grand, and Mandarin. The Sands Cotai Central Casino Resort opened last year (2012). This $4.4 billion extravaganza is the 35th casino to open in Macau, the world's biggest gambling market. The Venetian Macao Resort is the largest casino in the world with 546,000 sq. ft. and 3400 slot machines and 800 gaming tables. The way things are going and growing, this record will be surpassed very soon.

Hong Kong is one of the most stunning cities in the world, with skyscrapers ringing Victoria Harbour and ferries, cruise liners, and cargo ships bustling about, and all of this set against a backdrop of gently rounded mountains. The best views of all this, night or day, are from the bars and lounges located in hotels on the Bay.

The **Peninsula Hong Kong** is Hong Kong's most famous hotel. Built in 1928, among other luxuries, it has one of the largest limo fleets of Rolls Royces in the world. The top floor bar and restaurant, **Felix,** offers magnificent views.

Hotel Intercontinental Hong Kong, located on the water's edge, probably has the best views of the harbor. It is also the location of **Spoon** by Alain Ducasse, one of the very top restaurants in the city.

The **Sky Lounge** in the Sheraton Hotel offers spectacular views as the name implies.

As part of the modern scene, and typical of current Asian trends from Japan to Singapore; karaoke bars are popping up like mushrooms following a rain.

SHANGHAI is an immense city with different neighborhoods, offering totally different classes of bars. The Maoming Nau Lu has three avenues of solid bars, many noted for their "fishing girls," prostitutes, that will take your money and run.

The Bund area is home to many, many upscale drinking establishments.

Hotel bars include the famous **Cloud Nine Bar** on the 88th floor of the Grand Hyatt. For a while this place claimed to be the highest bar in the world at 1358 feet. It certainly has marvelous views. **The Sky Dome Lounge** on the 47th floor of the Radisson Hotel and the well-known **Jade Bar** on the 36th floor of the Shangri-La Hotel offer spectacular views. Two other established bars frequented by Westerners are the **Glamour Bar,** a must visit, and **Bar Rouge,** one of only a few places in China with a dress code.

In SINGAPORE, world luxury is still available at the historic **Raffles** Hotel and the legendary "**Long Bar,**" where the globe's "movers and shakers" have been conversing for more than 125 years. Raffles is the home of the "Singapore Sling" and is quite possibly the most famous hotel in the world.

Just as the favorite drink in Hong Kong is cognac, Huangjiu is the number one brew in Shanghai. Huangjiu, literally "yellow liquor," looks and tastes like whiskey with a lower alcohol content. Price and quality depend upon age; two, five or 10 years old. This drink is served warm and sometimes ginger or dried plums are added.

Beijing still has many traditional Chinese cafés, which often have an arrangement that includes a bookstore. The idea was always to be able to sip tea, China's number one non-alcoholic beverage, and browse through books. Many of these old cafés now serve alcohol.

The Yin Bar on the rooftop of the Emperor Hotel offers the finest view of the Forbidden City. This is indeed a classy experience.

The World of Susie Wong bar is named after the 1957 novel about a Hong Kong prostitute living in the 1930s. The bar is designed like a 1930's opium den with chic beds overrun with plush pillows. This is another special experience. The **"No Name Bar"** has been the favorite of foreigners for a very long time.

CZECH REPUBLIC

"I like beer. On occasion I will even drink beer to celebrate a major event, such as the fall of Communism or the fact that the refrigerator is still working." – Dave Barry

It was decided to include the Czech Republic, consisting of Bohemia and Moravia, in this discussion of drinking cultures around the world because it has played such an important role in the history of beer production. And the Czechs still produce some of the finest beers in the world. By most measures, the Czechs drink more beer per capita, most all of it produced in the Czech Republic, than any other nation on earth – Irish and Germans included. The most recent numbers show 156.9 liters consumed annually per capita, or about 338 U.S. pints of beer – that's about 1 pint per day for everyone! Czechs drink more beer than water. The history of beer is deeply embedded in the Czech national culture.

The first mention of brewing in the Czech territories is in the charter for the Vysehrad Church, dating from 1088. In this document, the first Czech King, Vratislav II, decided that his estates should pay a hop tithe to the Church.

In the early days, only citizens in the Czech lands had the right to brew beer, and only for their own consumption; so most citizens had a little brewery in their home. It wasn't long before some of these people banded together to form a co-operative central brewery. The first record of one of these breweries dates to 1118 in the town of CERHENICE.

Eventually, every town had at least one brewery, and much of the early brewing history is centered around monasteries. Much of the brewing history of the Czech capital, PRAGUE, is associated with various monasteries in the city with brewing first recorded at the Benedictine monastery in 993 A.D. Today, however, there are very few Czech monasteries brewing and selling beer to the public.

King Wenceslaus, 907–940, played his part, by convincing the Pope to revoke an order banning the brewing of beer – which may be one reason he is renowned as "Good King Wenceslaus" in the ancient Christmas Carol.

The Czech brewing industry expanded for almost 500 years until the 30 Years War devastated most of Europe. This war was one of the most destructive of all time, which is quite a feat in itself. At one point beer was used to pay-off a Swedish Army to prevent the plunder of Kunta Hora in South Bohemia.

The Czech Nation and its beer did not begin to recover from this blow until the "national awakening" movement of the 19th century, when the Czech language, Czech culture, and Czech beer were reinvented after centuries of Germanization and decline.

In 1842, a brewery in Plzen (Pilsen) employed Josef Groll, a German Master Brewer, who was experienced in the Bavarian lager method of making beer. Groll developed a golden Pilsner beer, the first light colored beer ever made. It became an immediate success and was exported all over the Austrian Empire. A special train loaded with beer traveled from Plzen to Vienna every single morning. By 1874, exports of Czech beer had reached Paris and the United States.

Originally, Pilsner was a specific term for beers brewed

in Plzen with Pilsner Urquell being registered as a trademark by the first brewery, the brand name Pilsner Urquell literally means "the original source of Pilsner." Now, the term Pilsner has come to mean any pale, well-hopped lager, with crisp carbonation. It is believed that 80% of the beer produced in the world today is a derivative of the Pilsner style.

One of the primary factors behind the excellent quality of Czech beer is the unique character of the hops grown in the Country. The agricultural conditions are ideal for growing hops, and they have been exporting hops since 903 A.D. Hops were so prized that King Wenceslaus ordered the death penalty for anyone caught exporting the cuttings from which new plants could be grown. Today, as well as being a major beer exporter, the Czechs still produce the finest hops for Pilsner-style lager beer, and large volumes are sent to the United States and other beer-drinking nations. The difference is these countries do not generally use the hops so liberally in the brewing process as their Czech counterparts.

The city of CESKE BUDEJOVICE was for centuries also known by its German name, Budweiser. Brewing has been recorded in the city since the 13th century and today it has two main breweries: **Budvar** and **Budweiser Burgerbrau**.

In the latter part of the 19th century, Adolphus Busch, who owned a brewery in St. Louis, was traveling in Bohemia and was impressed by the local beer he tasted in the town of Ceske Budejovice. Mr. Busch liked the name and slogan for the beer so much (Budweis Beer of Kings), that when he returned to St. Louis in 1876, he introduced "Budweiser King of Beers." This led to the "Budweiser trademark dispute." The first dispute began in 1895 and was settled in 1911 by allowing the Czechs to sell Budweiser in Europe, but not in the United States. The disagreement flared up again and

Anheuser Busch almost purchased Budvar. This was prevented by the Czech government taking control of the brewery, which it continues to own today. As of 2007, Anheuser-Busch signed an agreement with the European Union giving Budejovicky Budvar exclusive control over the Budweiser brand name in Europe. In the United States and Canada Budvar is sold under the Czechvar label and distributed by Anheuser-Busch.

The most well-known beers in the Czech Republic today include Pilsner Urquell, Budweiser Budvar Gambrinus (a sister of Pilsner Urquell), Staropramen, Prague's favorite, and Cosell. Czechs are so satisfied with their beer choices that less than 1% of beer consumed is imported. Also, very little bottled or canned beer is sold in the Czech Republic.

One big step toward standardizing beer quality was the development of the Balling scale by Czech chemist Karl Balling in the mid-19th century. The number of Balling degrees on the beer label indicates the amount of malt sugar used at the beginning of fermentation. It has to do with the strength of the taste. Most Czech pubs still designate beer at 10, 12, or more degrees, referring to the sugar content of the beer. A higher degree means higher malt and a little higher alcohol content. A 10 -degree beer will have between 3 and 4% alcohol and a 12- degree beer will be between 5 and 6% alcohol.

A recent trend in the Czech Republic has been a revival of interest in unpasteurized beers. You will see it prominently advertised on the menu outside restaurants and pubs. Only a select few, high-volume, places are allowed to serve this beer. The beer is kept in pressurized tanks and delivered fresh weekly. Pasteurizing beer helps beer to last longer, but heating the beer damages the flavor. The unpasteurized beer is slightly cloudy and has a more pronounced hops flavor.

Following the fall of Communism, 1989, the Czech breweries began a period of modernization and consolidation. By the mid-1990s, there were just 60 breweries left, with most of the biggest owned by multinational companies. However, in the last decade, a new breed of micro-breweries has sprung up all over the Country, and now there are over 100 operating breweries. Some of these micro-breweries in the smaller towns are wonderful combinations of brewery, hotel, pub and restaurant, in a beautiful setting.

The city of **Brno** is home to the **Starobrno Brewery** and the place is filled with pubs and bars, all serving the local brew. Two outstanding places are the **Pegasus Pub** and the **Pivovarska** family restaurant with an outdoor stage and entertainment.

The tiny hilltop town of LOKET has the **Svaty Florian**, a family-run brewery, hotel, restaurant, and pub in a beautiful setting.

The village of HARRACHOV has had a glass works operating continuously since 1712, and tours are available. What is unique here is the **Novasad Restaurant,** which is located in the glass factory and serves superb unfiltered, unpasteurized beer to guests and to the factory workers.

Regent Beer has been made in the town of TREBON since 1379. The brewery was founded by Augustinian monks, and expanded in 1482 by the Rosenberg family, which explains the five petal rose on the label.

The Czech Republic is very proud of its beer; it is like wine to the French. As a result, it is important to know some of the customs and etiquette associated with drinking in the Republic.

First, it is a surprise to learn that most pubs serve only

one brand of beer. Because each pub sells only one brand, that brewery provides pretty much everything required for the place's functioning: table cloths, coasters, umbrellas for outside, even the taps and the tap handles come from the brewery. Whatever is on the sign out front, that is what the pub serves, and don't waste time by asking for something different. It was this type of marketing in the United States, with big brewers buying up all the bars that caused the downfall of the saloon during the late 1800s and early 1900s. After Prohibition in the U.S., the government prohibited breweries from participating directly in the wholesale distribution and retail sale of alcohol.

Just because the Czech pub only offers one brand of beer doesn't mean there is only one choice available. You are likely to encounter a number of beers from light to dark and with varying degree designations. As explained earlier, the Czech degree system indicates the amount of malt in the brew, a higher degree means higher malt, and a little higher alcohol content, 10 degrees to 12 degrees is the most common.

The most traditional, and the most popular beer in the Country is a light Pilsner, this is what almost everyone drinks. Darker beers are available; but they are not like the normal porters and stouts, these are much sweeter and are considered inferior to their lighter counterparts.

When you sit down in a pub it is not necessary to wave the waiter down or shout across the room; the waiter assumes you want a beer and will bring one to you without asking. Subsequent rounds will appear without asking and the waiter will make small marks on a strip of paper for each round. Do not lose the strip of paper or decide to doodle on it, this is your bill. A short mark is a small beer and an "X" is a larger one.

It seems odd to Americans and British visitors to have

a beer delivered to their table with an inch of foam on top and be called "full." This head of foam is thick, so thick that some experienced drinkers can lift it off with a knife and place it on the table. This is only done as a demonstration since the foam is very important to the quality of the beer.

Once you have the beer in front of you, toasting your companions becomes an important ritual. The typical toast is "to your health." As we have seen in some other countries, it is very important to touch glasses while looking your companion directly in the eye. Always look them in the eye; it is a sign of severe disrespect to avoid eye contact.

Because of another drinking custom, toasting becomes a little tricky in large groups. No matter how many people are toasting and looking each other in the eye, no one is allowed to cross over or intersect anyone else's arms. The penalty for violating this rule is seven years of bad sex. The good news is that you only have to observe this tradition on the first drink. It would be nearly impossible to keep observing these rules as the evening draws on.

It's interesting that most Czechs don't sip their beer; they gulp it, taking a full mouthful each time, and then putting their glass down for a few minutes before repeating the process. For a group that reveres their beer, it seems like they should be sipping, not gulping. It's hard to explain, but somehow the beer seems to taste better, more refreshing when you gulp it.

As soon as you are about to finish your glass another will arrive. And remember, one of the positively worst things you can do is to leave a beer unfinished, for any reason. This is the highest insult you can offer to a server, a bartender, even to the bar itself. Drink up, or get a friend to finish it, but don't leave an unfinished beer on the table.

Beer is relatively cheap in the Czech Republic, and tipping is limited to the major cities; elsewhere, rounding the bill up to the nearest 5 or 10 is the custom.

The drinking age in the Czech Republic is 18, and the driving while intoxicated laws are strict. The blood-alcohol limit for drivers is zero, no alcohol in the blood stream. Since random breathalyzer stops are common, and if convicted, the sentence is one year in jail, you simply cannot drink and drive.

Beer is definitely the national drink in the Czech Republic; but there are a couple of other favorite spirits that are unique to the Country.

Slivovitz is a fiery, potent plum brandy that originated in MORAVIA, where the best brands still originate. This is known locally as "Moravian Moonshine."

Common or garden variety Slivovitz is crystal clear and is traditionally drunk straight from a shot glass. Slivovitz distilling became a cottage industry in 1835, when the Hapsburg Empire relaxed the excise tax laws. Every farm had its own pot still and "Slivovitz season" was part of the agricultural calendar. Some natives insist that the best brew is still homemade.

The biggest brand in the business is R. Jelinek, based in Vizovice in South Moravia. Some of the brands offered by this distillery have been aged in oak barrels, take on a golden color, and are much smoother in taste than the regular version.

Although illegal in some parts of Europe and the United States, absinthe has enjoyed something of a renaissance in the Czech Republic. Absinthe was a popular item with Parisian artists and poets in the 19th century. The ban stems from the potentially lethal green wormwood from which the product is distilled. Distinctively anise flavored, at 170 proof, the stuff is bitter, green, and virtually undrinkable straight. To make it vaguely palatable, you can dilute with water, or traditionally ignite an absinthe-soaked spoonful of sugar and then mix the caramelized mess with the absinthe.

Becherovka is herbal liquor made from a secret recipe in the Bohemian spa town of Karlovy Vary. This drink is supposed to have medicinal properties, and indeed, has a pronounced medicinal taste. Despite the unusual taste, it can be great when mixed with tonic and other mixers.

Beer overshadows wine totally in the Czech Republic, but there have been vineyards in southern Moravia since the 14th century. One Czech specialty is "Burcak" a very young, sweet, fizzy, misty wine of varying alcoholic content, often very strong.

Plzen or Pilsen, 55 miles west of Prague, the capital of West Bohemia, was founded in 1295 and has been built on beer and bombs. The huge Skoda Ironworks was the second largest European armaments factory (second only to Krupps in Germany). It is also home to the Pilsner Urquell brewery, producer of what many consider to be the best beer in the world. The excellent quality of the beer is allegedly due to the combination of the soft local water and the world-renowned Zates hops.

Tours of the brewery are available, and at the finish you can settle into the vast **Na Spike pub**, the Czech Republic's largest, for a sampling of the brew. You will notice the triumphal arch built in 1892 to commemorate the beer's 50th birthday; note that it has been depicted on every bottle of Pilsner Urquell ever since.

There is also the Pivovarska Brewery Museum. Hundreds of exhibits testify to the history of brewing and the culture of drinking beer from the earliest times to the present day. Exhibits include the smallest beer barrel in the world (a mere 1 cm cubed), and a huge collection of Baroque beer mugs.

U Salzmann Hotel houses **Pilsen's** oldest and world-famous pub. The wood-paneled historical site is located at Prazska 8, downtown.

Ceske Budejovice (Budweis in German), in South Bohemia, is famous for its local brew, Budvar, also, confusingly known by its German name, Budweiser, except in the United States. The Budvar Brewery has a modern pub located on the premises and tours are offered daily. The brewery also operates the **Budvarka Pub** in the downtown Maly Pivovar Hotel.

The best Czech pubs, known as "pivince," from the Czech word for beer "pivo," are straightforward affairs: wooden tables, benches, beer nuts, and an endless supply of beer. The clientele are mostly male, there's rarely any music, and apart from an occasional game of cards or dominoes, drinking is the main pursuit. And getting drunk is rare. Most pubs serve inexpensive Czech food, which goes well with all the beer. In addition to these traditional drinking spots, the larger cities like Prague have a variety of places to consume alcohol, including fancy bars, hotels and nightclubs, as well as the ever-present European Irish pub.

PRAGUE, **U Fleků** (224-934-019). This brewpub is a Prague institution dating from 1499, making it one of the oldest brewpubs in the world. Only one beer is served, oddly enough, a dark lager, home-brewed, 13° black beer known as Flek. This place is big and seats over 1,200 people, and is truly one of the world's most spectacular taverns. Paintings of brewing, drinking, and enjoying beer are everywhere. There is a trademark clock out front and an attractive courtyard with an oompah band. Don't miss the Swedish cannonball embedded in the wall in the courtyard. It found its way there during the last year of the Thirty Years' War in 1648.

Na Slamniku claims to be the oldest pub in Prague, serving beer to customers for over five centuries. Originally a coaching inn, this historic pub is located on Stromovka Park, which was originally the Kings Deer Park and was only open to the public one day a year, the Tuesday after Easter.

Budvarca (222-960-820). Owned by Czech brewer Budvar and serves several very special and rare, Budvar brews. These include Budvar pale ale and Bud Strong. In addition to the excellent beer selection, this place has outstanding traditional Czech food.

U Medvidků (224-211-916). Located in a former brewery dating from the 13th century. This pub has decor from the turn of the 20th century. Beer is shipped here directly from the Budvar Brewery in Ceske Budejovice.

U Rudolfina (222-313-088). This place has old-fashioned charm, making it one of the most authentic Czech pubs. This was one of the first places in the world to offer unpasteurized beer from pressurized tanks rather than from kegs.

U Zlateho Tygra (222-221-111). This spot is old, crowded, smoky and famous. It is renowned as the hangout of one of the Country's best-known and beloved writers, Bohumil Hrabal, who died in 1997. Locals consider the Pilsner Urquell served here on tap to be the best in the Country.

Pivovar Staropramen (257-191-200). Staropramen means "the source" and this is the brewery for Staropramen beer and includes a restaurant and bar on the premises. Several varieties of beer are sold here, including one that is not available anywhere else.

Provarsky (296-216-666). This brewpub has only been around for a decade, but the quality of the beer makes it a big hit with the locals. Czech lager (in light, dark, and mixed varieties), wheat beer, and a range of flavored beers (coffee, banana and cherry) are all brewed on the premises.

DENMARK

"The mouth of a perfectly happy man is filled with beer." Ancient Egyptian Proverb, 2200 BC

The drinking culture in Denmark is much more open-minded than in Sweden, Norway, and Finland. Buying alcohol in shops is legal at age 16 and in bars at 18. There is no minimum drinking age. There is a tradition of allowing teens to begin drinking alcohol after Confirmation, normally 13 to 14 years old. This custom dates back over 200 years. In another liberal twist, beer is available from vending machines. Beer, wine, and spirits are sold in regular grocery stores – no government monopoly here. On the conservative side, the blood-alcohol limit is .05 versus .02 in Sweden and .08 in most countries, including the U.S.

The earliest archaeological evidence of a potent kind of beer consumed by the Danish Vikings is 700 A.D. The drink called "Miod" was produced by fermenting a solution of water and honey with grain mash; the result was a drink with very high alcohol content.

The Danes continue to be big consumers of pale, lager type beer known in Danish as Pilsner. The best known Danish brands of beer are Carlsberg and Tuborg, which merged in 1970, creating a near monopoly for Carlsberg. Denmark holds the lead for having the most breweries per capita of anywhere in the world. And let us not forget, in survey after survey, the Danes are chosen as the happiest people on earth. This is despite, or perhaps because of, paying the highest taxes in the world. Interesting fact, highest taxes, happiest people. And remember, these high taxes do not include taxes on alcohol.

Danish industrialist, J. C. Jacobsen revolutionized the world of brewing when his brewery, Carlsberg, bred a pure strain of lager yeast. This enabled Carlsberg to achieve a large and consistent output, and lager has been the most popular style of beer in Denmark since 1847.

In spite of Carlsberg's dominance for many years, recently the Danish beer landscape has included many new small breweries, brewpubs, and microbreweries. Wine is a very popular drink in Denmark, especially at dinnertime, and wine selections in stores and restaurants are extensive.

Carlsberg Breweries is owned by the Carlsberg Foundation, which is a major supporter of Danish art, science, and humanities – things that touch every aspect of Danish life. Carlsberg's scope and commitment to the culture of a single country is unique in the world. The financial support includes the Copenhagen Art Museum, Tivoli Gardens, the History Museum and scores of annual musical events.

The Carlsberg brewery was constructed in 1847, and produces three million bottles of beer per day. Self-guided tours are available every day, and free beer at the finish. You would have to say that Carlsberg and Tuborg are Denmark's national drinks.

The most popular spirit in Denmark is the Aalborg-produced aquavit. This is available in several dozen varieties. In Denmark, Aquavit is always swallowed in a single shot, not sipped, followed by a chaser of beer.

Another popular Danish drink is a liqueur, Peter

Heering, also known as Cherry Heering. This liqueur was invented in the 1830s by Peter Heering. It is ruby red and has a complex, black-cherry flavor that's not overly sweet. This drink is sipped straight or served over ice cream. Available world-wide, it's an important Danish export.

Glogg, a mulled wine in other Scandinavian countries, is a favorite at Christmas time.

COPENHAGEN is just loaded with bars, especially beer bars with happy people having a fun time. Supposedly, **Hviids Vinstue** is the oldest bar in Copenhagen. It certainly looks it, dating from 1723.

ENGLAND

Lady Astor: *"Sir, if you were my husband I would poison your drink."* Winston Churchill: *"Madam, if you were my wife I would drink it."*

England is the home of the pub, short for public house, and the pub is the home of British beer: bitter beer, lager and stout.

There are approximately 53,500 public houses in the Commonwealth (Britain, Northern Ireland, Australia, New Zealand and Canada). Public houses are socially and culturally different from places such as bars, saloons, brew pubs and nightclubs. In many places, especially in small villages, a pub can be the focal point of the community. Each pub generally has regulars, known as "locals," people who drink there regularly. The pub they visit most often is known as their "local."

The English have been drinking beer since the Bronze Age, 3000 BC, but it was the arrival of the Romans and the network of roads that established the first inns called tabernae. When the Romans left, the Anglo-Saxons established alehouses that grew out of normal domestic dwellings. The "Alewife" would put a green bush up on a pole to let people know her brew was ready. These alehouses became the place for locals to meet gossip and arrange mutual activities. This was the beginning of the pub. They became so commonplace that in 965 A.D. King Edgar decreed that there should be no more than one alehouse per village.

The tabernae, established by the Romans, became the tavern and eventually was called an inn. The thing that separates an inn from a pub is inns provide accommodations. Inns tend to be grander and more long-lived establishments and historically have provided not only food and lodging, but also stabling and fodder for the travelers' horses. There are many famous historical inns throughout Britain. Famous London examples of inns include "The George" and "The Tabard."

The alehouses continued to serve traditional English ale, and the practice of adding hops to fermented malt was introduced from the Netherlands in the early 15th century. Alehouses would each brew their own distinctive ale, but by the end of the 17th century, almost all beer and ale were brewed by commercial breweries.

Gin became very popular in England in the 18th century. By 1740, the production of gin had increased to six times that of beer, and because of its low price, it became popular with the poor. Over half of the 15,000 drinking establishments in London were so-called "gin shops." By the early 19th century, the "Gin Craze" had spread from London to most of the major cities and towns in Britain.

These "gin shops" or "gin mills" were mostly illegal, unlicensed, bawdy, low, and unruly drinking dens. Charles Dickens describes these places in his "Sketches by Boz" published in 1835-1836.

Beer, meanwhile, continued to be viewed as harmless, nutritious, and even healthy. To combat the gin problem and reduce public drunkenness, the Beer Act of 1830 established a new licensed and regulated alcohol outlet termed the "Beer House." The idea was cheap, readily available beer would wean the drinkers off the evils of gin. Any householder could secure a permit to sell beer or cider in his home, and even brew his own on the premises. The sale of spirits and fortified wines was strictly prohibited. Within eight years 46,000 Beer Houses had opened across the country.

Finally, in 1869, new licensing laws stemmed the tide and the public house began to appear. A vast majority of Beer Houses applied for the new licenses and became public houses.

After the development of the large London breweries in the late 18th century, the trend grew for pubs to become "tied houses," which could only sell beer from one brewery. Pubs not committed in this way were known as "Free Houses." The common arrangement for a tied house was for the brewery to own the pub and rent it to a private individual.

As the 20th century rolled in the trend was for the breweries to run their pubs directly using paid managers. In the 1980s breweries began exiting the pub business and corporations (public companies), formed pub chains, which own hundreds of pubs in a particular region of Britain.

Two of the most charming characteristics of British pubs are on the outside, the sign, and the name. Originally, because customers could not read, the sign was used to readily identify a pub. In 1393, King Richard II compelled all landlords to erect signs outside their pubs. The earliest signs were often not painted but consisted, for example, of paraphernalia connected with the brewing process, such as bunches of hops or brewing implements, which were suspended above the door.

The most common pub names in Britain are the following: **The Crown** - represents the King or Queen.

The **Red Lion** - James I ordered a red lion to be displayed outside all public houses.

Royal Oak - King Charles II escaped by hiding in the branches of an oak tree.

Swan - a heraldic symbol of powerful families.

White Hart - the white hart (stag) was the heraldic symbol of the King.

Other subjects that lent themselves to visual depiction included famous battles (Trafalgar, Waterloo); explorers' names, sporting heroes, and animals. All pubs granted their license in 1780 were called the Royal George after King George III, and the 20th anniversary of his coronation.

Most pubs still have decorated signs hanging over their doors and these almost always bear the name of the pub, both in words and pictorial representation. The Irish custom of displaying the owner's name is not used in Britain, since the pub is usually owned by a large corporation.

Traditionally, pubs in England were places to drink, and very little emphasis was placed on food, other than "bar snacks." Food did not begin to appear on a widespread basis until the 1960s. The quantity and quality have gradually improved, and since the 1990s, most pubs serve lunch and dinner. Now, there is a pub category termed "the gastropub" that concentrates on quality food. The concept of a restaurant in the pub has served to reinvigorate both pub culture and British dining.

You have to be 18 years old to order a drink in a British pub. Some pubs will allow people over 14 years old to go inside if they are with someone who is over 18, but they are not allowed to go to the bar or to have an alcoholic drink.

Sometimes 16- or 17-year-olds are allowed to have an alcoholic drink with a meal at the table.

Smoking is banned in enclosed public places throughout the UK since 2006 (including pubs, bars and restaurants).

Opening and closing times depend on the conditions of the pub's license. Standard times are 11 AM to 11 PM, about 10 minutes before closing time the landlord will ring a bell, and announce "Time, gentlemen, please." The pub is not allowed to serve drinks after closing time; but, of course, you have 20 minutes to a half hour to finish your drinks.

British pubs have been disappearing at a rapid pace and over 6000 have closed since 2005. More than half the villages in Britain now have no pub at all. The village church can close, long since the preserve of the flower-arranging ladies; the local grocery may go, eclipsed by the distant supermarket's prices; but the disappearing of a pub means the loss of the beating heart of the village. Pubs are the preserve of history; they hold trophies and memories both sad and glad. Gone are the pub games: darts, skittles, marbles and quoits, and the marvelous quiet corner to tell your stories, or listen to someone else's. At the Widow's Son in Brawley-By-Bow there is a hanging bundle of hot cross buns to which another bun has been added every Good Friday for the past 150 Years.

In a highly stratified society, the pub was open to everyone; the worker, the merchant and the Lord. You were able to meet and mingle and discuss opinions with people you otherwise would not encounter.

The pub is vanishing for many separate reasons. Some blame the smoking ban, but this hasn't been true in other countries. Almost half the pubs, 40%, are tied to the giant chains or "pubcos," and must buy their beer from one brewer at premium prices. In addition, the tax on beer is ten times as high as Germany. It all makes buying a supermarket six-pack and drinking at home attractive. In addition, alcohol consumption has been declining in Britain for the past five years, and is now below the European Union average.

Perhaps the biggest source of the decline in pub attendance is the trend away from communal imbibing. Just as in other countries around the globe, people are spending time alone in front of the computer, television set, iPad or whatever. Community engagement in all forms has been declining world-wide for the past 30 years; but the explosion of electronic devices has really accelerated the disappearance of sociability among younger people. Just observe any public event and you'll be overwhelmed by the number of people using their cell phone, iPad, BlackBerry or Kindle - they have retracted into a solitary online world. This is not the form of social engagement that gave the pub its charm or reason for being. A French poet, Hilaire Belloc, once remarked, "*When you have lost your inns, drown your empty selves, for you will have lost the heart of England.*"

Prince Charles and others, including the "Campaign to Save Rural England" are now striving to save Britain's pubs. Pubs are needed, even when every social and economic indicator is running hard against them. In some rural villages the local population has banded together to buy the local pub and allow it to re-open.

The drink of choice in the pub has always been beer; however, wine and cocktails are beginning to take over. British beers come in three main varieties. Bitter is traditional British beer (also known as ale). It is quite strong, and leaves a bitter taste in your mouth and is served at room temperature.

There are light ales (mild), strong ales, and real ale. Real ale is a term used for a beer brewed from hops, malted barley, yeast and pure water, then stored in wooden casks until served. Stout is very dark brown and bitter, an example is the Irish brew called Guinness. Lager is a lighter-colored type of imported beer and is served cold. Examples are Australia's Fosters, German Becks, and Belgium's Stella Artois. When ordering a beer in Britain always specify whether you want a pint or a half-pint, otherwise you will get a pint.

The English have a drinking routine described as "session drinking." It focuses on the community aspect of drinking, rather than the amount of alcohol consumed (binge drinking). With session drinking the goal is to drink a variety of alcohol that has very low proof so that it can be drunk all night without resulting in intoxication. These "sessions" typically take place at family gatherings, celebrations, and other socially minded events.

Cider is a traditional English alcoholic beverage, and sales have been increasing for the past several years. There are two broad types of cider in the UK - the West tradition and the East Anglia tradition. The cloudy, unfiltered ciders made in the West Country are often called "scrumpy," a local term for small apples. There are a host of small cider producers in the West; but Gaymer Cider Company is also located here and it is the largest cider plant in Europe.

The mass-produced commercial cider is clear in appearance from filtration, and is usually pasteurized and carbonated. This cider has an alcohol content of about 7.5%. It is the cheapest way to buy alcohol in the UK.

Wine has become a very popular drink in Britain and a limited selection can be found in most pubs. The younger population has made a relatively new addition to the drinking scene very popular, wine bars. Very little wine is produced in England, so the selections are all imported.

Whisky, spelled without an "e," means Scotch in the UK. Canadian and Irish whiskey (spelled with an "e") are readily available; but American bourbon and rye are found only in the best-stocked bars.

In summertime, a popular British drink is Pimms, a mixture developed by James Pimms, owner of a popular London oyster house in the 1840s. It can be served on the rocks, but it is usually consumed as a Pimm's Cup. This drink can be made with a variety of ingredients including citrus fruits and lemonade. A typical recipe follows: take a tall glass, fill it with ice, add a slice of lemon or orange, cucumber spike, two ounces of Pimm's liquor, and finish with a splash of club soda, 7-Up or Tom Collins mix.

Keep in mind the English drink everything at a warmer temperature than Americans are used to. So if you like ice, be sure to ask for lots of it, otherwise you will get a measly cube or two.

A source of famous pubs is the annual "Famous Grouse Famous Pub" contest sponsored by Famous Grouse scotch. The drinking public is invited to nominate their favorite pub based on history and character. Each year the top 100 famous pubs are selected. As stated earlier, Britain has thousands of pubs, and many of them are hundreds of years old. The following is a brief list of some of the more interesting ones and why they are worth a visit.

As in almost every country a number of pubs claim to be the oldest surviving establishment in the UK, although in some cases original buildings have been demolished and replaced on the same site. Others are ancient buildings that have seen uses other than as a pub during their history.

Ye Olde Fighting Cocks – St Albans Hertfordshire This pub holds the Guinness World Record as the oldest pub in England. It is an 11th century structure on an eighth century site.

Ye Olde Trip to Jerusalem – NOTTINGHAM. This place claims to be the oldest inn in England. It was built on the site of the Nottingham Castle Brewhouse, dated 1188; the present building dates from 1650.

The Nags Head – BURNTWOOD. There has been a pub on this site since at least 1086, since it is mentioned in the Doomsday book. The present pub dates back to the 16th century.

The Old Ferryboat Inn, HOLYWELL, CAMBRIDGESHIRE. The foundations of this place date to 905 AD and there is archaeological evidence of ale being served as early as 560 AD.

The Cott Inn – DARTINGTON, near TOTNES, DEVON. Constructed in 1320, this place is considered the second oldest inn in England. This is a low, stone building with a thatched roof.

Man and Scythe – Bolton. This pub is mentioned by name in a charter of 1251, but the current building is dated 1631. The cellars are the only surviving part of the older structure.

A few more ancient pubs include the **Bingley Arms** in LEEDS, 905 A.D.; **The Old Salutation** in NOTTINGHAM,

1240, and the **Adam and Eve** in NORWICH, 1249 A.D.
Here are some other record-holding pubs in England.

Largest – **The Moon Under Water** in MANCHESTER is located in a converted cinema.

Smallest – There is quite a list of pubs claiming to be the smallest, but a few with clever names are the following:

The Nutshell – Bury Street - EDMONDS.

The Little Gem – AYLESFORD, KENT.

The Signal Box Inn – CLEETHORPES.

The *longest bar* in all of Britain is at the **Cittie of Yorke** – 22 High Holborn, LONDON. This place resembles a giant medieval hall; the pub has existed at this location since 1430.

Naturally, there are many pubs that have been featured in English literature and poetry, and others that have played a role in British history.

Dun Cow Pub – Sedgefield, COUNTY DURHAM. U.S. President George W. Bush had lunch here with Prime Minister Tony Blair during his state visit in 2003.

Ye Olde Cheshire Cheese – 145 Fleet Street, LONDON. Charles Dickens was a frequent visitor here, and was also a customer at **Ye Olde Cock Tavern,** and many others in London. This pub dates from 1667, the year after the great fire of London. This pub was the most regular of Dr. Johnson and Dickens many "locals."

Fitzroy Tavern – 16 Charlotte Street, LONDON. This was a major intellectual hangout during a period from the 1920s to the mid-1950s. George Orwell and Dylan Thomas were patrons.

The Red Lion – Parliament Square, LONDON. This pub is used by political journalists and members of Parliament. The pub is equipped with a bell alarm that summons members of Parliament back to the chambers when a vote is required.

Crown Tavern – Cleckenwell Street, LONDON. Vladimir Lenin and a young Joseph Stalin met here in 1902 when it was known as the Crown and Anchor.

Prospect Whitley – 57 Wrapping Wall, LONDON. This is one of London's most historic pubs. Charles Dickens used to stop by and the famous watercolorist J.M.W. Turner came for weeks at a time to study views of the Thames River. In the 17th century the notorious hanging Judge Jeffries used to get drunk here while overseeing hangings at the adjoining execution dock.

The Grenadier – 18 Wilton Row, Belgrave Square, LONDON. Probably London's best-known pub. This place was frequented by the Duke of Wellington's officers on leave from fighting Napoleon. The basement houses the original bar and a skittles alley used by the officers. The bar counter has an original pewter top and the walls are filled with military memorabilia.

The Salisbury – Covent Garden, LONDON. This place resembles a big Victorian gin-parlor – cut-glass mirrors, soft velvet banquettes, and lighting fixtures of bronze girls in togas. Dates from 1892.

Pickerel Inn – 30 Magdalen Street, CAMBRIDGE. This is a wonderful old inn dating back 600 years.

The Eagle – Bene't Street, CAMBRIDGE. This is where Francis Crick interrupted customers' lunchtime to announce on February 28, 1953 that he and James Watson had discovered the secret of life, "The DNA double helix." The place has been famous ever since. Also, the ceiling is covered with signatures of RAF pilots serving in World War II.

The Ship Inn – EXETER, DEVON. This was a hangout for Sir Francis Drake and Sir Walter Raleigh.

The Turks Head – PENZANCE, CORNWALL. Dating from 1233, this place is filled with artifacts. Pirates and smugglers used an underground tunnel to transport their bounty from the harbor to the inn.

The Eagle and Child Pub – 49 St. Giles Street, OXFORD. From the 1930s to the 1960s this was the meeting place of C.S. Lewis, J.R.R. Tolkien, and their circle of literary friends who called themselves the "inklings." It is owned by the college, but open to the public.

Sherlock Holmes – 10 N. Cumberland Street, Trafalgar Square, LONDON. Arthur Conan Doyle was a regular here. It figures in "The Hound of the Baskerville's," and you can see the hound's supposed head and other Holmes' memorabilia in the bar.

The Mayflower – 117 Rotherhithe Street, LONDON. This 17th century riverside inn is on the very spot where the Pilgrims set sail for Plymouth Rock.

Lamb and Flag – 33 Rose Street, Covent Garden, LONDON. This 17th century pub was once known as the Bucket of Blood, because the upstairs room was used as a ring for bare-knuckle boxing matches.

All these pubs continue to operate today. What a wonderful treat to be able to have a beer in a place that has been serving customers for hundreds and hundreds of years. To be able to sit in the same pub that was used by Charles Dickens, Arthur Conan Doyle, Joseph Stalin, George Orwell or Wellington's officers - such a wonderful opportunity.

The current brewpub concept, which is so popular in the United States, began at the **Litchborough Brewery** founded in 1975 in the Northhamptonshire village of the same name. Of course pubs brewing their own beer go back to the medieval times in England, but commercial breweries had forced almost all of these to close over the last several hundred years. By the mid-1970s, only four remained operating in the Country: All Nations, the Old Swan, the Three Times, and the Blue Anchor. **The Blue Anchor** in HELSTON, CORNWALL, was established in 1400 and is regarded as the oldest brewpub in England. Now the brewpub has returned to favor, and there are many fine examples throughout the Country.

Some current examples of small, independent brewpubs include the following: The **Ministry of Ale** in Burnley, The **Masons Arms** in Headington, Oxford, The **Brunswick Inn,** Derby, **The Old Cannon Brewery** in Bury, St. Edmunds.

NORTHERN AND SOUTHERN EUROPEAN CULTURES

"The people of the Mediterranean began to emerge from barbarism when they learned to cultivate the olive and the vine." –

Thucydides, Greek historian (460 BC – 395 BC)

The northern and southern regions of Europe have traditionally been seen as having different drinking cultures. The southern European (Mediterranean) drinking patterns are typically found in Italy, Spain, Portugal, southern France and Greece. The northern European patterns tend to be found in Scandinavia, the Netherlands, Britain, and Germany. A blend of these two norms exists in northern France, Austria, and Switzerland.

The southern drinking culture accepts wine, the most commonly consumed alcoholic beverage, as a normal part of the daily diet. Wine is generally consumed with meals, drunkenness is not accepted even at celebrations, and children are given diluted wine at meals. A few other characteristics are prevalent throughout this region; there are very few strict control policies concerning the use of alcohol;

there is little social pressure to drink, Latin-based languages are spoken, the viticulture is a major industry, and all of these countries were once provinces within the Roman Empire.

There is quite a contrast to these Mediterranean patterns when we examine the characteristics of northern European countries. First, wine is not the beverage of choice, grain-based drinks and beer are the commonly consumed beverages, and they are most often consumed on occasions other than with meals. The northern attitude toward drinking is one of ambivalence (extremes of heavy drinking versus abstinence). Heavy drinking occurs on weekends or special occasions and some people drink for the sole purpose of getting drunk. Public drunkenness is more or less accepted; but a high percentage of the population does not drink alcoholic beverages at all. Control policies are numerous, and include both the selling and consumption of alcohol. Drinking age limitations are often established and alcohol for children is prohibited, even at family functions. It is interesting that throughout history, temperance movements have primarily occurred in these northern cultures.

Two other traits symbolize this region. First, there is no viticulture industry due to the cooler climate, and second, with the exception of Britain, none of these countries was a former Roman province, and the languages spoken are non-Latin.

There are several theories as to why the drinking cultures of Northern and Southern Europe are so different. First, of course, grapes grow naturally in the southern Mediterranean, and cannot be grown normally in northern Europe. Second, the role of the Roman Empire appears to be significant in the areas it dominated. As they conquered these regions in the period from the late third century BC through the mid-first century A.D., they brought urbanization, Latin language and viticulture. Although we are all familiar with drawings and descriptions of the drunken Roman banquets and orgies, historians claim the more normal drinking culture for Romans was one of moderation, and drunkenness was a rarity.

The viticulture industry and the wine trade were important parts of the Roman Empire. Wine was considered an integral part of civilized life, and by 100 BC wine in some form was the daily drink of all Romans, both rich and poor. Wine taverns and cafés were common throughout most of Roman history. These establishments were found in urban areas and along country roads from the third century until the end of the Empire, and many examples remain today, particularly in Pompeii and Herculaneum.

Historians believe that infrequent, but heavy drinking, developed among northern Celtic and Germanic tribes in ancient times because alcoholic beverages were not always available due to variations in the weather.

Beer (malt liquor), cider, and Mead were the common alcoholic drinks of northern Europeans. History is filled with descriptions of heavy "feast drinking" among these people, while on the other hand, there are few descriptions of drunken Italians or Gallic Franks.

Unlike the southern region, northern areas of Europe had a "hierarchical" system in which only the very rich were able to consume alcoholic beverages on a regular basis. In southern areas, wine was available year-round for everyone, and was even used as payment to fulfill social obligations. Malt liquor produced in ancient times, without preservatives, tends to spoil quickly, thus people had to consume it while it was fresh. Mead, which depends on the honey supply, was a scarce item and grain and fruits, which were seasonal and also used for food, were also limited. It is felt that this limited supply of alcohol combined with a climate that forced people indoors, and also included extremes of seasonal light and dark cycles – all this contributed to heavy episodic drinking in northern Europe.

Thus we have the Germans with their beer festivals, Scandinavians with their alcoholic reputation, and the British Isles with their dark, enclosed pubs, and the Irish with their formidable drinking reputation.

Over the past 20 years these established drinking patterns have begun to change among the younger people. Particularly in the South, wine is being replaced by beer, and drinking in moderation at meals is being displaced by "binge" drinking. Meanwhile, in the North there's been a significant growth in the use of wine.

FRANCE

Eating is for the stomach, drinking is for the soul." — Till

A single national alcoholic drink, French wine, has been defined as a "national treasure." Through its soil, its people, its history, its culture, its customs, literature and songs; France is inextricably linked to the vine and to wine. For French people, wine, or more precisely, the love of good wine, characterizes Frenchness in much the same way as being born in France, fighting for liberty, or speaking French.

For countries from which statistics are available, France has consistently had the highest annual per capita alcohol consumption. This is largely due to the amount of wine consumed in the country. However, recent trends have shown a decrease in drinking since World War II, and a general convergence of total alcohol consumption among the European Union nations. There exists major differences between the consumption of wine between men and women in France, and this is linked to the idea of masculinity within the French culture. Women tend to drink both lower quantity, and lower quality wines, including wine mixed with water as a lighter drink. Wine drinking is comparatively heavier in the wine producing regions of France.

The French are not part of the northern European tradition of "guilty pleasure" (anything that's fun must be sinful). The French attitude of "faire plaisir" (to give pleasure), whether to oneself or to others, is embedded in the French culture in the idea of "the civilization française." It permeates every aspect of their lives, including enjoying drinking. Hence, wine is served at every meal, and is on the menu at McDonald's and Disneyland.

It is incomprehensible to the French mind that if something like wine gives you pleasure - how would guilt even fit into the equation? As a result, the French learn to drink at a young age and drunken behavior is rarely a problem. There has never been an effort to bring about Prohibition in France.

As outlined earlier, France, especially southern France, considers wine a normal part of the daily diet and viticulture is a major industry. In fact, measured by value, France is the largest wine producer in the world. Northern France, in the area adjoining Germany, Alsace and Strasburg, produce notable wines and beers. There are strong German influences here and the wines are mainly whites, Riesling, Pinot Blanc and Muscat. This area is home to Kronenbourg, one of Europe's biggest sellers in the beer market.

French "cider" is an alcoholic drink produced predominantly in the provinces of Normandy and Brittany along the English Channel. Until about 1950, cider was the second most popular drink in France, after wine, but an increase in the popularity of beer displaced cider's market share outside the traditional cider-producing regions.

Calvados is produced throughout Normandy. It is made by a process called double distillation of cider. In the first pass, the result is a liquid containing 28 to 30% alcohol. In the second distillation, the amount of alcohol is increased to about 40%. The product is similar to applejack in the

United States.

A popular aperitif in Normandy is Pommeau, a drink produced by blending unfermented apple juice and apple brandy in the barrel (the high alcoholic content of the brandy stops the fermentation process of the cider and the blend takes on the character of the aged barrel).

Another popular cocktail is Kir Breton (or Kir Normand) made with cider and Cassis, rather than white wine and Cassis for the traditional Kir. Cassis is a black currant liquer.

French wine originated in the sixth century B.C. with the colonization of Southern Gaul by Greek settlers. Grapes soon emerged with the founding of the Greek colony of Marseille. The Roman Empire arrived later and licensed regions in the south to produce wines.

St. Martin of Tours (316-397 A.D.) was actively engaged in both spreading Christianity and planting vineyards. St. Martin proposed that every church and monastery become self-sufficient by establishing its own vineyard for sacramental, medicinal and beverage purposes. During the dark and turbulent period of the Middle Ages, monasteries preserved and improved the skills for making wine.

Wine production followed a bumpy road through history encountering the French Revolution, followed by crop disease across Europe that left vineyards desolate. Then came an economic downturn in Europe, followed by two world wars and the French wine industry did not recover for decades.

Meanwhile, competition had arrived and threatened the treasured French brands like Champagne and Bordeaux. This resulted in the establishment in 1935 of the "Appellation d'Origine Contrôlée" to protect French interests. Consequently France has one of the oldest systems for protected designation of origin for wine in the world, and strict laws concerning winemaking and production.

Beginning in 2012, French law divided wine into three categories:

- Vin de France – a table wine category.
- Indication Geographic Protégé (IGP) – an intermediate category.
- The Appellation d'Origine Protégé (AOP) – the highest category, wine from a particular area with many other restrictions, including grape varieties and winemaking methods.

The basic premise of this classification system is the concept of "Terroir." It refers to the unique combination of natural factors associated with any particular vineyard. It includes such factors as soil, underlying rock, altitude, hill slope, orientation towards the sun, etc. In other words, when the same grape variety is planted in different locations, it can produce wines that are significantly different from each other.

Labels on French wine bottles will include classification, name of the producer and region of origin. The higher classification will include details of where the wine was bottled and the specific vineyard of origin. Variations of this classification system have been copied around the world and adopted by the European Union.

If there is one thing that most French wines have in common, it is that most have been developed as wines meant for accompanying food. The French tradition is to serve wine with food; wines have seldom been developed or styled as "bar wines" for drinking on their own. This, however, is also changing. From a private and domestic activity organized around the family meal, wine drinking has been transformed into a social, public and ritualized act. Only recently have wine bars begun to appear in metropolitan areas where even some top-of-the-line restaurants have sprouted a bar annex. The French have finally accepted wines by the glass.

The drink of choice has always been wine, but just as with the rest of Europe this is a changing market. A recent poll showed 68% of those over 50 preferred wine as their favorite drink, while only 24% of those aged 14 to 29 gave that response; most young French people chose beer as their preferred drink.

As a result, the French wine industry has been influenced by a decline in domestic consumption, as well as world-wide competition from Chile to Australia to South Africa, Spain, and the United States. To counter these trends, the French wine industry has begun to consolidate and to concentrate on high quality vintages. It is interesting that the French language dominates the vocabulary attached to wine.

When it comes to style, art, culture, food, and drink, the French are the undisputed kings, and Paris is the crown jewel, a city bursting at the seams with fabulous sidewalk cafés, bars and restaurants full of history and renowned for their famous clientele – authors, artists and celebrities.

In addition to cafés, we have two other French dining and drinking establishments whose names have become part of the English language – the "bistro" and the "brasserie." The bistro developed out of the basement kitchens of Parisian apartments where tenants paid for both room and board. Landlords could supplement their income by opening their kitchen to the paying public. The food was simple and wine and coffee were included.

Today, a bistro is still a small restaurant serving

moderately priced meals in a modest setting. A brasserie in France is a restaurant with a relaxed, upscale setting. A brasserie can be expected to have professional service, printed menus and, traditionally, white linen – unlike a bistro, which may have none of these. The word "brasserie" is also French for brewery. The origin of the word stems from the fact that beer was brewed on the premises, rather than brought in; thus, an inn would brew its own beer and supply food and lodging. Now, in northern France, especially near the Belgian border, there has been a welcome revival of old breweries, which had been connected to hotels and restaurants, brewing their own beer as micro-brewers.

Lyon is the birthplace of traditional French cuisine, and the food here is definitely among the finest in the world. The casual, smaller restaurants here are known as "bouchons." The term bouchon originated as a description for the bundles of straw that hung over the entrance of early bouchons, indicating the availability of food and drink for horses, as well as humans.

Today, many restaurants call themselves bouchons, but do not fit the original small, family-run tavern description. For the real thing look for a little plaque at the door showing "Gnafron," a drunken marionette with a red nose and a wine glass in hand. He signifies that the establishment is part of the official Bouchon Association.

"Champagne in victory, one deserves it; in defeat one needs it," a quote from Napoleon.

The European Union has ruled that for a sparkling wine to be called champagne it must originate in the Champagne region of northeast France. Even within France, wine can be made the same way, with the same grapes, but if it isn't produced in CHAMPAGNE, it cannot be called champagne.

While REIMS is the official capital of the region, the self-proclaimed "capital of champagne," for both the region and the wine, is Épernay. The Rue de Champagne is lined with opulent buildings bearing the names of the most treasured brands: Moët and Chandon, Perrier Jouët, Pol Roger and others. Mumm, the third largest champagne producer, is located in Reims. As a result, some champagne snobs do not consider it as authentically "French" as the other brands.

In 1668, a young monk arrived at the Abbey de Hautvillers monastery to revive their decrepit vineyards. His name was Dom Pérignon, and he found a way to add carbonation to the "still wines" that were produced in the region. He also found a way to bottle the highly pressurized product with a wire-caged cork, and a concave bottom for the bottle.

Not much was known about Dom Pérignon until Moët and Chandon acquired the rights to his name and placed it on one of their brands back in 1936, 200 years following his death. Today, Dom Pérignon is synonymous with the very best champagne. Just as a point of information, higher-quality, expensive champagnes have smaller bubbles than champagnes of lower quality. The smaller the bubbles, the smoother the champagne.

Champagne producing standards are set forth and enforced by the CIVC, "the Comite Interprofessionel du Vin de Champagne organized in 1827. Growers must adhere to strict guidelines dictating such things as planting, pruning, harvesting, pressing, and how it is produced and aged.

Champagne is made by a double fermentation process. The first occurs in the vat, like regular wine, the second fermentation occurs in the bottle, when yeast and sugar are added. The bottles are aged upside down in chalk caves for at least one year and a half, during which they are shaken and rotated regularly. Once the aging has been completed, the inverted bottle neck is frozen, the bottle opened and the sediment, known as "lees" is removed. The bottle is then quickly re-corked until opened for consumption.

There are over 100 miles of chalk caves and tunnels under Reims and Épernay. These were invaluable before refrigeration, since they were the only way to maintain a constant cool temperature throughout the year.

The CIVC allows only three grapes to be used for champagne: Pinot Noir, Pinot Meunier, and Chardonnay. Blanc de Blanc champagne is made exclusively from Chardonnay. A rose champagne gets its pink color from a small amount of red Pinot Noir or Pinot Meunier added to the Chardonnay.

The sweetness of the champagne, called the "doux," is controlled by adding sugar during the second fermentation. The more sugar added, the less "dry" the champagne becomes. The dry varieties are labeled "brut." Since champagne is usually made with a blend of several years, it is not as important to keep track of a certain year as with most wines. The vintage only has to be 80% for that particular year. A final note on champagne. Oscar Wilde sipping champagne on his death bed announced: "Alas, I think I'm dying beyond my means."

Paris cafés are very special places, and have served an essential social function in Parisian life for centuries. Paris cafés are a meeting place, a neighborhood pub, a place to relax and refuel; they are the social and political pulse of the city. Although different in many ways, the Paris café echoes the American neighborhood saloon or the Irish or English pub. Some cafés are really a home away from home for a built-in clientele of people who all know each other.

Whether you live in a cramped apartment and need to get outside to preserve your sanity, or you are just hungry for some human contact, Paris cafés have always been the solution for all that ails you. Typical cafés are not "coffee shops." The Paris café comes with a complete kitchen offering a regular restaurant menu, sit-down service, a full bar, and a good wine selection. Most of these cafés are businesses handed down from generation to generation.

Many Paris cafés have gained fame and notoriety, and have become sightseeing destinations in themselves. But keep in mind there are simply wonderful cafés all over the city.

The following is a list of the more recognizable names among PARIS Cafés. These are places where you can sit at a table and soak-up the artistic vibes from past generations.

Les Deux Magots, 170 Boulevard, Saint-Germain. This is the most famous café in Paris, a Paris institution. Les Deux Magots has long had the reputation of being the place for a rendezvous among the literary and intellectual elite. It has hosted several famous patrons, among them Jean-Paul Sartre and Simone de Beauvoir, as well as Hemingway, Camus and Picasso. The café has been featured in many films and, like **Café de Flore;** it also has an annual literary prize for French novels every year since 1933. Inside are two Asian statues that give the café its name.

Café de Flore, 172 Boulevard Saint-Germain. While there are dozens of bars that claim to have hosted famous literary and artistic clientele, there are a few places in Paris that hold a special place in café culture and literary legacy in the City of Lights. Café de Flore is one of these places. Like its main rival **Café Les Deux** (who knew bars could have rivalries?), Café de Flore has long been celebrated for its intellectual clientele and gives its own annual literary prize, called the "Prix de Flore." This is where John-Paul Sartre wrote his trilogy "Les Chemins de la Liberté" (The Roads to Freedom).

Le Fouquets. As a Paris institution on the Champs Élysées since 1899, Le Fouquets is known as a place to see-and-be-seen, and has boasted patrons like Charlie Chaplin, Chevalier, Winston Churchill, FDR and Jackie Onassis. Not only will you be surrounded by the history of the famous guests who have sat and sipped here before; the sidewalk seating is perfect for spending a few hours nursing a cocktail and watching people stroll by on the Champs Élysées.

Café de la Paix, 12 Boulevard des Capucines. A popular meeting spot for after-opera, and dinner and drinks. It is said that if you sit at Café de la Paix long enough, you are bound to run into someone you know. Café de la Paix opened in 1862, and has attracted many famous clients since its opening, including Emile Zola and Guy de Maupassant. On opera nights, the Café de la Paix will fill with the "Who's Who of Paris"; while certainly not a budget place to eat or drink, it is guaranteed to provide you with prime Parisian people watching.

Le Rotunde. Yet another bar once patronized by Ernest Hemingway, this famous Café was immortalized by the author in "The Sun Also Rises" when he wrote, "No matter what café in Montparnasse you ask a taxi driver to bring you to from the right bank of the river, they always take you to Le Rotunde." Le Rotunde is known as one of the many rallying sites for the Lost Generation, surrealists, and existentialists living in Paris after World War I. Le Rotunde and its Art Deco interior have seen patrons like F. Scott Fitzgerald, Matisse, T.S. Elliott, Sartre, Gertrude Stein, Alice B. Toklas and others who sought out the Montparnasse bar during a time when the neighborhood was known for its Bohemian vibe.

La Closerie de Lilas. Another famous Montparnasse bar, **La Closerie** has been an important Paris institution since its opening in 1847, serving as a magnet for the social and culinary avante-garde. The famous people who have sat in the "Lilac Garden," include Stein and Toklas, Ingress, Henry James, Picasso, Hemingway, and Lenin and Trotsky (at the chessboard). There is definitely something to be said about sipping a glass of wine where it is rumored Hemingway once wrote much of "The Sun Also Rises."

Café le Procope. A plaque on the wall proclaims Café le Procope as the oldest café in the world having opened in 1686, 20 years after coffee had been introduced from Austria. Over time this place drew some illustrious patrons, including Napoleon, Victor Hugo, Benjamin Franklin, and the French Revolution icons, Robespierre and Marat. We must note, there are several other cafés in Paris that claim to be the oldest – all dating from the 17th century.

Harry's New York Bar. 5 Rue Daunou. This is arguably the most famous bar in the world. The bar was acquired by former American star jockey Tod Sloan in 1911, who converted it from a bistro and renamed it the "New York Bar." Sloan had gone into partnership with a New Yorker named Clancy, who owned a bar in Manhattan. That bar was dismantled and shipped to Paris. Sloan then hired Harry MacElhone, a barman from Dundee, Scotland, to run the place. At the time, American tourists, and members of the artistic and literary communities, were beginning to show up in Paris in ever-increasing numbers, and Sloan hoped to capitalize on his fame and make the place a spot where expatriates would feel at home. His bar did become a popular spot for members of the American Field Service Ambulance Corps during World War I; however, financial problems, from Sloan's overspending on a lavish personal lifestyle, forced him to sell the bar, and in 1923 it was acquired by MacElhone, its former barman, who added his name to the bar, and would be responsible for making it into a legendary Parisian landmark over the years.

Harry's New York Bar was frequented by a number of famous expatriates and international celebrities such as Knute Rockne, Sinclair Lewis, Ernest Hemingway, Bill Tilden, Coco Chanel, Jack Dempsey, Aly Khan, Rita Hayworth, Humphrey Bogart and even the Duke of Windsor occasionally showed up. The "Ivories" piano bar at Harry's is where George Gershwin composed "An American in Paris." Harry's New York Bar is also the birthplace of several classic cocktails, including the Bloody Mary, French 75, Side Car and The Monkey Gland.

Moulin Rouge founded in 1889 and the birthplace of the "can-can" dance. Posters painted by Toulouse-Lautrec secured rapid and international fame and the Moulin Rouge is now the most famous cabaret in the world.

GERMANY

"Give me a woman who loves beer and I will conquer the world."
Kaiser Wilhelm

Beer is a major part of German culture. The Germans are behind only the Czechs and the Irish in their per capita consumption of beer. Only 5% of Germans consider themselves teetotalers. Beer soup was the standard German family breakfast till the end of the 18th century, the toast and coffee of its day.

As towns were established in the 12th century, Germany granted the privilege of brewing and selling beer in their immediate localities as a means of raising money. A flourishing artisan brewing industry developed in many towns, about which there was much civic pride. The Benedictine Abbey Weihenstephan Brewery (established in 725) is reputedly the oldest existing brewery in the world (brewing since 1040), and is located in Freising 19 miles northeast of Munich.

Germany has had for centuries a very strict set of regulations governing the production of beer. The Reinheitsgebot (literally "purity order," sometimes called the "German and Beer Purity Law," or the "Bavarian Purity Law"), dates back hundreds of years. Some say it originated in Bavaria in 1516; others trace it to a document written in

1434 in Thuringia. The original text allowed only water, hops and barley-malt as ingredients in beer. After its discovery, yeast became the fourth legal ingredient. Before its repeal in 1987, it was the oldest food quality regulation in the world. Since 1993, the production of beer has been governed by the Provisional German Beer Law, which allows a greater range of additives.

Today there are approximately 1300 breweries in Germany, producing over 5000 brands of beer. While production is closely regulated, the German laws governing the use and sale of alcohol are some of the least restrictive ones in the world. The legislation is not designed to keep young people away from alcohol completely; but rather to teach them an appropriate way to consume alcohol. With this in mind, the drinking age follows a three-step process.

At age 14, minors are permitted to consume and possess fermented alcoholic beverages, such as beer and wine, in the company of their parents. At age 16, fermented beverages may be drunk without parental company. At 18, people are allowed to consume distilled alcoholic beverages, since they are considered adults. This step-by-step approach is similar to acquiring a license to drive a vehicle in countries like the United States and Canada.

Unlike many other countries, drinking in public is legal in Germany and it is not uncommon to see people drinking in parks, on the streets, and even on public transportation. Also, consuming alcohol during the day is more accepted in Germany than elsewhere.

The two most common German toasts are "Prost" (Cheers) or "Zum Wohl" (Your Health). It is especially important to look each person at the table in the eye while you clink glasses with them. According to local myth, those who drop their eyes are destined to seven years of bad sex – a heavy price to pay for one poor toast!

Drinking places in Germany range from the Eckkneipes to the Biergartens, with everything from rathskellers, sidewalk cafés, nightclubs and Irish pubs in between.

The Eckkneipe is probably as close as you can get to a German pub. The term is a shortening of "Kneip Inn" which described very narrow premises in the 18th century. Today Eckkneipes could be translated as "corner pubs." These places are small bars, often situated on street corners in cities, which cater to local and regular clientele, usually men. Eckkneipes are normally quite small with dark and somewhat closed off interiors, and a lot cheaper than the more common café bars. These are places where working-class folks gather and socialize. Unlike the classier café-bars, the customers know each other, and they know the bartender and the wait-staff. People are allowed to sit at the bar, in fact, sitting at the bar is normal, and there is usually singing and loud conversation.

Many mainstream Germans do not approve of the Eckkneipes and would not consider having a drink in one. The most common German drinking places are café-bars, which serve a wide range of beverages, including tea, juices, hot chocolate and snacks; as well as beer, wine and spirits.

Cafés and bars in the larger German cities have a relatively homogeneous clientele. It is rare to find a broad mixture of ages, social classes, or lifestyle choices in a single location; executives choose a bar and manual laborers "hang out" somewhere else.

There are a few drinking places that are peculiar to Germany, even though they are imitated around the world. These include the "biergarten" (beer garden), "Hofbrauhaus," and the famous Oktoberfest.

The biergarten, or beer garden, is an open-air area, serving drinks and food, and is usually attached to a beer hall of some sort. Beer gardens in Germany developed in the Kingdom of Bavaria in the 19th century. King Ludwig the First decreed that beer had to be brewed during cold months, since fermentation had to take place between 4° and 8°C (39° and 46°F). To provide this during the summer, large breweries dug cellars in the banks of the River Isar in Munich for the storage of beer. To help keep it cool they covered the banks with gravel and planted chestnut trees to provide shade.

Eventually, the beer cellars were used not only to store the beer, but also to serve it. Simple tables and benches were set up among the trees, creating "beer gardens." Smaller breweries in Munich complained about the loss of business to these larger outdoor beer gardens, and as a result, Ludwig the First forbade them to serve food. To counter this measure, the beer gardens allowed their customers to bring their own food – – this continues to be a common practice today. Munich now has 36 beer gardens which are crowded in summer months with people enjoying a mug of beer and a typical BYO picnic of white radishes, pretzels, obatzda (a savory mash of cheeses, onions, and spices).

The largest traditional beer garden in the world is the Hirschgarten in Munich, which seats 8000 patrons. The name Hirschgarten means "deer garden" and about 30 deer occupy a park adjacent to the beer garden. The beer is dispensed directly from the cask at five separate beer stations. One liter mugs are provided and when you finish a beer you are obliged to rinse the mug in a cold-water basin before embarking on the next mug-full.

The setting is gorgeous, dating back to 1770, when it was a preserve for pheasants. Most of the tables and chairs sit under the leafy chestnut trees. Some areas of the sprawling beer garden offer table service, including foods such as roast pork, spareribs, rotisserie chicken, baked pretzels, and homemade desserts.

The "beer hall" is another special feature of the German drinking scene, and the most famous one is the Hofbräuhaus am Platzl in MUNICH. Founded in 1589 by the Duke of Bavaria, Wilhelm, the Fifth, this ancient beer hall is managed by Hofbräuhaus München.

Hofbräuhaus has quite a lot of history attached to it, and was originally a brewery; the beer brewed here became world-famous and once saved the city from annihilation. When King Gustavus Adolphus of Sweden invaded Bavaria during the 30 Years War in 1632, he threatened to sack and burn the entire city of Munich unless the citizens surrendered some hostages and 600,000 barrels of Hofbräuhaus beer. The citizens of Munich made a wise decision!

Some famous and infamous individuals are associated with Hofbräuhaus, including Amadeus Mozart who lived around the corner and claimed to have written the opera Idomenco after being fortified for the task at the Hofbräuhaus.

Prior to World War I, Vladimir Lenin lived in Munich and was a regular customer at the Hofbräuhaus. In 1920, Adolph Hitler and the National Socialist Party held their first meeting in the Festsaal Room on the third floor. At the Hofbräuhaus in February 24, 1920, Adolph Hitler proclaimed the 25 theses of the National Socialist program, which became known as the Nazi Party. Although these political events took place at the Hofbräuhaus, Hitler was not a frequent visitor.

Since Hitler did not drink alcohol, eat red meat or smoke, the beer hall was not his scene. In fact, his favorite Munich restaurant was an Italian place near Ludwig-Maximilian University. One of Hitler's watercolor paintings is of the Hofbräuhaus. It is interesting that Hitler did not drink alcohol while his three adversaries: Roosevelt, Churchill and Stalin, were all considered major consumers of alcohol.

Following World War II, the Hofbräuhaus became Munich's major tourist attraction, and the famous clay mugs with the HB symbol are collectors' items. Eventually, franchises began spreading throughout Germany and across the world. There is a full-scale replica in Las Vegas. Other locations include New York City, Pittsburgh, Chicago, Milwaukee, Stockholm, Bangkok, and Genoa, Italy. This is a German version of the explosion of Irish pubs around the world.

If you are going to "bar hop" in Germany and get the full flavor and experience, you must be there for the annual Oktoberfest. It is named Oktoberfest because it lasts 16 days and ends on the first Sunday of October. For example, the dates for 2013 were September 21 through October 6. There are exceptions when the first Sunday of October falls on the first or second, the event is extended until the third, which means the festival lasts 17 days when the first Sunday is October 2nd, and 18 days when it is on the first.

The original Oktoberfest dates back to October 12, 1810, when crowds were invited to a meadow in the center of Munich to celebrate the wedding of Prince Ludwig of Bavaria and Therese of Sachsen-Hildburghausen. It subsequently became an annual fair that included horse races and agricultural events. Local businessmen working with city breweries created the first massive beer tent in 1896, and the festival has been all about beer ever since.

By 1960, the Oktoberfest had turned into the world's largest fair, with about 6 million people attending each year. The major attraction involves the 15 huge tents, each one sponsored by a local brewery, only beer which is brewed within the city limits of Munich, with a minimum of 13½ percent Master Spice, is allowed to be served at the festival. This special beer is designated Oktoberfest beer and has an alcohol content of 5.82 to 6.3 percent, compared to a normal German beer with alcohol content of 5.2 percent. As you might expect, enormous quantities of beer are consumed, usually averaging over 7,000,000 liters during the 16-day festival. In 2011, a liter or mug of beer cost about nine Euros, or $12.

In addition to beer, the massive tents have varied musical entertainment and serve mountains of food – sauerkraut, sausage, pork knuckles, grilled fish, roast pork, pretzels, potato dumplings and Brathaenchen (most popular). There is also a fun fair at the festival with a Ferris wheel, roller coaster, and many, many games.

A final word about the all-important tents. These 15 tents are large, the largest seating over 10,000 people, and most of the others accommodating 8 to 10,000 guests. In addition, there are about 20 smaller tents with seating for 400 each. The most important tent is probably the Schottenhamel sponsored by the Spaten-Franziskaner. This is where the festival begins when the mayor of Munich taps the first keg at noon on opening day. This tent seats 6000 inside and an additional 4000 outside. An interesting concept, to accommodate older people and families; music is limited to 85 dB until 6 PM each day. The party atmosphere is enhanced by many of the guests wearing traditional German attire, including the famous Bavarian hat with a tuft of goat hair, the women in Dirndl skirts, and the men in Lederhosen.

Oktoberfest has spread around the globe and is celebrated in countries from Canada to Russia. The largest Oktoberfest outside Germany is held each year in Cincinnati, Ohio, where close to 700,000 people jam the streets to listen to music from seven large entertainment stages. Known as Oktoberfest Zinzinnati, details can be found on www.OktoberfestZinzinnati.com. Other major Oktoberfest celebrations in the U.S. can be found in San Francisco, St. Louis and Milwaukee.

The world's largest beer competition is the annual Great American Beer festival held in Denver, Colorado. There are 3100 beers entered from 624 brewers and attendance exceeds 50,000. The huge success of craft beers is a major reason for the proliferation of Oktoberfests and beer festivals around the world.

Although beer has been the German beverage of choice since the 16th century, wine has been produced in the southwestern German states since the first century. The Romans founded the oldest city in Germany, Trier, on the River Moselle in the heart of today's wine region.

At one point in medieval times, the Catholic Church controlled vineyards in Germany, and quality was very good. In the 1800s Napoleon took control of all the vineyards from the Church, and divided and secularized them.

Today, Germany produces about 1.2 billion bottles of wine per year, which places it as the eighth largest wine-producing country in the world. Almost all, two thirds, of this total is white wine. Although much of this production consists of cheap, mass-market, semi-sweet wines, such as Liebfraumilch, high-end wines made from the Riesling grape variety have a very good reputation worldwide. Mark Twain remarked, "You can tell German wine from vinegar by the label." Wine is the second most popular drink in Germany, but it is second by a wide margin, and is usually consumed only on special occasions.

In Germany, schnapps is a general term for any type of beverage that warms you up on the inside. "Schnapps" in German means "mouthful." Schnapps covers a wide range of alcoholic drinks made from grains or potatoes. Sweet peppermint schnapps is undoubtedly the most widely known version, but the flavorings include a variety of ingredients and can vary from sweet to dry.

Denmark is the leading producer of schnapps, with Germany coming in second. The majority of schnapps distilleries are located in the Freiberg region of Germany on Black Forest farms. The best Black Forest schnapps is made from cherries; Kirsch, the German word for cherries. Other varieties include Pflümli from damsons (plums) and Williams made from pears. Schnapps is usually served in small measures, like a shot glass.

Somewhat of an unusual twist, there has been a virtual explosion of Irish pubs opening in Germany over the past several years. Germans seem to have a special interest in all things Irish. Many own vacation properties on the coast of Ireland.

It is difficult to list the best drinking spots in any country since it's a moving, changing target. The following is a list of a few of the outstanding, traditional drinking places in the major German cities.

BAMBERG: **Schlenkerla Inn**. There are over 90 breweries in and around Bamberg, the highest density of breweries in the world. The local favorite is Rockbier, the dark, red ale with a smooth, smoky taste! Try it at Schlenkerla, the traditional inn in the old town. Also, there is an interesting beer brewing museum; the Fränkisches Brauereimuseum in the rebuilt, historic caves of the former Benedictine monastery's brewing cellars.

BERLIN: Hackescher Market. Known as the world's oldest brewery, the **Weihenstephan** brewery has long been revered as a giant among German beer makers – and fortunately for Berliners, the brewery's **Weihenstephaner** restaurant and beer hall transports this famous taste of Bavaria right to the center of the city. Located on Hackescher Market, this charming spot specializes in all things Bavarian, from weisswurst (white sausage) to schnitzel.

The oldest beer garden in Berlin, **Prater Garten,** has been around since 1837 and features its own unique beers, Prater Pils and Prater Schwarzbier (black beer). The establishment's long history – Prater survived bombing raids during World War II and the Soviet rule of East Berlin – has made it a local institution, and its thousand seats are usually packed. This is a wonderful outdoor German beer garden with bright yellow picnic tables under a canopy of majestic, old chestnut trees. During inclement weather everyone retreats to the adjacent beer hall.

BREMEN

Ratskeller. This is one of the most famous ratskellers in Germany. A ratskeller by definition is a bar and/or restaurant below street level. The German "rat" meaning council and "keller" meaning cellar. This place has been in business since 1408.

COLOGNE

Kolsch is the name of the dialect spoken by natives of Cologne. It is also the name of the city's traditional beer, which is served in every bar, bistro and restaurant in town. It is a light, refreshing beer, and is served in special small, narrow glasses. The name is protected by law and can only be used for beer brewed in or near Cologne.

FRANKFURT

Haus Wertheim. This is the oldest inn in the city and it was one of the few buildings to survive the Allied bombing raids of World War II. Inside, it appears as if nothing has changed for several centuries.

HEIDELBERG

Zum Roten Ochsen. "The Red Ox" has hosted beer drinkers from Mark Twain to Bismarck. Students of the University have been drinking here since 1703.

LEIPZIG

Auerbachs Keller. This is where Goethe staged the debate between Faust and Mephistopheles in his play "Faust." The tavern dates from 1530. There are a series of murals depicting the Faust legend.

MUNICH

Probably the beer drinking capital of the world. In addition to the Hofbrauhaus, discussed earlier, another favorite is **Agustiner Brau**, known for its golden lager "Helles." Tourists who roam Munich's taverns and beerhalls are routinely surprised to see German patrons accompanied by their pet dogs. Typically, they lie by the side of their owners and behave perfectly...in keeping with their masters' discipline. It is not unusual to see a group of local folks in traditional lederhosen and Alpine caps imbibing happily, surrounded by a dozen dogs in silent peace.

GREECE

"He was a wise man who invented wine." – Plato

Greece has been around a long time; Greek is the second oldest, continuing language after Chinese, and the Greeks have been celebrating the virtues of alcohol for thousands of years. Among the many Greek Gods was Dionysus, son of Zeus and Semele, and the God of wine and revel; and there were many festivals to honor Dionysus. Drinking was central to ancient Greek culture and vases and drinking cups from the period usually show images of people drinking. Drinking wine in Greece predates the written word and the Bronze Age – 3000 BC.

There were drinking parties for the elite that consisted of a ritual with formal rules and elaborate ceremonies. The parties, known as symposiums, began with a banquet followed by a regimen of toasting the divinities. These were all-male events and when the singing and poetry portion arrived, the music was provided by a "flute girl" who was especially attractive and scantily attired. The wine was passed around the room in a particular order, each guest taking his turn, singing and drinking, and eventually everyone was drunk. This type of entertainment was reserved for the upper classes; but the women and slaves had their own neighborhood taverns.

We must keep in mind the "Golden Age of Classical Greece" was around the fifth century BC, over 2500 years ago. This was the time of the Acropolis and great men like Sophocles, Euripides, Socrates, and Plato, all of whom drank wine.

"The wine urges me on, the bewitching wine, which sets even a wise man to singing and to laughing gently and rouses him up and to dance, and brings forth words which were better unspoken." Homer (800-700 BC, the Odyssey).

Ouzo is Greece's most famous alcoholic beverage. No other drink is as uniquely Greek or as closely linked to a culture as Ouzo is to Greece. In 2006, the Greek government won the exclusive rights to use the product name Ouzo.

Ouzo is distilled from the residue, grape skins and seeds, left in the wine press after the juice is removed to make wine. It is crystal clear, 40% alcohol, potent and fiery; usually flavored with spices, primarily aniseed, which gives it the intense licorice flavor. Ouzo turns milky when mixed with water.

The best Ouzo is produced in Lesvos Mytilini, including the top brand, Plomari, named after the region where it is made. Better known brands outside of Greece are Ouzo 12, Sans Rival, and Ouzo Mini.

Ouzo is usually served neat, without ice. The Greeks will add iced water to dilute the strength, causing the liquid to turn milky white. The Greeks use only water with Ouzo, no other mixers are recommended.

Greeks love this drink so much that there are countless Ouzo bars across Greece called Ouzeries. These are casual places that specialize in many types of Ouzo, but are even more importantly popular for their tantalizing array of appetizers, known as "mezethes." In a typical Ouzerie patrons will linger over their drinks and food, sipping slowly and nibbling at their food. Greeks very rarely drink any alcohol without some sort of food accompaniment.

As with so many long-term customs, more Ouzo is drunk in Germany these days than in Greece, where Johnny Walker scotch dominates, and the trendy youth are drinking mojitos.

Retsina is the wine with the biggest name recognition in Greece. Retsina is a white wine with a distinct resin taste. Its unique flavor is said to have originated over 2000 years ago from the practice of sealing wine barrels with pine resin to keep oxygen from spoiling the wine. The pine resin kept the air out, but infused the wine with a resin aroma.

The Romans were able to produce airtight barrels by 300 AD, and stopped using the resin. However, the eastern regions of the empire developed a taste for the strong, pungent wine and continued to produce resinated wine long after the Roman Empire had stopped the practice.

Today, local Retsina is produced throughout Greece. The European Union treats the name "Retsina" as a protected designation of origin in traditional appellation for Greece and parts of Cyprus. Modern Retsina is made following the same wine-making techniques for wine or rose with the exception of adding small amounts of pine resin to the "must" during fermentation. Although not as strong as the old Retsina, enjoying a glass of this wine is definitely an acquired taste.

By the way, the term "must" is used to describe the freshly squeezed grape juice that contains skins, seeds, and stems of the fruit. The solid portion of the "must" is called "pomace." The length of time the pomace stays in the juice is critical for the final character of the wine. When the winemaker judges the time to be right, the juice is drained off the pomace, which is then pressed to extract the remaining juice. Yeast is added to the juice to begin fermentation, while the pomace may be distilled to make drinks like Ouzo or Italian Grappa.

Two other alcoholic drinks similar to Ouzo are made throughout Greece, especially in the home. Raki and Tsipouro are distilled from white grape skins and served chilled in a shot glass. These are fiery and very potent drinks made for sipping, not gulping.

Beer is not a big item in Greece and consumption is about half the European Union per capita average. The big names dominate the market, Amstel, Heineken, Beck's, Budweiser; but there are a few local breweries.

One special Greek custom is that if you are seated at a table, you will not order your own bottle. Instead, the whole group will order a number of bottles that are placed in the middle of the table and shared by everyone using their own glass.

As in most countries, there are a variety of establishments that serve alcoholic beverages, and each has its own special character. Almost every village has at least one Kafeneio, or coffeehouse. These are one of the oldest institutions in Greece, and serve coffee and spirits, and little else; and remain largely the domain of men. Men drop by, play a game of cards, and nurse a cup of coffee or glass of Ouzo for hours.

The taverna is the most common and casual drinking place. Usually family-owned and operated and has wine by the barrel. These are down-home places with plenty of food and appetizers.

Estiatorio is an upscale restaurant similar to a taverna with a nicer setting and more formal service.

Ouzeries traditionally serve plates of mezedhes

(appetizers) with rounds of Ouzo. You can have a full meal here or the mezedhes. These places are similar to Kafeneios, with more emphasis on Ouzo and better food selection.

A more recent addition to the drinking scene is Greece's lounge-bar which is usually a café with elaborate decor, lots of TVs and loud music. These are the places to see and be seen.

Regardless of your choice of drinking establishment, a combination of a generally sunny climate and Europe's lowest urban crime rate have fostered a bustling outdoor café culture. Having a drink and meal on the street is a way of life.

The drinking age in Greece is 18, in reality there is no age limit and no one checks IDs. The blood alcohol limit for drunken driving is .05%, compared to .08% in the U.S. and the United Kingdom.

Alcohol is available just about everywhere, including liquor stores, kiosks on the street, and grocery stores. Cafés and coffee houses, which are plentiful, are a little tricky, since some serve alcohol, as well as coffee, and others are limited to coffee.

Greek nightlife, much like Spain, has the reputation of just getting started when the rest of Europe has gone to bed. Every neighborhood in Athens has its fair share of bars and there are endless barhopping opportunities. It is a common procedure to begin your night downtown and head for the large coastal clubs later. This is very convenient on the weekends, using the inexpensive, 24-hour tram service.

Some of the very best bars and lounges in Athens are located in hotels. The top-floor Galaxy at the Hilton offers an amazing view of the city. Other hotel bars with wonderful views include the Hera Hotel's Peacock Lounge and the Fresh Hotel's Air Lounge.

During the summer months, most of the bars and

restaurants spill out onto the sidewalks in Athens, which makes it easy to have a drink and watch the city go by. You can linger all night long at some of these wonderful cafés.

The seaside clubs are huge. **Akrotiri Club,** phone 210-985-9147, holds 3000 customers with a huge pool, dance floors, deck seating near the beach and good, pricey food. **Summer Mao** is another beachside club with a capacity of over 5000. **El Pecado,** 2010-324-4049, **"The Sin,"** came about from the unusual union of a medieval Spanish-style church and erotic murals inspired by various Bible themes. El Pecado moves to its beach location for the summer in a beautiful seaside mansion.

The current European economic crisis, especially in Greece, has taken much of the fun out of the drinking and bar scene. But we all know, and hope and pray, that the fun in this great country will return soon, as it has for centuries.

IRELAND

Only Irish coffee provides in a single glass all four essential food groups: alcohol, coffee, sugar, and fat. – Alex Levine

Thanks to Irish emigrants, Irish pubs, Irish whiskey and Guinness beer; Ireland and drinking are practically synonymous. With the decline of Waterford Crystal, and the world-wide fascination with everything Irish, Irish pubs are probably Ireland's best-known export.

The Irish have been drinking alcoholic beverages for what seems an eternity. It is claimed that Dublin's oldest pub, the Brazen Head, dates back to 1198. The oldest pub in Ireland is Sean's Bar in Athlone, 900 A.D.

Historians trace ale brewing using wild barley to 800 years ago in Irish monasteries. The ruins of the St. Francis Abbey can still be seen on the grounds of Smithwick Brewery in Kilkenny. The first confirmed written record of the distillation of whiskey comes from the year 405 in Ireland.

The Irish pub, always privately owned, has been the center of Ireland's social life for centuries. The term "spirit groceries" was first applied to Irish pubs in the mid-18th century when a growing temperance movement in Ireland forced publicans to diversify their businesses to compensate for declining spirit sales. Many rural pubs in Ireland still resemble grocer's shops of the 19th century, with groceries occupying shelves on one side, and spirits on the other, and little room for the customers in between.

Most of the pubs in Ireland use signage bearing the owner's name. This is in contrast to England where the pub is usually owned by a large conglomerate or brewery and the generic sign uses the name of an animal, general, or famous battle.

The Irish public house, pub, has been a social and community hub for the people of Ireland from the very beginning. It serves not just as a place to consume alcohol; but as a place to meet and greet people locally. Virtually all the regulars will know each other very well and there will be a very close relationship with the bar staff and the customers. The Irish people refer to their favorite pub as their "local." The Irish sometimes have several "locals." Irish pubs are happy places and known worldwide for welcoming strangers.

The etiquette in Irish pubs varies from place to place; but a few rules apply across the board. Keep in mind that unlike most other countries, the Irish do 94% of their drinking outside the home.

First, it is not necessary to tip the bar staff, unless they're serving food. Second, the practice of buying "rounds" is widespread. Drinking in "rounds" requires each person to buy a round until everyone has bought at least one round. It is considered very rude and cheap to drink in a round without paying for a round.

Smoking has been banned in pubs since 2002. Despite the "gloom and doom" prediction of the majority of pub owners, the ban has been very successful. Many rural pub owners thought they would just ignore the law, since they have disregarded many of the other regulations; but the severity of the fines and the strict enforcement, quickly changed their minds. Many pubs do offer outdoor smoking areas equipped with heaters for the cold evenings. Finally, Irish pubs require a level of decorum that considers loud and boastful behavior very rude.

Aimed directly at the tourist industry a couple of major changes have occurred over the past 25 years. The original pubs in Ireland never served food because "eating out" in Ireland was uncommon. Rural pubs still do not serve food; but all the traditional bars in the major urban areas of Dublin, Galway, Cork, etc., serve meals.

Entertainment in pubs (music, singing) was another rarity; and, of course, this has changed "big time" in the populated areas. These newer types of pubs, however, continue to be conspicuously absent in the countryside where the old- style typical pub still exists.

In the latter part of the 20th century, a fascination with all things Irish swept around the world – Irish themed movies, Irish dancers (Riverdance), Guinness beer, and especially, Irish pubs.

Guinness, the world's leading producer of Irish beer, located in Dublin, inaugurated an Irish Pub Concept program to capitalize on the popularity of the Irish pub. The goal, of course, was to sell more Guinness Stout.

Through its relationship with designated designers and builders, Guinness has assisted in the opening of several thousand "so-called" Irish pubs around the world, and over 100 in the United States.

The Guinness affiliates, the Irish Pub Copany, and the Irish Pub Design and Development Company, have built these pubs and shipped them to over 40 countries, including the **Matsumote Irish Pub** in JAPAN and **Shanghai O'Malley's** in CHINA.

The Irish Pub Design Company lets customers select which "authentic" version they prefer; the cottage pub, the old brewery house, the grocery shop pub, the Gaelic pub, Victorian pub or the contemporary pub. The bars and accompanying decor for these pubs are built in Ireland, shipped to the U.S., and assembled by a crew sent over from Ireland. When the pub opens, Guinness provides an Irish bartender to help set the proper Irish tone for the pub.

Of course, not all the Irish-themed pubs opening in America are built in Ireland – most are constructed here to look like an Irish pub. The accompanying decor, menu, music, and television are usually the same. The menu will have a traditional Irish breakfast served all day – eggs, rashers (a traditional Irish bacon), bangers, (a sausage), black and white pudding, tomatoes, and brown bread. Dinner options include salmon and fish and chips (sounds British), shepherd's pie and lamb stew. The TV will offer sporting events directly from Ireland; Gaelic football, soccer and hurling. The whole idea is to make you feel as though you are at a real Irish setting when you step through the door.

Another well-financed group of Americans is going one step further; they are actually purchasing pubs in rural corners of Ireland, and shipping the interiors to America for re-assembly in Irish "hot spots" like Boston, New York City, Savannah and Chicago.

There is even an Irish pub in downtown Disney at Disney World in **Orlando,** Florida, called "**Raglan Road.**" The pub features Irish food, an Irish band and six dancers. This place is so popular that there is a line outside the door seven nights a week year-round.

There are over 8,000 pubs in Ireland, one for every 300, men, women and children. So it is difficult selecting the "best," but it can be a lot of fun trying.

The oldest pub in Ireland, according to the Guinness Book of World Records, is **Sean's Bar** on the road from Dublin to Galway. In fact, Sean's Bar is the oldest bar in Europe, perhaps the oldest in the world, dating from 900 AD. Many of the artifacts from Sean's Bar are on display in the National Museum of Ireland; a section of the wall is displayed in a glass case in the pub. It is wonderful to imagine that this pub has been serving weary travelers crossing the Shannon River for over 1000 years.

The Brazen Head Pub in DUBLIN claims to be officially Ireland's oldest pub dating from 1190. This is a pub that has retained the charm and character of the past. Its patrons have included James Joyce, Brendan Behan, and Jonathan Swift. Brendan Behan, noted author and drinker, claimed to have been thrown out of 720 Dublin pubs. Revolutionary heroes patronizing the Brazen Head included Robert Emmet, Daniel O'Connell, and Michael Collins. Pictures and scrolls cover the walls.

Grace Neills certainly is one of the oldest pubs in Ireland. The bar today sits on its original site on DONAGHADEE'S High Street where it opened in 1611, as the King's Arms. Grace Neill ran the pub from 1842, when her father bought it for her as a wedding present. She was a real character, hugging and kissing the customers as they entered and departed the pub. Grace ran the pub right up to 1916, when she died at the grand age of 98 years old. Two snugs in the original area contain antique glass and stone bottles from days gone by (including Comber Whiskey and Belfast Mineral Water bottles).

In the 1800s, when Donaghadee was the main seaport to both the Isle of Man and Portpatrick, Scotland, the pub was a sanctuary for the many smugglers and horse thieves that frequented the area. There are many reminders of this criminal element throughout the bar.

There are several alcoholic beverages that are unique to Ireland. The most famous today is Guinness stout – a dark, creamy stout with a foamy head, first produced by Arthur Guinness in 1759 in his brewery on the Liffey River in Dublin.

Guinness stout is available in a number of strengths and variations, but the main product is Guinness draft sold in kegs, bottles and cans. The distinctive feature is the burnt flavor, which is derived from the use of roasted, unmalted barley. The thick, creamy head is a result of being mixed with nitrogen when being poured. The alcohol content is usually between 4.1 to 4.3%. Stout was originally the name given to the strongest or stoutest porter beers.

Guinness is so popular worldwide that it has acquired nicknames "the dark stuff," "the blonde in the black skirt," or simply "I'll have a pint, please." Despite this popularity, anyone who has tried it knows it takes an acquired taste for drinking a full pint of the heavy stuff.

By 1986 the brewery at **St. James Gate** had become the largest in the world. Part of the success of the Guinness brand has been due to the distinctive taste of the stout; but also because of the many highly innovative advertising campaigns it has launched throughout the years.

The early campaigns touted the medicinal qualities of the brand with slogans, "Guinness is good for you," and "Guinness for strength." In March 2010, Guinness announced it would no longer promote alcohol as medicine, or simply that it can be used as a treatment or cure. This was after 75 years of using "Guinness is good for you" as their major slogan. In 1935, the artist John Gilroy developed the animal posters that became part of the Guinness promotions for the last half of the 20th century. The Toucan bird was closely identified with Guinness for over 50 years.

Another clever Guinness promotion involved a worldwide contest to win an Irish pub or $250,000. The contest involved completing a sentence beginning "I love Guinness because blank, blank, in 50 words or less. Finalists were flown to Ireland where they competed in a dart throwing contest, and a "pulling a pint challenge." Pulling a proper pint of Guinness is considered a high skill in the bar trade. The glass must be at a precise angle, the flow halted at a precise point, and topping-up completed carefully. A typical beer is carbonated with 100% carbon dioxide, which is released when the beer is poured. Guinness is pressurized with 75% nitrogen and only 25% carbon dioxide. When the pressure is released from the Guinness it creates a much creamier head that settles slowly.

An acquaintance of mine won this contest many years ago, and actually owned and operated the pub with his wife in BANTRY, Ireland for several years. I visited the pub once and it was a delightful place in downtown Bantry, three bars, and living quarters upstairs.

One of the very best places to enjoy a pint of Guinness is the **Gravity Bar** at the end of the Guinness St. James Gate brewery tour. This is a circular bar with views of all downtown DUBLIN from the seventh floor. The bar is located on the top level of the Guinness Storehouse where they used to add the yeast to the beer for fermentation. Now the "Home of Guinness" is Dublin's most popular tourist attraction acting as a museum, incorporating elements from the old brewing equipment to explain the history of Guinness Stout. Guinness is now owned by Diageo PLC.

Today, Guinness is one of the most successful beer brands in the world. It is brewed in over 50 countries, and sold in over 150. Every day, over 10 million glasses are served, and 1.8 billion pints are sold every year. The largest selling national beer in Ireland is Southwick's, an Irish red ale.

A few other Irish drinks include the following: a "black and tan" is a special drink consisting of Harp beer, topped off with Guinness. The Guinness is poured over the back of a spoon so it doesn't mix with the Harp.

Bailey's Irish Cream is a delicious blend of Irish whiskey, cream and caramel. The original problem was preventing the alcohol and cream from separating in the bottle. A secret process solved the problem, and Bailey's was introduced in 1974. Today, there are numerous competitors.

The "Irish Car Bomb" was a popular title during "The Troubles" between Ireland and Northern Ireland. To make this drink, fill a glass with Guinness, fill half a shot glass with Jameson's and top it off with Bailey's. Drop the shot glass in the Guinness and drink in one fell swoop.

Ireland once dominated the global market for whiskey, producing 90% of the world's whiskey at the beginning of the 20th century. At this time, whiskey was the second most popular spirit in the world, after rum. Irish whiskey, which Queen Elizabeth II once called her only true Irish friend, made from barley, is sweeter, and not as smoky, with more sting than Scotch whiskey.

The Anglo-Irish Trade War of the 1930s resulted in tariffs on Irish whiskey across the British Empire. Shortly thereafter, Prohibition in the United States excluded Irish whiskey from its largest market for a dozen years. Meanwhile, Scottish brands were available throughout the British Commonwealth, including Canada, where it was easy to ship it into the United States across the Canadian border. Also, Scottish blenders had introduced basic grain whiskey production using column stills, versus pot stills, at far lower cost.

In 1908, there was a large legal battle concerning what was to be considered true whiskey. The Irish lost and Scottish blends became recognized in law as being whiskey. This was a huge victory at the time. Jameson whiskey still produces a large proportion of its brand by pure pot still practices. By the middle of the 20th century sales of Irish whiskey fell to a meager 2% of total volume replaced mainly by Scotch. Irish whiskey, however, remains popular in Ireland and recently, once again, has grown in popularity internationally.

Irish whiskey was one of the earliest distilled drinks in Europe, dating to the 12th century. The Old Bushmills Distillery claims to be the oldest surviving licensed distillery in the world (received a license from King James I in 1608). The other major Irish whiskey distiller is Jameson located in Cork and known as the New Middleton distillery. Jameson Irish whiskey was founded by John Jameson in 1780 in Dublin. It's interesting that John Jameson was a Scottish lawyer who had married a sister of the Haig brothers, who founded Haig and Haig Scotch whiskey. All Jameson whiskey is produced at the Cork distillery using a mixture of malted and unmalted "green" barley, all sourced from a fifty mile radius around the distillery. It is distilled three times in copper pot stills to create its famous smoothness and flavor. A tour of the distillery is absolutely a delightful experience.

The final stop on the tour is in the store-museum-bar.

As far as I could tell, you could order as many drinks as you wished – free! Participants are chosen from each tour group to join the contest to identify different whiskeys by drinking a shot of each one. Probably the only tour in Ireland that requires a designated driver. Reminds me of a field trip to a distillery in Indiana that my senior chemical engineering class took many years ago. At the end of the tour the distillery wanted to take a photo of the class in front of the office building. They were unable to get a suitable shot because several members insisted on lying down in the front row.

As an added note, the largest pot still in the world is in the Old Middleton Distillery in Cork, holding 31,618 gallons. It's a shame it is not in use anymore.

The Irish Whiskey Act of 1980 set down the regulations defining Irish whiskey. Irish whiskey must be distilled and aged in the Republic of Ireland or in Northern Ireland. The contained spirits must be distilled to an alcohol volume of less than 94.8%. The product must be aged three years in wooden casks. If the spirits comprise a blend of two or more distillates, the product must be referred to as "Blended" Irish whiskey.

For a taste of the very finest in Irish whiskeys try a shot glass of Middleton's – this stuff is expensive, and the bottles are sold in their own wooden containers. It is difficult to find Middleton's in ordinary liquor stores, but it is always available in "duty free" shops.

The bar that sells the most Jameson Irish whiskey annually is located, not in Ireland, but in MINNEAPOLIS, Minnesota. Named the "Local Irish Pub," it sold 671 cases in 2010, 22 bottles a day. The Local, owned by two Irish expatriates, has held the top-selling title for four consecutive years.

Pernod, the French giant, has taken the 230-year-old Jameson brand to new heights. Using clever advertising and cultivating bartenders across the world, sales in the United States increased 27% in 2011. Sales have increased for seven consecutive years and Irish whiskey remains one of the fastest growing segments of the liquor industry in America. Annual world-wide sales are over 22 million bottles. Although Jameson is the number one Irish whiskey worldwide, it is not the most popular brand inside Ireland, Powers Gold Label is the leader, and they are also owned by Pernod.

Poitin or Poteen is a traditional drink distilled in a small pot, and the term comes from the Irish word "pota" meaning "pot." It is distilled from barley grain or potatoes, and is one of the strongest alcoholic beverages in the world with an alcoholic content of from 60 to 95%, or 120 to 190 proof.

Poteen was declared illegal in 1661; but has been produced in remote areas of Ireland ever since. The operation was much like moonshine in the United States. Smoke from peat fires used to heat the still frequently alerted the Irish Gardai and the still was confiscated.

Producing poteen was a source of income for some, while for others it was a cheap alcoholic drink. It was very popular at weddings and wakes, and also as a medicine for relieving aches and pains in farm animals and people. It is an alternative for deep heat and is commonly rubbed on muscles to warm them. Today, two distilleries in the Republic of Ireland are licensed to produce poteen; it remains illegal in Northern Ireland. Poteen is mentioned throughout Irish literature and music.

It is difficult to find a country or culture more

associated with drinking than Ireland and the Irish. What a place, less than 4 million people and over 8,000 bars. And these aren't just bars; these are Irish pubs with all their charm, character, and personality. The pubs of Ireland are not just a place to have a drink. They are theaters for storytelling, homes away from home, keepers of the spirit of the town, music houses, and places to be revered and admired. It is summed up by the Irish phrase "the craic," which in Ireland means "having a good time." What better place to do this but in a pub. It is especially rewarding if you are able to go to the same pub several nights in a row, so the local crowd gets to know you and, of course, you get to know them.

The "Celtic Tiger" was the name given to the unprecedented growth in Ireland between 1995 and 2008. Ireland had historically been an exporter of people, but the economic boom reversed this trend and immigrants were attracted to Ireland; now the country is, once again, losing more people than it is attracting. The collapse of the housing bubble in 2008 has brought on a deep recession with resulting high unemployment and government austerity measures.

The Irish pub has been a very conspicuous victim of these tough times, and is now closing at a rate of one every other day. Prior to the recession, there were over 10,000 pubs in Ireland. By 2012 this had dropped to 8,300.

To add to the misery, the pub is beginning to fall out of favor with the Irish youth. For years and years almost all Irish drinking took place in the bar; now alcohol is purchased at the grocery store and consumed at home before heading out to the "club," which has replaced the pub as the center of young people's social life.

The pub is far from dead and the government is very aware how important it is to the economy as a tourist attraction. In addition, in the rural areas of central Ireland, it is an essential part of daily lives. KILRICKLE is a village in eastern County Galway with a pub, a church, a store, an elementary school, and a police substation. In many ways **Dessie O'Brien's Pub** is Kilrickle. Whether it's a christening, first communion, wedding, birthday, or funeral, the pub is central to the occasion. Everything takes place at the pub, whether it's celebrating or mourning, and this is repeated in hundreds and hundreds of villages across the country. Thank the "Good Lord in Heaven" **Dessie's** is not closing.

To enjoy the pub experience you need to know a few rules and regulations. The legal drinking age is 18. Closing time mid-week in Ireland is 11:30 PM with a half-hour "drinking up" time. Friday and Saturday closing is at 12:30 PM, most nightclubs stay open until 2:30 AM. Alcohol is not available two days each year, Christmas and Good Friday. It is also difficult to find a drink before Mass on Sundays. The legal limit for alcohol in the bloodstream while driving is below .08%. This law is vigorously enforced, which is why in every village in Ireland you will see a crowd at the taxi stand at the end of the evening.

There are many noteworthy pubs throughout Ireland, including **O'Donoghue's,** located at 15 Merrion Row in DUBLIN. The pub is historically significant, and is the most famous pub in Ireland. Built in 1789 as a grocery store, this pub is closely associated with Irish traditional music. "The Dubliners" started out here along with a long list of other prominent Irish groups. Live music seven nights a week makes this place crowded and popular.

The Temple Bar is a cultural and entertainment district in Dublin. There are numerous bars and pubs in the busy Temple Area and you can hear great Irish music in pubs like the **Oliver St. John Gogarty** on the corner of Fleet and Angelea Streets. One pub named "**The Temple Bar**" is frequently featured in photographs of Dublin and Ireland. Other good traditional pubs are **Doheny** and **Nesbitts** on lower Baggot Street, the **Palace Bar** on Fleet Street, **O'Neills** on the corner of Pearse and Shaw Streets, and old-fashioned **Mulligans** on Poolbeg Street.

A cozy spot south of St. Stephen's Green at the corner of Camden Street Upper and Harcourt Road is the **Bleeding Horse,** formerly a blacksmith shop and a church. For an upscale experience, try the famous **Horseshoe Bar** in the Shelburne Hotel.

"Bloomsday" is a commemoration observed annually on June 16" in Dublin and elsewhere to celebrate the life of author James Joyce; and relive the events in his novel Ulysses, all of which took place on the same day in Dublin in 1904. The name derives from Leopold Bloom, the main character in the novel. Tracing Bloom's steps that day around Dublin include stops at pubs like Davy Byrne's and others. Ulysses is considered by many as the greatest novel of the 20th century. Should you choose to read it, allow plenty of time because it is written in the "stream of consciousness" style of James Joyce, and as a result, understanding the travels and travails of Leopold Bloom is not easy!

The following is a "short" list of some other pubs spread over Ireland that are worth a visit. Keep in mind there are over 8000 pubs in Ireland and over 1000 in Dublin.

Abbey Tavern (Dublin): a short distance from Dublin center, the Abbey Tavern is the perfect place to recover and refuel after spending the day exploring Dublin. The Abbey is known far and wide for its ballads, as well as its brew.

The Long Valley (County Cork) for anyone who

knows and loves Cork, this is a place of pilgrimage. The bar runs the full length of the room, and the doors are taken from an ocean liner, the food is "delectable," and the whole place is a "slice of heaven."

McGann's (County Clare) DOOLIN, a dot of a town on the Clare Coast, is home to many traditional Irish musicians, and a wonderful spot to hear impromptu sessions. **Gus O'Connor's,** down the road, is the more famous pub; but thicker with tourists, and **McGann's** remains the genuine article without the hype.

Moran's Oyster Cottage (County Galway): famous for its seafood, this cozy thatched-roof cottage pub on The Weir draws a perfect pint of Guinness. This place could well be the capital of Ireland. It's 12 miles out of Galway, and well worth the trip.

Crown Liquor (BELFAST) - this National Trust Pub, across from the Parliament House, is a Victorian gem. Your mouth will drop open at the interior splendor even before you lift your first pint.

In addition to drinking, Ireland is famous for its toasts and jokes; so we end this chapter with a few of each.

"May your glass be always full, may the roof over your head always be strong and may you be in heaven a half-hour before the devil knows you're dead."

"Here's to a long life and a happy one. A quick death and an easy one. A pretty girl and an honest one. A cold beer and another one."

An Irishman was terribly overweight so his doctor put him on a diet. "I want you to eat and drink regularly for two days, then skip a day, then eat and drink regularly again for two days, then skip a day – and repeat this procedure for two weeks. The next time I see you, you should've lost at least 5 pounds." When the Irishman returned, he shocked the doctor, having lost nearly 60 pounds! "Why, that's amazing," the doctor said. "Did you follow my instructions?" The Irishman, nodded, "I'll tell you, though, by Jesus, I thought I were going to drop dead, on that third day." "From the hunger, you mean?" asked the doctor. "No, from the fucking skippin.'"

The following was voted "Best Joke in Ireland" last year:

John O' Reilly hoisted his beer and said, "Here's to spending the rest of my life between the legs of my wife!" That won him top prize at the pub for the best toast of the night. He went home and told his wife, Mary, "I won the prize for the best toast of the night." Mary said, "Did you now. And what was your toast?" John said, "Here's to spending the rest of my life sitting in church beside my wife."

"Oh, that is very nice indeed, John," Mary said. Mary ran into one of John's drinking buddies on the street corner. The man was laughing and said, "John won the prize the other night at the pub with the toast about you, Mary." Mary said, "Yes, he told me and I was a bit surprised myself. You know, he's only been there twice in the last four years. Once I had to pull him by the ears to make him come, and the other time he fell asleep."

A recent article in The New York Times described a pub in a tiny seaside village in County Clare called BALLYVAUGHN. The pub opens at 8 PM every evening unless Margaret happens to get her act together sooner. It specializes in whiskey with a stock of over 400 brands; but she only serves around 50. The rest, crowding the shelves behind the bar, are for show. Margaret says, "It's taken me years and years to collect them, be a shame to open them now." This is a place to talk, laugh, listen, and sip whiskey;

keep in mind, the Irish drink the whiskey straight, or "neat," no water. Surprisingly, Margaret does have an ice machine, with a hand crank, must be 100 years old.

This pub, called **O'Lochlainn,** is essentially one room with a grandfather clock ticking, crammed with antiques, old pictures, older maps, bric-a-brac, and run and ruled by Margaret. The wonderful news is that this scene is repeated in little towns and villages all over Ireland.

Drinking whiskey straight out of a shot glass reminds me of a true story about my father, who drank several shots every day of his life. These drinks were never close together, and never, not once, did I ever notice he had had too much to drink.

The doctor in the small town of Olean, New York, another Irishman, asked my father during a regular checkup, "How much do you drink now that you are older and retired?" Whatever the answer was, I am sure the wise old doctor increased it at least a little. So the doctor replied, "John, here's what I would like you to do from now on. When you bring that bottle of Four Roses home just put half of it in another empty bottle and fill both bottles with water. Keep drinking your shots of whiskey, only now you will be drinking half as much." Worked like a charm! What a great piece of advice, the doctor knew the alcohol wasn't a requirement, the shots had just become a habit. My father followed this advice until his death from a broken hip at age 93. By the way, my mother never touched a drop of alcohol; she died at 89.

ITALY

"Bring more wine." – Response by Roman emperor Claudius upon learning of the execution of his wife Messalina for conspiracy, 48 A.D.

Wine pervades most spheres of life in Italy and is an important part of the Italian culture. As discussed earlier, wine was a valuable ingredient of the Roman Empire, and has played a key role, both as an industry and as the most popular beverage ever since.

Drinking without eating has always been rare in Italy. Drinking has never been an activity in itself. Italians do not drink simply because friends are getting together, unless, of course, food is involved. With meals it is normal to serve wine with every course. Wine is considered nourishment and a normal part of everyday life; so no special circumstances are required to bring a bottle of wine out of the liquor closet.

Italians have more of a "sipping" culture than a "drinking" culture, and traditionally wine has been served at the dinner table for centuries, with boys and girls often getting their first taste of alcohol around age 12. The national minimum drinking age of 16 is often ignored, and rarely enforced.

Italy is the largest, by volume, wine- producing country in the world. It is said that more land in Italy is used to grow grapes then to grow food. In 1965, laws were passed to guarantee regular consistency in winemaking. Wines regulated by the government are labeled "DOC" (Denominazione d'Origine Controllata). If you see "DOCG" on the label the "G" means guaranteed, that means even better control. It is considered an honor, and certainly helps profitability, to own vines with these designations.

A recent Wall Street Journal poll of European drinking habits had some surprising results. In Italy, where wine has been the drink of choice for thousands of years, 88% of the survey respondents over 50 said their favorite drink was wine. But among Italians aged 14 to 29, only 29% prefer wine, while 43% say they prefer beer. Similar results were found for other Mediterranean countries (France, Spain and Portugal).

A few other characteristics of Italian drinking tend to affect bar hopping in this country. Cocktails are not common in Italy, and cocktail hours are short or nonexistent. Italians do not appreciate hard drinking, and even mild intoxication is frowned upon. In major cities like Milan, it is customary to end the day with an aperitivo or aperitif, a pre-dinner drink. During the day, thousands of outdoor chairs bask empty in the sun in expectation of aperitivo hour. At 7 PM the patios are teeming with men and women downing fruity, red concoctions served in oversize wineglasses. The drink might be a frageno (prosecco, fresh strawberry juice, and vodka) a spritz, (aperol, prosecco and club soda), or an Americano (Campari, sweet vermouth, and club soda). The hotspot in Milan for aperitivo has been Bar Bacso for the past 35 years.

Unlike most other parts of the world, where a

coffeehouse is called a café, in Italy it is called a bar, and in some cases a caffé. Caffé is the Italian word for coffee; and the preparation, selection of blends and the use of accessories are all part of a special Italian culture focused on coffee.

A bar or caffé in Italy is a place where patrons may purchase coffee drinks, wine, liquor, gelato (really more like soft ice cream), pastries and small sandwiches called Panini. The bar is the center of social life, not a place to go and consume large amounts of alcohol. When you are in Italy, you will come to depend on the bars or caffés: in the morning go to your local caffé for cappuccino and pastry. Midday, when you're out touring, drop into a caffé and pick up a panino (sandwich) and an espresso to get you through until lunchtime. Midafternoon, drop into a caffé for an espresso and a chance to sit down and rest awhile. Because they serve gelato, you could have a nice ice cream with your espresso. During the day, if you need to find a restroom, you can always find one in the caffé. In the early evening, before heading out for dinner, drop into your local caffé for an aperitivo to stimulate the appetite. Sit outside and watch the evening passeggiata. After dinner return for a final grappa, to help with digestion. Going to the caffé is almost medicinal!

Daily visits to the caffé will provide you with some of the nicest times in Italy, the people who run caffés are usually very friendly and used to tourists. They make you feel comfortable and at home, as well as giving you the best coffee you have ever had. By the end of your trip, you may long for the large cup of American coffee with its endless refills, but you will never have espresso as good as what you get every day in Italy. And, of course, the caffés are excellent places for people watching. As Yogi Berra would say, "You can observe a lot by watching."

In VENICE **Harry's Bar** is a place with a lot of history. There are Harry's Bars all over the world, including **Harry's New York Bar** in PARIS; but the one in Venice is special. Harry Pickering, a rich, young Bostonian had been a daily customer at the hotel Europa bar, where Giuseppe Cipriani was the bartender. Eventually Pickering ran out of money and explained that his family had cut him off financially after learning of his drinking habits. Cipriani loaned Pickering 10,000 lire (about $5,000 U.S.) because he thought he was such a fine young man. For two years Cipriani never heard a thing from Pickering and pretty much gave up hope of ever seeing his 10,000 lire again. Then one day in February, 1931, Harry Pickering showed up at the hotel bar, ordered a drink, and gave Cipriani 50,000 lire. "Mr. Cipriani, thank you," he said. "And to show my gratitude, I'm giving you an extra 40,000 lire, enough to open your own bar. We will call it Harry's Bar." The Italian Ministry for Cultural Affairs declared Harry's Bar a national landmark in 2001.

Harry's Bar was a favorite of famous people from the day it opened in 1931. The first and only guestbook it ever had bears the names of Toscanini, Marconi, Somerset Maugham, Charlie Chaplin, Alfred Hitchcock, Truman Capote, Orson Welles, Aristotle Onassis, Woody Allen, Peggy Guggenheim and Barbara Hutton.

During the long, cold winter of 1949–50, Ernest Hemingway established himself in his own corner table in Harry's Bar overlooking the Grand Canal. He was finishing the novel "Over the River and Into the Trees" in which Harry's Bar is mentioned many times. Cipriani claims Hemingway was generous to a fault, and filled more pages in his checkbook than in a medium length novel. Harry's Bar is famous for the Bellini Carpaccio and its dry martini. The martinis are very dry with a ratio of 10 parts gin to one part vermouth. This is an adaptation of the Montgomery Martini, which has a ratio of 15 to 1. The Montgomery is named after British Field Marshall Bernard Montgomery, who liked to have a 15 to 1 ratio of his own troops against the enemy before entering the battlefield. Harry's Bar today is a global brand positioned around the Cipriani name with three restaurants in New York City, and three more in Buenos Aires.

While coffee and red wines are still the drinks of choice in Italy, beer and ale are beginning to flow in the larger cities. **The Open Baladin** in Rome offers 100 craft brews and a grand display of bottled Italian beers.

Ma Che Siete Venuti A Fá ("What the hell are you doing here") has a great selection of pilsners and ales, and down the street at the **Bir & Fud** the barkeep helps you pair your food with your beer.

Limoncello is now considered the national drink of Italy and can be found in bars, stores, and restaurants all over the country. An absolute natural product made by the infusion of lemon skins in pure alcohol; it has become Italy's second most popular drink, after Compari. This lemon liqueur is served chilled, and is wonderful as a pallet cleanser or as a light after-dinner drink. Other uses for Limoncello include mixing it with champagne or fruit juice, or simply drizzling it on ice cream, salads, or fresh fruit.

Authentic Limoncello is made from Sorrento lemons, which come from the Amalfi Coast. The ingredients for Limoncello are simple: lemons, alcohol, water and sugar. A problem arises because in most recipes the lemons must steep for 80 days.

Compari is probably the most well-known Italian

drink. Red in color and flavored with herbs, it has a genuine bitterness to it. It's customary to serve it with ice cubes and soda. This beverage was created in the 19th century in Milan by restaurateur Gaspari Compari.

Grappa is a uniquely Italian drink, and has been around since the Middle Ages. Grappa was originally made in Bassano del Grappa, a town of about 40,000 in Italy's Northern Veneto region, hence the name.

Similar to France's Brandies and Portugal's Sherry, Grappa is a clear, 40% alcohol, distilled beverage. Grappa is made by distilling the skins, pulp, seeds and stems leftover from winemaking after pressing the grapes. These leftovers are called the pomace. Grappa is now a protected name in the European Union. To be called Grappa the following three criteria must be met:

1. Manufactured in Italy, or the Italian part of Switzerland.
2. Produced from pomace.
3. Fermentation and distillation must occur on the pomace – no added water.

Criterion number two rules out the direct fermentation of pure grape juice, which is the method used to produce brandy.

Criterion number three has two important implications. First, the distillation must occur on solids, which requires steam distillation; otherwise the pomace may burn with direct flame distillation. Second, the woody seeds and stems are co-fermented with the juice producing wood alcohol (methanol), which is poisonous and must be carefully removed during distillation.

Today, there are hundreds of highly individual, markedly different styles of this fiery distillate, which can have great character and depth. There are also aged Grappas that are complex in flavor due to being aged in barrels made of oak, birch, or juniper. These aged Grappas are not clear and take on a yellow or red-brown hue from the barrel in which they are stored.

The Nonino Distillery in Percoto, Italy, has been producing Grappa since 1897. In the early 1970s, Giannola Nonino began making Grappa from a single grape variety instead of the usual practice of using a mixture of grape leftovers. This approach elevated the quality and consistency of the Grappa made by Nonino. Today, this woman, Giannola Nonino, is given great credit for her efforts over many years to establish the single grape Grappa as an upscale beverage. In Italy, Grappa has been used for generations as an after-dinner drink to aid in digestion of heavy meals. It also is added to espresso coffee to "correct" it.

Once considered an acquired taste, popular only in Italy, Grappa, today is known around the world. Distilleries from Austria to Oregon are producing Grappa with surprisingly good results.

It's been more than 100 years since the first espresso machine was invented by an enterprising Italian named Luigi Bezzera. Since then, espresso has become a way of life for Italians. No true Italian kitchen is without a "moka" pot, and no day in Italy is complete without taking a moment to sit and enjoy one of the finest discoveries this Country has ever brought the world.

Whether you're traveling to Rome for the tenth time, or making your first trip through Tuscany, it's impossible to truly experience Italy without spending time in a classic Italian caffé . . . Even if espresso isn't your cup of tea, per se, it's worth it just to sit and relax with a homemade treat as you let the Italian sun wash over you. In the spirit of taking things slow and fully living in those little Italian moments, the following is a list of some of the most interesting caffés in Italy. These places also have alcohol; but their reputation is founded on espresso and other coffee beverages.

Il Caffé di Sant'eustachio – This 70-year-old landmark is located in the heart of ROME's historic district, and remains much the way it was when it got its start back in the 1930s. With outdoor tables that face an open piazza, this is the place we all imagine when we fantasize about whiling away the hours on a gorgeous Roman holiday. The caffé's specialties include a signature blend espresso with a secret recipe known only to the caffé's owners.

Giolitti, ROME– Located on the Uffici Del Vicario, just up from the Pantheon, Giolitti isn't technically a caffé, but no trip to Italy would be complete without gelato. And if you are going to try it, you might as well have it here in the city's oldest gelato shop. Open at 7 AM daily, coffee buffs will enjoy kicking-off their morning with a combination of their caffé flavor and the sumptuous chocolate hazelnut gelato.

Caffé Greco – Located on one of the most exclusive shopping streets in Rome, Via Condotti, this literary caffé is one of the oldest. Marble tables, upholstered chairs, gold and crimson damask walls, jacketed waiters, and countless mirrors reflect an age of elegance that's remained suspended in time since 1760 in this classic caffé. Decades of travelers on a Roman holiday have made this a must-stop. Goethe, Byron, Dickens, Keats, and Mark Twain – each of them whiled away the hours in one of the oldest coffeehouses in this Eternal City.

Caffé South Eustachio – Despite its discreet facade and location (near the Pantheon), this is THE espresso institution in ROME. Actually, there are two caffés bearing more or less the same name: choose the most crowded and less glittering of the two.

Caffé Della Pace – Located in a beautiful small square, just off Piazza Navona, is known for its show business clientele.

Caffé Rosati – Located on the famous Piazza del Popolo, founded in 1923, attracts elegant, heterogeneous clientele. This place becomes more interesting as the night wears on, and is more famous for its sandwiches than for its cappuccino.

Caffé Biffi, MILAN– Located in an unassuming two-story building, Caffé Biffi is surprisingly one of the most famous in Italy. Asserting itself as the birthplace of Italian Pancetta and the ever-popular Spritz, it once played host to a string of movie stars and business leaders. Now it is more popular with the many tourists who pass through the beautiful Galleria while sightseeing around the City. You will enjoy the ambience of the historical surroundings as well as the traditionally served cappuccino and espresso.

Caffé Florian St. Mark's Square, VENICE– Operating for over three centuries, **Caffé Florian** lays claim as Italy's oldest caffé. And over time it has expanded the vast repertoire of coffee beverages offered. From modest beginnings as a simple caffé, it has developed as a center for culture and coffee, attracting both royalty and celebrities alike. Eminent for its history as a crossroads of art, politics, and entertainment, the modern Florian is also known for its elegant trademark products, luxurious decor and location. Situated opposite the Basilica de San Marco, visitors can admire the amazing Byzantine, Gothic, Romanesque, and

Renaissance architecture, as they receive the same impeccable coffee and service that has been enjoyed by patrons for hundreds and hundreds of years.

Caffé Quadri, VENICE– With an enviable view of St. Mark's Square creating the perfect backdrop, this is without a doubt, the quintessential Venetian caffé. Best enjoyed at night when the tourists are elsewhere and the pigeons are tucked in their nests, Caffé Quadri's personal orchestra lulls late-night coffee sippers into a romantic end of the day. Come for the atmosphere and stay for the history – this place has been entertaining coffee drinkers since the late 1600s and hasn't changed much since then.

Caffe Quadri, VENICE

Ye Olde Fighting Cock, St Albans, ENGLAND

Café Smalle, AMSTERDAM

Grace Neills's Pub, IRELAND

Bazen Head, DUBLIN

O'Donoghue's Pub, DUBLIN

Gravity Bar, Guinness Brewery, DUBLIN

Trappist Monastery, BELGIUM

Cafe de Flore, PARIS

Carlsberg Brewery, COPENHAGEN

HofbrauHaus, MUNICH

Ocktoberfest, MUNICH

Temple Bar, DUBLIN

McSorley's Old Ale House, NEW YORK CITY

Oktoberfest, MUNICH

St. James Gate, Guinness Brewery, DUBLIN

Terry W. Lyons

Carnavale, RIO de JANEIRO

Café Greco, ROME

York Hotel, Kalgoorlie, AUSTRALIA

Westmalle Beer, BELGIUM

Les Deux Margots, PARIS

Harry's Bar, PARIS

La Lafitte Saloon, NEW ORLEANS

21 Club, NEW YORK CITY

Last Chance Saloon, OAKLAND

Brown Café, AMSTERDAM

The Eagle Tavern, Cambridge, England

U Fleku Brewpub, Czech Republic

JAPAN

"The problem with the world is that everyone is a few drinks behind." – Humphrey Bogart

The manufacture and consumption of alcohol are serious businesses in Japan. With its exceptional bars and drinking culture, many "experts" claim "it is the best place to drink alcohol in the world"; others call it a drinker's paradise.

The consumption of alcohol has contributed to the development of giant Japanese corporations employing tens of thousands of people, and with world-wide operations. There are almost 2000 manufacturers of sake in Japan; but sake has been replaced by beer as the most popular drink in Japan.

National beer breweries include Sapporo, Suntory, Asahi, and Kirin. Suntory started out by producing wine, but is now the oldest and the largest distiller of whisky in Japan. It also produces wine, beer and soft drinks. Asahi, Suntory's main rival, brews Asahi Super Dry, Japan's most popular beer.

Japanese men enjoy drinking together, and this has led to a wonderful selection of drinking establishments all over Japan, not just in major cities. Drinking, although not confined to men, is mainly the province of the male population.

In addition to recreation, relaxation and entertainment, drinking is a very important element of the Japanese business culture. Business relations and negotiations have two totally different worlds, one of daytime or "dry" relations, and the other at night, termed "wet" relations. The daytime world consists of strict business associations and formal negotiations. The evening "wet" relations take place in the bars, restaurants and nightclubs where business negotiations are successfully concluded.

Even in rural areas the conclusion of any kind of business – a land deal, forest clearing, barn sale, or whatever – is followed by sharing of a drink, usually sake, among the participants.

Japanese consume about 8 liters of pure alcohol per person per year. The French are the largest consumers of alcohol, about 12 liters per year per person, and the Americans consume about 7 liters.

Drunkenness is an accepted form of behavior in Japan, and many feel it is the only time they can let themselves go and say what they think. Some Japanese believe that the only way to really get to know someone is to get drunk with them, and regard people who won't drink as arrogant and having something to hide.

The earliest written reference to alcohol use in Japan is recorded in the "Book of Wei," and it appears sake originated in the period 710-794 A.D. Sake production was a government monopoly for a long time. Around the 10th century, sake began to be used in religious ceremonies and temples and shrines began brewing sake; they became the main source of production for the next 500 years.

In the 16th century, distillation was introduced and

shochu became available with a higher alcohol content of 20-40%. Today in Japan, sales of sake and shochu are about equal. In the 1700s, laws were passed that allowed anyone with the money and expertise to operate their own sake brewery, and around 30,000 breweries sprung up in about a year. Over the ensuing years, the government continued to levy more and more taxes on the industry, and the number of breweries dwindled down to about 8,000.

During the 20th century sake brewing technology grew by leaps and bounds. Wooden barrels were replaced by enameled tanks, and yeast strains with special brewing properties were isolated in government research laboratories. By the beginning of the 20th century, the Japanese government was getting about one-half its total revenue from the levy on sake. Obviously, there was a whole lot of drinking going on. In order to increase revenue even more, the home-brewing of sake was banned during the Russo-Japanese War in 1904-1905. This was the end of home-brewed sake, and the law remains in effect today, even though sake taxes now make up only 2% of government income.

When World War II brought rice shortages, the sake industry began adding pure alcohol and glucose to small quantities of rice mash, increasing the yield as much as four times. A majority of sake continues to be made this way today. After the war, breweries began to recover, and the quality of sake improved; but new competition had finally arrived on the scene – beer, wine, and spirits. By 1970, beer had surpassed sake as the number one beverage in Japan.

So now, while the rest of the world is drinking more sake, consumption in Japan is continuing to decline. In 1975, there were over 3000 sake breweries; now there are less than 1800.

Sake is a rice-based alcoholic beverage of Japanese

origin. There is a little confusion because the drink is called sake in English, but in Japanese sake refers to alcoholic beverages in general, and the term for this particular beverage is nihonshu, meaning Japanese alcohol.

Unlike champagne, Scotch, or tequila, which are "region-specific" with very clear laws and regulations, sake can be produced anywhere. There are sake breweries all over the world. Sake in English is also often referred to as a "rice wine"; however, unlike wine, in which alcohol is produced by fermenting sugar from fruit, like grapes, sake is made through a brewing process more like beer, thus it's more like a rice brew than a rice wine.

The sake brewing process differs slightly from beer brewing because to produce beer requires two steps to convert starch to sugar and sugar to alcohol; for sake this conversion occurs simultaneously in one step. As a result, sake has an alcohol content of 18-20%, while beer is around 3-9%, and wine about 9-16%.

Like French wine, nihonshu (sake) is a complex beverage, and it is officially separated into four different grades depending on how much of the rice grain remains after polishing. More polishing of the rice results in better sake. Polishing, or milling in this sense, means removing the outer portion of the grain. The highest grade of nihonshu (sake) is dai-ginjo shu, where the rice is polished so only 50% of the grain remains. There an endless variety in the methods of making and aging sake, resulting in thousands of different products. These sakes are complex, light and crisp. If you only try one nihonshu, make sure it is dai-ginjo shu.

Like wine, sake, can be sweet or dry. Dry sake has a positive number, while sweet sake has a negative number on the label. The average grades may be drunk warm, while the higher grades will be served chilled. Sake is the only drink that is commonly served across a wide range of temperatures. Sake is brewed throughout Japan and brewery tours are common. Few breweries allow guests to enter the actual brewing area; however, the Kobe Shushinkan Brewery has been in business since 1751 and it does open its brew house to visitors. Call ahead for reservations: 078/841-1121. Sake is only brewed from October to March, but the breweries remain open all year for guided tours of the facilities.

Nada, one of Kobe's western suburbs, is home to Hakatsura Sake Brewery. The brewing process is demonstrated using life-size figures of traditionally clad brewers using ancient tools and equipment. Videos are available in English, and there is a free tasting at the end of the tour.

The southern side of Kyoto has a district of old white-walled sake breweries and warehouses dating to the 17th century. Gekkeikan was founded in 1637 and it is still operating. They have tours and a museum that details the brewing process.

While sake is the essential Japanese drink, beer is the most popular beverage in Japan. In fact, Japan is the world's seventh largest beer market. Beer in Japan dates back to the early 17th century, when the Dutch opened a beer hall for sailors. By the late 19th century brewers from Germany had arrived and production increased notably. The major producers today are Sapporo, Asahi, Kirin and Suntory. In addition, the micro-brewing industry has begun to take a portion of the market.

Due to the Japanese taxation system, the varieties of beer are classified into three categories. The system is based on the amount of malt used, and the term "happoshu" is used to describe low-malt brews. Japanese law prevents brews containing less than 67% malt to be called beer. A third category titled "happousei" contains no malt at all, and is taxed at the lowest rate.

Vending machines are a big deal in Japan with the highest density of vending machines per capita in the world, one machine for every 23 people. Beer and other alcoholic beverages are sold in these machines, and some have small TV screens that play commercials seen on television or heard on the radio. It is considered bad manners to eat or drink while walking down the street, so beverages obtained from a vending machine are gulped down on the spot and the container thrown away before moving on. There's been much concern over these outlets due to underage drinking. Japan is quite liberal when it comes to selling and consuming alcohol and beer can be purchased at convenience stores, supermarkets, and at kiosks at train stations. Japan is experimenting with an ID system to help with the underage drinking problem. Japan has very strict laws against drinking and driving, or even riding a bicycle and drinking. You are not allowed even one drink.

Japanese beers are now available around the world, but many of them are not produced in Japan. For example, for the U.S. market, Asahi is produced by Molson in Canada, Kirin is brewed at an Anheuser Busch facility in Los Angeles, and Sapporo is made at a Sapporo-owned brewery in Guelph, Ontario, Canada.

The city of Sapporo is home to the Sapporo beer brewery and the Sapporo beer museum. The museum is housed in a former red brick factory. The main attraction here is the neighboring, huge beer garden. Every summer for three weeks, Sapporo hosts an outdoor beer festival that attracts thousands of people. Tours of the Sapporo brewery are available year-round with tastings offered at the conclusion of the tour.

Other major Japanese alcoholic beverages include plum wine, Shochu, whisky, and Awamori.

Plum wine is made from Japanese plums and is very popular with people who normally do not drink alcohol. It has a sweet, fruity, juice-like aroma and is commonly made at home but is available anywhere alcohol is sold. It is usually served on the rocks mixed with soda.

Shochu is an alcoholic beverage produced mainly in southern Japan, and generally made from rice; but wheat, sweet potatoes, and sugar cane are also used. It was once considered a lower class drink but sales now approach sake and whisky. A clear liquid, similar to vodka, it is usually mixed with soda water or fruit juices. Shochu production is often seasonal because fresh ingredients are considered important. The use of koji mold spores to break down the starches to sugar is fundamental in all traditional Japanese alcohol products. The koji is mixed with water and yeast and left to ferment for about a week. This is then added to the main ingredient (rice, sweet potatoes, barley, etc.) and a second fermentation takes place for another week. At this point, distillation produces the final product.

There are two main types of Shochu. Korui, which is right from the still and is inexpensive, neutral alcohol. The good stuff is Honkaku Shochu made in pot stills and aged with a variety of added ingredients.

Awamori is a type of Shochu produced in Okinawa. It differs from Shochu in that it must be made from long-grained Thai-style rice instead of short-grained Japanese-style rice. Two other distinguishing features are that all Awamori is made with black Koji mold spores indigenous to Okinawa, and all of the rice is cultivated with Koji mold from the beginning, rather than the two-stage process used for Shochu. Awamori is allowed to mature for years in earthenware pots, stainless steel vats, or wooden oaken casks. The classic way to drink Awamori is straight, or on the rocks. Alcohol content is about 20-50%, so water is often added.

Whisky was first introduced to the Japanese by the Americans when Commodore Perry arrived in 1854 to negotiate the opening of Japan to foreign trade. Commodore Perry arrived with a barrel (110 gallons) of American whisky as a gift for the Emperor and his subjects. Apparently a good time was had by all, and the stuff was an instant hit. But when everyone stopped hugging and the Commodore and the ships had departed, the Japanese had no idea how to make the wonderful stuff. Feeble attempts were made and shabby product was produced over the next 70 years without much success.

Today, Japan is regarded as one of the five major whisky-producing countries, along with Canada, Ireland, Scotland and the United States. The Japanese have won a series of major tasting awards for both single malt and blended whiskies over the past decade.

In 2008, at the world whisky awards in Glasgow, Scotland; Japan won the prize for the best single-malt whisky (Yoichi, 20-year-old), and the best blended whisky (Hibiki, 30-year-old). Like scotch, the Japanese products are spelled "whisky," without the "e." Japanese whiskies have close ties to Scotland.

In 1918, Masataka Taketsuru, a 24-year-old chemist was sent to Glasgow, Scotland; to study the secrets of Scottish distilled spirits. He returned to Japan two years later with a Scottish wife and the know-how to produce quality whisky. He is credited with founding Japan's two great rival whisky empires, Suntory and Nikka. It was not until after the Second World War that whisky became popular in Japan.

Japanese whiskies have stayed remarkably loyal to

their Scottish roots. The award-winning Hibiki produced by Suntory is a blend of more than 30 individual whiskies with the final blend topped off with a whisky aged over 30 years. Hibiki uses mild plum liqueur casks for aging, and a bamboo charcoal filter that mellows out the flavor.

There are seven major distilleries in Japan producing both single-malt and blended products. Suntory and Nikki are the heavyweights and competition is tough in a declining market, as the popularity of beer and Shochu continues to rise.

Japanese dining and drinking etiquette is quite formal. One of the strictest rules involves the pouring of drinks. The main thing to remember is that you never pour your own glass. If you want (or need) a drink, be sure to hold up your glass when someone else is pouring. Because each person in the group is continually filling everyone else's glass, you never know how much you had to drink. This can be good, or very, very bad. It is especially polite if you hold the bottle or your glass with both hands.

Japanese usually do not begin drinking until someone offers the toast "kampari," meaning "drain your glass," or "dry glass." Another toast often used is "bonsai" meaning "live 10,000 years," sort of like "hip, hip, hooray." It does not mean "charge" or "fix bayonets: as those familiar with the Second World War might think.

Unlike Western bars and pubs that tend to open early and close early (11 PM in Britain), Japanese bars open later and stay open almost all night. For the uninitiated, this type of drinking can exact a heavy toll.

The legal drinking age in Japan is 20, and beer, wine and spirits are readily available in grocery stores, convenience stores, liquor stores, kiosks and vending machines.

If you intend to drive in Japan, you are not allowed even one drink or you will be over the limit. Japan has some of the strictest drunk driving laws in the world. And if you have been a witness to the traffic you can understand why they must have the strictest laws in the world. You can be imprisoned and heavily fined, not only for drunk driving yourself, but for being in a car with a drunken driver, lending a car to someone who has been drinking, or serving alcohol to a driver who is drunk.

The legal limit is less than .03% blood alcohol content, much lower than in many other countries. One small beer can put you over the limit. In addition to the jail sentence, Japanese law routinely enforces large fines on people who cause harm to others.

Japan not only has its own unique types of alcohol (sake, Shochu, Awamori), it also has a varied and unusual variety of drinking establishments. One reason Japan has so many bars is because people have so little room in their own homes that they go out when they entertain and socialize. Another reason is the bars tend to be small, so there are lots of them.

Izakayas are the main drinking places in Japan and serve alcohol and food. Customers can sit at the bar, at a table or on a tatami floor mat. There's usually a lot of interaction between the staff and the customers. The Izakayas are often identified by red lanterns outside their doors. These are the places where company employees drink with their friends and workmates. The range of Izakayas is great: some are cheap, some are very expensive, some are classy and some are really grim, and many charge a small entrance fee.

Tachinomiya (standing drinking shop) are places without seating and drinks are served to standing customers. These places are particularly popular in Tokyo, where property is very expensive.

Sunakki (snack) are small, neighborhood bars that serve food and alcohol. Often, the drinks are poured from bottles the customers bring with them, or from bottles they keep at the restaurant. Some of these places have less than a dozen seats. The bars are typically run by women, known as mamas, who are known for cheering up customers and lending a sympathetic ear to their problems. A sunakki or "snack" is never a cheap place to go for a little bite to eat.

Other specialized bars include Yakitori bars that concentrate on grilled chicken; Robatayaki bars feature grilled meat; Karaoke Boxes are singing rooms serving alcohol. The list continues with beer gardens and beer halls, nightclubs, Irish pubs and jazz clubs.

In Japan, there are about 220,000 "hostess bars," where young women entertain, chat up, pour drinks, and generally flatter male customers. The women generally do not have sex with the male customers. This is certainly a drinking custom that is a little difficult for foreigners to grasp. By the way, there are also host bars where women are flattered by men – not the world's worst job!

The words "pub" and "bar" can refer to an enormous variety of drinking and non-drinking establishments. The general advice is not to regard the word "pub" or "bar" as a guarantee of something familiar.

In recent years, large, chain Izakayas have become a force on the Japanese bar scene. You miss all the character, charm, service, and individuality in these places, but you do gain consistency and reassurance, particularly in unfamiliar locations. The most successful chain is Watami, with over 600 outlets.

A recent book, "Drinking Japan – Guide to Japan's Best Drinks and Drinking Establishments," by Chris Bunting, is a wonderful guide to Japanese spirits and bars. This book gives detailed reviews of unusual bars, each complete with an excellent photograph, menu and detailed map and directions on how to get there. The bars are categorized by what they serve: sake bars, Shochu bars, wine bars, single-malt bars, beer bars, etc.

The following list includes only a few very special drinking spots in this crowded country of over 128 million people; the world's most densely populated country. Tokyo alone has 12.5 million people, and it would take a lifetime to explore. Japanese addresses get very complicated, so only phone numbers are listed.

In September 2008, the U.S. gourmet magazine, Bon Appétit declared Tokyo to be the "cocktail capital of the world." They claim the city had displaced New York and London, at the cocktail game. It's not just the bars; it's the highly skilled and disciplined cadre of bartenders that make the city special. Just the often noted bartender's skill in shaping and handling ice is special. The bartenders have all been to school and serve apprenticeships before taking charge; the result is the typical Japanese dedication and attention to detail.

The New York Grill – TOKYO (03-5323-3458). One of the top dining and drinking experiences in Tokyo, The New York Grill is located on the 52nd floor of the Park Hyatt Hotel.

Kamiyor Bar –TOYKO (03-3841-5400). Established in 1888 as the first Western bar in Japan, this place is famous for a drink, "Denki Bran," a mix of gin, wine, brandy, Curacao liqueur, herbs and spices. Although the claim of being the first Western bar in Japan may be dubious, the place was definitely the first to popularize Western drinks in Japan.

Akaoni –TOYKO (03-3401-9918). The best-known premium sake pub in Tokyo with over 100 types of sake available. Sake is becoming so specialized that quite a few manufacturers all over Japan play music to their fermenting alcohol in the belief that it influences the fermenting process of the better grades.

ShuSaRon –TOYKO (03-5449-4455). This is, quite simply, the best place in the world to drink aged sake. The owner here has written the definitive book on Koshu or aged sake, and believes these richer tasting sakes will revolutionize the business over the next few years. The aging over a period of 4 to 10 years in a variety of containers, including wooden barrels and enamel pots, imparts all manner of taste, fragrances and colors to the sake.

Tokyo Shochu Bar Gen – TOKYO (03-5485-8316). Bar Gen claims to have more types of Shochu on the shelves than any other bar in the world – over 5,000 at last count.

A Sign Box – TOYKO (03-3481-5353). An "A" sign could mean the difference between ruin and making a livelihood in post-war Okinawa. It stood for "U.S. Military Approved," and American GIs were forbidden from entering bars without the "A." Since Americans were the only ones with any money, it was all-important to get the blue "A" daubed over the bar entrance. The sign has come to symbolize an entire era in Japanese history. A boom in post-war nostalgia combined with a feeling for all things Okinawan, has brought a return of the "A" signs all over Japan.

Katakura – TOKYO (03-3260-4504). The Katakura family has been running a bar here since the 1800s. The emphasis is on Japanese alcohol: 200 types of Shochu, 80 kinds of sake, and 90 kinds of Awamori. There is an extensive collection of antique drinking vessels; and, strangely enough, the food menu is pretty much Italian, which goes well with sake.

Popeye – TOKYO (03-3633-2120). This is the spot for beer drinkers. Popeye's has the largest range of beers in Japan, and the biggest range of Japanese beers in the world. There are 17 beers on tap, mostly micro-brews. The owner is one of Japan's leading authorities on beer. The place is always packed.

Bar Argyll – TOKYO (03-3344-3442). As the name suggests, the emphasis here is on Scottish single malts, but an excellent selection of Japanese whiskies is also available. The owner claims to have over 250 premium brands. This sounds like a lot, but many Tokyo establishments offer thousands of bottles.

Cask – TOKYO (03-3402-7373). This is one of those upscale places where you don't want to begin carelessly ordering when you have had too much to drink. The whisky collection is extensive by any measure, thousands of bottles and hundreds of brands. A few examples of the high-end stuff: Yamasaki 50-year-old single malt, ¥90,000 yen (about $1,000); White Bowmore, 1964, ¥35,000 yen per glass ($400), or Black Bowmore, ¥50,000 yen ($500).

Shot Bar Zoetrope – TOKYO (03-3363-0162). Zoetrope is the best place in the world to drink Japanese whiskies. There are over 250 whiskies from every distillery in Japan. In addition, there are off-beat Japanese alcohols like Japanese rum, Japanese vodka and Japanese mead.

MEXICO

"Take life with a grain of salt, a slice of lemon and a shot of tequila."
- Anonymous

Mexico has close ties to Spain dating back to 1519 when Cortez and 500 adventurers were able to conquer the Aztec Empire that had existed in one form or another for 3000 years. The Mexicans traded one emperor for another. Today, the last Aztec emperor, Cuauhtémoc is an official national hero; and Cortez, the Spanish conqueror, is considered a villain. Beginning in the 1800s, a non-stop series of rebellions and wars plagued Mexico for the next 100 years, including an attempt by Napoleon III to rule Mexico in 1864, and the Mexican-American war (1846-1848). The Mexican-American war resulted in Mexico ceding what is now Texas, Colorado, California, Utah and parts of Arizona and New Mexico to the U.S.A.

Today, crime and large drug cartels continue to torment Mexico, along with wide disparities between rich and poor. Most Mexicans still despair of the Country ever being governed well; but they remain a proud people, proud of their families, their villages and towns, and proud of Mexico.

As a result of these centuries of turmoil, these long-suffering people work hard at enjoying the leisure side of life.

This may take place in bars or clubs, at festivals, or most likely, with their closely-knit families at parties and celebrations.

Much like the Spanish, festivals play a major role in Mexican society on both a local and a national scale. Some intellectuals have written that the Mexican love of color, noise, music, and crowds is merely a mask to offer a temporary escape from the ever present doom and gloom of society in general. As a result, festivals fulfill a need to celebrate, have fun and enjoy a bit of life. There is at least one national holiday each month, and some of these last for days. In addition, each town has many local Saints Days, regional fairs, art shows and festivals.

One of the biggest events, and one of the most unusual, is All Saints Day, November 1, and Day of the Dead, November 2. This is based on an old Indian belief that the dead could return home one day each year. Every cemetery in the Country comes alive as families visit graveyards to commune with the dead on the night of November 1st and the day of November 2nd.

A week or more of celebrations lead up to the Day of Our Lady of Guadalupe, December 12. This is Mexico's patron saint who appeared to Juan Drago, an Aztec pottery maker, on a hill outside Mexico City in 1531.

September 16 marks the anniversary of the start of Mexico's 1810 failed attempt for independence from Spain. This is a major holiday and big celebration throughout Mexico. Cinque de Mayo (5 May), a very popular Mexican holiday in the United States, is not a big deal in Mexico.

Before the Spanish conquest in 1521, two of Mexico's most important drinks were tapped from the magney (agave) plant. Aquamiel is the non-alcoholic sweet juice that comes direct from the plant. After fermentation, it becomes pulque, a beverage with alcohol content similar to beer. This drink was used by the Aztec Indians for 1000 years. The first bars in Mexico City were called "pulquerias" and these existed for over 400 years before other drinks, such as tequila, mescal and beer forced pulque aside.

Pulque was widely consumed in Mexico City during the colonial period of Spanish rule. In contrast to North America, which was colonized by Northern Europeans who favored beer, the Spaniards brought a taste for wine. Unfortunately, Mexico's climate and soil did not lend themselves to the successful cultivation of wine grapes. The Spaniards quickly learned they could roast the hearts of the agave plant, ferment the juice, and then apply their distilling know-how to produce a fiery, alcoholic beverage called tequila and another called mezcal.

True pulque is homemade, not bottled, and therefore not viable for large-scale commercial production. Today, just a few pulquerias remain in business, and these are extremely small, rustic places. You may have the white liquid straight up or in the more palatable flavored form using coconut, pineapple or mango juice.

Tequila is Mexico's national drink. The agave, a cactus-like plant, is grown for at least eight years until its heart, called a "pine," reaches the size of a beach ball and weighing up to 300 pounds, is harvested. It is then chopped into pieces and oven-roasted for up to three days. The next step is fermentation and distillation.

Mexico has strict rules governing what can be labeled tequila. Premium tequilas must be made from 100% blue agave plant with no additives. Lesser tequilas may contain sugar, flavoring and coloring agents; but by law, the mixture can contain no less than 51% blue agave if it is to be called tequila. In addition, tequila must be produced from agave plants grown in a specific area around the city of Tequila, a small town about 30 miles northwest of Guadalajara. A total of five states are permitted to grow the blue agave plant for tequila production.

There are four varieties of tequila, and which is best is a matter of personal taste. White, or silver tequila, is not aged and no colors or flavors are added; it has a distinct agave flavor. Gold tequila is not aged; but color, caramel, and flavor are added. An example is the best-selling tequila, Cuervo Gold. Tequila reposado, "rested," has been aged from 2 to 11 months in oak barrels. The taste is sharp and peppery. Tequila anejo has been aged at least one year in oak barrels, and is the smoothest tasting variety. Recently a more expensive option of tequila has become popular. These tequilas are aged 3 to 8 years and become as mellow as an aged Scotch or cognac.

Although hundreds of years old, the Spanish conquistadors first cultivated the blue agave plant around 1550, tequila never became really popular until Prohibition took over in the United States from 1922-1932. Just as whiskey from Canada supplied the northern states of the U.S., tequila from Mexico helped serve the drinking needs of the South and West. Another unusual fact is that margaritas, which are extremely popular in the Southwestern part of the U.S., are not a favorite drink in Mexico. The recipe for a margarita, by the way, includes 1½ ounces of tequila, ¾ ounce of fresh lime juice, a half ounce of Cointreau, triple sec, and a lime wedge. Finally, there is no worm in a bottle of tequila. The traditional worm is sometimes found in bottles of mezcal, or mescal, a close cousin of tequila. This is merely a marketing gimmick for the lower-priced mescals, and swallowing the worm won't make you any higher or hornier.

Thirty-five miles northwest of Guadalajara lies the town of Tequila, surrounded by fields of blue-green colored agave. The Jose Cuervo distillery opened in 1795 and is the oldest tequila distillery in the world. Every day, 150 tons of agave hearts are processed into 80,000 liters of tequila. Tours of the facility are conducted several times a day and tastings are included. The National Tequila Museum is also located here and is worth a visit, along with the Sauza Museum, which contains memorabilia from the Sauza family, a tequila-making dynasty, second only to the Cuervos. The Sauza tequila is produced at the Perseveranda distillery, which also has tours.

The "Tequila Express" is an all-day train trip from Guadalajara that visits distilleries and offers plenty of sampling time. This way to try all these tequilas and allow someone else to drive costs about $100 for the day. There is a lot of interest in tequila these days and the tourist business here is strong. Tequila sales in the U.S. have increased 45% in the past five years.

Mezcal, or Mescal, the pride of Oaxaca, is often thought of as a less-refined version of tequila. Quite the contrary, while tequila is only made from the heart of the blue agave plant, cooked in steam chambers and distilled in large batches; mescal is produced from dozens of varieties of agave plants, roasted over a wood fire pit, and distilled in small quantities. The result is a soft, smoky and complex liquor meant to be sipped and savored.

A law passed in 2005 set standards on mescal production, and now you know what you are getting when you see a certified bottle that has been aged in oak barrels (reposado) for two months to one year, one to three years, more than three years, and some are aged up to ten years. The major mezcal brands include El Senorio and Beneva. If you are visiting Oaxaca City, stop by La Cava for a good choice of mescals.

Beer in Mexico has a long history and is a very big business today. Over 63% of the population drinks beer, and it is one of the Country's major exports. The native Indian cultures of Mexico were fermenting corn into alcoholic beverages long before Hernán Cortés and the Spanish arrived in 1520. The Spanish began to brew beer using barley; but the government placed heavy taxes and regulations on the product to protect the markets in Spain by forcing the colonials to import alcoholic beverages from Europe. The beer industry finally began rolling when the Spaniards left and German immigrants began arriving. Many breweries were established in the latter half of the 19th century, and by 1918 there were 31 beer companies in Mexico. Prohibition in the U.S. in the 1920s helped establish the Mexican beer industry with Americans crossing the border to drink, and beer being smuggled into the U.S.

Mexican beer producers also began a campaign at home to discredit the native drinks, such as pulque. They claimed these drinks were produced by unsanitary methods, including the use of feces as a fermenting material. The strategy was quite successful and today pulque is regarded as a second-class drink and Mexican beer is extremely popular.

The 20th century saw a major consolidation of the Mexican beer industry; now there are only two major producers left standing: Grupo Modelo and Cerveceria owned by FEMSA.

Mexico now ranks third in global beer exports with

most of the product shipped to the U.S. The major brands include Corona and Corona Light from Grupo Modelo and Dos Equis from FEMSA. Dos Equis was first brewed in Mexico in 1897.

Mexican beer is distinctive for its lager-like properties, being generally light bodied with a mild taste and is meant to be drunk cold. Most Mexican beer is sold in return bottles and very little is sold on tap. Many trends in the U.S. are adopted in Mexico; but on-tap beer is not a big hit. Another trend that has not proven successful in Mexico is light beer. Despite Corona Light being the best-selling imported light beer in the U.S., sales in Mexico have been dismal. The number one selling premium beer in Mexico is Bohemia. This beer has reached the status of being one of the finest beers in the world. It is produced by Cerveceria Brewers and is its longest aged product, and is made from a special variety of hops, giving a significant hops flavor.

Beer is commonly drunk with lime juice in Mexico. A beer cocktail, called a "michelada," consists of light beer with lots of lime juice, salt, Worcestershire sauce, and tomato juice. As with the margarita, the salt is usually placed on the rim of the glass. Another common college drink in the U.S. is to fill the top of the neck of the bottle with rum or vodka, turn the bottle upside down slowly, return to the upright position, and drink the contents. This is called a "Loaded Corona."

Rum is an incredibly popular drink in Mexico, and much of it is imported, although some is now manufactured in the Valley of Mexico.

Kahlúa is Mexico's most exported liqueur and has been produced for over 60 years. Rum based, mahogany-colored, coffee-flavored, with hints of vanilla and semi-sweet chocolate; Kahlúa is a favorite after-dinner drink around the world.

Alcohol is a controlled substance in Mexico and there are laws governing both the production and consumption. The age for legal drinking is 18 and driving while intoxicated is illegal. Drinking on the street is also technically illegal, but the custom is widespread. The reality is that any of the laws regarding drinking are rarely enforced. Checking ID is rare and drinking under the age of 18 is not a problem in most bars and restaurants. The problem is, if your behavior does warrant encountering the police, the punishment and penalties can be severe. So, as a tourist, it is definitely best not to drive at all if you plan to have a drink. Another problem involves the blood alcohol level defining "drunk driver"; the levels seem to vary at the discretion of the arresting officer.

Cantinas are Mexico's pubs and these places have been traditionally male forever, but women are welcome nowadays. MEXICO CITY founded in 1325, and with today's population over 22 million, has lots of bars. Until recently, most of the cantinas were rather seedy places, and hardly worth a visit. The result is, unlike Europe, there are not a lot of wonderful old, historical pubs for bar hopping.

El Nivel, in the central historic district, is Mexico City's first cantina and proudly displays its license (number one), dating from 1855. It has been a tradition for every Mexican president, except Vincente Fox, to drop in for a drink. The drinking snacks here, known as "botanas," are especially good. Unfortunately, bars, nightclubs, and discos have forced most of the old cantinas out of business in the big cities; but in the smaller towns and villages, the cantina and its Mariachi music, small wooden tables and male domino games are very much alive. El Nivel closed in 2013; but will undoubtedly reopen with new ownership.

La Opera Bar was established in the early 1900s, and only opened its doors to women in 1970. The original booths are dark walnut and the ceiling is the original ornate tin. Look for the bullet hole made by Poncho Gonzales. Phone: 5512-8959. Address: Avenue 5 de Mayo 10.

La Guadalupana, dating from 1932, is definitely a traditional cantina. The stuffed bull's head on the wall adds a dash of flavor to the place's bull fighting theme. In the past, this place was frequented by Leon Trotsky and Diego Rivera. Phone: 55-5554-6253. Address: Calle Higuera 2.

Salon Tenampa opened in 1923 and is over-the-top tacky and quite wonderful. Most of the great singers of Mariachi music have at least struck up a tune in the Tenampa, and many have their portraits painted on the walls. Address Plaza Garibaldi #12.

Before cantinas, Mexico had "pulquerias," named after the pulque drink they all served. These low-brow hovels were the watering-hole of the working-class for well over 400 years. During the colonial period (Spanish occupation) there were over 200 pulquerias operating in the central district of Mexico City. There are only a few remaining in business today. They are extremely rustic spots, and pretty much male-only enclaves. The pulque is generally served straight up, or in the somewhat more palatable flavored form. For a taste of this life, try Las Duelistas where pulque is dispensed right out of the barrel in flavors ranging from pine nut to pistachio. No reservations. Address: Calle Aranda 30 in the historic district.

GUADALAHARA has an interesting old cantina opened in 1921. **La Fuente** attracts all types with its combination of music, cheap drinks, and unpretentious charm. Be sure to notice the bicycle hanging over the bar. It was left by a customer in 1957 to pay for his drinks. No phone. Central Historic District.

OAXACA has emerged as Mexico's food capital, and along with great restaurants it has some wonderful bars.

La Casa de Mezcal is a cantina with mostly male patrons. Dating from 1935 it is one of Oaxaca's oldest bars. One room has a large stand-up bar and shelves full of mezcal, the other room has tables where snacks are served. Address: Flores Magón 209.

La Cucaracha. This place has over 40 varieties of mescal available along with the best live music in town. Address: Porfirio Diaz 301.

MONTERY is Mexico's third-largest city, after Mexico City and Guadalajara and the home of the oldest brewery in Mexico, dating back to 1890. The Cuauhtemoc produces the Bohemia, Dos Equis, and Tecate brands, and tours are offered hourly.

NETHERLANDS

"I'll stick with gin, Champagne is just ginger ale that knows somebody" ~ Hawkeye from *MASH*.

When we think of the Netherlands or Holland, Dutch people, windmills, dikes, wooden shoes, drugs, and tulips, all come to mind. When it comes to drinking in Holland, the special item is the **"brune kroeg"**, or **"Brown Café."** These traditional Dutch bars, many dating from the 1600s, are unpretentious, unpolished places, filled with camaraderie, much like a British pub or an American neighborhood bar. These brown cafés are found throughout Holland and on almost every corner in Amsterdam. Inside you will find the smoky, brownness that's unique to these cafes; the result of centuries of thick smoke, dark stained wood and dim lighting. These places are as much a part of Amsterdam's charm as its canals and special architecture. Unfortunately these charming cafes are no longer popular with the younger generation and are beginning to close their doors. In addition, smoking, a mainstay of the cafes is banned in public places throughout the Netherlands.

There are over 500 cafés in the center of AMSTERDAM and most of these are brown cafés. These are social centers for the regulars who use brown cafés as an extension of their living rooms. Open from early in the morning to around 2 AM, these are places that serve breakfast, lunch and dinner. You will feel welcome as soon as you enter through the door. A few booths may be along the wall and small tables sprinkled around, and a back bar with an extensive range of beverages. Customers linger for hours sipping beer or coffee and reading a newspaper or book. Consider the fact that Rembrandt was a frequent patron of these places almost 400 years ago. Rembrandt's most famous painting "The Night Watch" was completed in 1642, and hangs in Amsterdam's Rijksmuseum.

There are a few things you need to know about brown cafes. First, very few accept credit cards, bring cash. Most have outdoor seating for sunny days and some are self-service at the bar. Brown cafés are not the places to go to find entertainment and live music...what a blessing! Three types of beer are normally on tap. The pils, or lager, is usually from the Dutch Amstel or Heineken breweries. The two other commonly tapped beers are "blonde" and "dark", or brown beer. These types are imported from Belgium. Beyond beer on tap, the choice of bottled beer is almost endless, with choices from countries around the world.

Another drinking spot unique to Holland is the "tasting house." There are three differences between a Brown Café and a "proeflokaal", or tasting house. The age of these places, sometimes surpasses the Brown Cafe, and the decor is still basically brown. The first difference is what you drink. The tasting room serves jenever gin, taken "neat" (without ice or additives). These places are owned by a distillery, and generally only serve product produced by that particular distillery, as opposed to a café that is usually owned and run by an individual. The third difference is how you consume your drink. This involves the ancient drinking custom known as the "kofs stoop." The following are the directions to perform the "kofs stoop" or "kopstoot."

1.) Pour a small glass of beer (6 to 8 ounces)

2.) Fill a small shot glass or tulip glass to the brim with chilled jenever; so full that the top bulges.

3.) Bending from the waist with your hands behind your back take your first generous sip of the jenever.

4.) Straighten up and have a healthy sip of beer.

The Dutch are famous for their jenever, or genever, sometimes called "the spirit of the Netherlands" and the forerunner of gin. A Dutch chemist is credited with the invention of gin about the middle of the 17th century, and by 1663 there were over 400 distillers in Amsterdam, and many more throughout the Country. The blue-green juniper berry obtained from the low-growing juniper bush was added to hide the strong taste of the raw alcohol. At this time, the drink was thought to have widespread medicinal properties, and was sold in pharmacies to treat gallstones, gout, kidney problems and stomach ailments. It was found in Holland by English troops who were fighting against the Spanish in the 80 Years War. Drinking gin before a battle seemed to have a calming effect and is the origin of the term "Dutch Courage."

As mentioned in the chapter covering Britain, the introduction of cheap gin in England resulted in the period known as the "Gin Craze" (1740), and the resulting wave of alcoholism almost ruined the nation. Several different varieties of gin have evolved since its origin 400 years ago. The European Union recognizes four individual categories, with two of these officially established in the United States (Distilled Gin and Compound Gin).

1.) Distilled gin is produced exclusively by re-distilling grain, ethyl alcohol, in the presence of juniper berries or other natural botanicals. Distilled gin cannot be produced by simply adding the flavorings.

2.) Compound gin is made by flavoring ethyl alcohol, adding flavors or essences without re-distillation.

3.) London gin is similar to distilled gin with a higher alcohol content and no additives. It is usually distilled in the presence of accenting citrus elements, such as lemon and bitter orange, as well as a subtle combination of other spices, including cinnamon, licorice, etc. This category includes Gordons London Dry Gin, founded in 1769, Tanqueray London Special Dry, founded in 1830, Beefeaters London Dry Gin, 1820. The Beefeaters label reads as follows: "the botanicals in Beefeaters Gin are steeped for 24 hours prior to distillation, resulting in a complex, yet perfectly balanced gin of depth and integrity. Wild juniper combines with the subtle spice of coriander and the citrus freshness of lemons and oranges for a vibrant gin."

There is a renaissance occurring in the production of old-style, higher-alcohol "navy strength" gins. Navy strength must be 57 percent alcohol or 114 proof; versus regular Beefeaters etc., at 47 percent alcohol. The term "Navy strength" comes from the requirement that the Royal British Navy had for gins in the 1800's. Gunpowder could still be fired if 114 proof or higher gin was accidentally spilled on it.

This was the same era when the gimlet was invented by a Royal Navy doctor, Sir Thomas Gimlet, so sailors could mix their gin ration with their daily lime ration to prevent scurvy. These "navy strength" gins are becoming more available today.

4.) Juniper-Flavored Spirit Drinks. This classification represents the earliest form of gin, which is produced by pot distilling alcoholic grain wash, and then re-distilling it with botanicals to extract the aromatic compounds. Due to the use of pot stills, the alcohol content is relatively low. This is the gin that is known as Geneva Gin, or Holland Gin in the UK and US, and as jenever or genever in France and Holland.

Traditional jenever is still very popular in the Netherlands and Belgium. The European Union regulations specify that only liquor made in these two countries, two French provinces and two German federal states, are allowed to use the name "jenever." There are two types of jenever, old and young. This is not a matter of aging, but of distilling techniques.

Around 1900 it became possible to distill a high-grade type of alcohol almost neutral in taste, regardless of the origin of the spirit. A world-wide tendency for a lighter and less dominant taste and lower prices, led to the development of blended whiskey in the United Kingdom and to "young jenever" in the Netherlands. Young jenever is distilled from grain and sugar-based alcohol and is aged for a few years in oak casks. The result is young jenever has a neutral taste, like vodka, with a slight aroma of juniper and old jenever has a smoother, aromatic taste, with malty flavors.

The Dutch also love beer, and they've been cultivating their taste for the brew since the 14th century. At one time Holland could lay claim to over 500 breweries.

Heineken is the Netherlands best-known beer and claims a substantial export market. The old Heineken brewery in Amsterdam offers a tour called the "Heineken Experience" where you can view the operations and sample three glasses of the brew at the finish. Freddy Heineken was quite a ladies man about town, and often stationed himself at the bar and when an attractive lass announced, "I'd like a Heineken please" he'd offer "I'm right here." Heineken beer, like Foster's in Australia, is not a favorite at home. Amstel, also a well-known brand, is owned by Heineken.

Two other independent labels that are recognized internationally are Grolsch and Oranjeboom. These are pilsners and contain about 5% alcohol. The traditional 15.2 ounce Grolsch beer bottle with the re-sealable ceramic cap is still available in Dutch supermarkets. The design was introduced years ago to accommodate those thrifty Dutch drinkers who considered the contents of a bottle too much to drink in one sitting. Grolsch dates from 1615!

Belgian beers with their great reputation are popular in Holland; but the Dutch have scores of brewers turning out creditable beers. There are only seven Trappist monasteries producing beer in the world, six in Belgium and one in Holland, La Trappe is the Dutch Trappist beer brewed at Koningshoeven monastery near Tilburg on the Belgian border.

White beers are popular in the summer and are served with a slice of lemon and a swizzle stick. A good choice is Hoegaarden. A glass of beer costs about two euros.

The Dutch National Beer Museum is housed in the old Da Boom brewery in Alkmaar, just north of Amsterdam, in the heart of cheese-making country. The antique brewing equipment is demonstrated using wax dummies. Here, you can see a video featuring Dutch beer commercials that is really hilarious. Choose from 30 different beers in the friendly beergarden tour. There are a few other drinks native to the Netherlands, including Advocaat, rich, creamy liquor made from eggs, sugar, and brandy. It has a smooth custard-like flavor and is similar to eggnog. The alcohol content is generally between 14 and 20%. The recipe may vary a little and contain a blend of egg yolks, sugar, or honey, brandy, vanilla, and sometimes cream. The Polish variety is based on vodka instead of brandy. Thick Advocaat is the type sold in Holland and Belgium and is often eaten with a small spoon or used as a topping for waffles or desserts. The export variety is more liquid and served in a wide glass as an aperitif or a digestif. The best-known cocktail using Advocaat is the Snowball, a mixture of Advocaat, sparkling lemonade and sometimes lime juice.

Amsterdam has no shortage of nightlife, including its well-known red light district where prostitution is legal and marijuana may be purchased at licensed outlets. In addition, there is a wonderful supply of ancient drinking establishments.

However, today's Amsterdam is only a pale shadow of the good old days known as "the Golden Age" (1602-1670), when the City had 518 taverns, one for every 200 inhabitants. Today, the ratio has slipped to one for every 725 dwellers. In addition, the free movement provided by the European Union has introduced wine as a substitute for the ever-popular beer.

Hoppe (020/420-4420) Dates from 1670 and still attracts standing room only crowds. This ancient brown café is worth stopping just to view the decor and the crowds.

Pilsner Club (623-1777) This is a genuine brown café from 1893. This typical hole-in-the-wall café serves beer straight from the keg.

Absinthe (320-6780) This bar is devoted to the brain-changing liquor that was reputed to be the source of van Gogh's problems. The staff will teach you all about their signature drink, and we hope you leave with your ears intact.

De Drie Fleschjes (020/624-8443) This is a tasting house, "The Three Little Bottles", that opened in 1620. This place specializes in liqueurs, and fifty-two wooden casks line the wall facing the bar

Brouwerij (020/622-83) This tasting house is a small brewery in a fascinating location at the base of an unused De Gooyer windmill in the city's old harbor area. There are guided tours of the brewery and you can follow-up with a tasting at the bar. A favorite is the Columbus wheat beer that's hearty, reddish in color, and 10% alcohol.

Wynand Fockink (020/639-2695) This old tasting house with the interesting name when pronounced in English, has been serving Dutch jenever since 1679. In addition to over 50 jenevers to sample, there is a collection of liquor bottles on which are painted portraits of every Amsterdam Mayor since 1591.

Ciel Bleu Bar (020/678-7111) Located in the Hotel Okura Amsterdam, this is not a historic site, but the view of the city from the 23rd floor rooftop lounge is worth a visit.

Café Chris (020/7624-5942) This is Amsterdam's oldest drinking spot, having opened in 1624. There are a lot of quirky things about this bar to grab your attention. For instance, the bathroom toilet flushes from outside the door and inside the bar. Seems like you could have some fun surprising people with this one!

De Druif (020/624-430) Opened in 1631, and is the third

oldest bar in the city.

De Karpershoek (020/6248-788) Serving sailors since 1629, the floor of this second oldest bar in Amsterdam is still covered, with sand, just as it was 400 years ago.

Cafe Gollem (020/626-6645) This is a very popular brown café and serves over 200 brands of beer. This is your best spot to obtain those scarce Trappist brews from Belgium.

Café't Smalle (020/623-9617) Located in the Amsterdam Jordan district, this bar is located in a former jenever distillery and tasting house that dates from 1786.

De Pieper (626/4775) This place is considered by many to be the best of the brown cafes. Established in 1665, the interior features stained glass windows, sand on the floor and antique Delft beer mugs hanging over the bar, and a working Belgian beer pump, dating from 1875.

Het Papenieland (624/1989) This 1642 bar features Delft blue tiles and a central stove. The name dates from the Reformation, when a tunnel linked the bar to a secret Catholic Church across the canal.

Until recently there was no minimum drinking age in Holland. For purchasing drinks that have less than 15% by volume, the minimum legal age was 16, for drinks over 15% alcohol, the minimum age is 18. Now the Netherlands has become very strict regarding the control of drinking and 18 is the minimum age for drinking or purchasing alcohol. And, as in every European country, driving under the influence of alcohol is an extremely serious offense.

POLAND

Polish legal drinking age – "I have 3 Euros."

Poland is on the border of the European vodka and beer cultures. The vodka belt runs from Oslo, Norway to Moscow, and includes Sweden, Finland, Lithuania, Latvia, Estonia, Poland, Russia and the Ukraine. The beer belt includes Ireland, England, Belgium, Holland, Czech Republic and Germany. Although Poland is considered the birthplace of vodka, beer is increasingly popular with the younger population. In spite of this strong trend, vodka remains the Polish national drink.

Vodka may have been produced in Poland as early as the eighth century; but according to the Gin and Vodka Association, the first distillery was documented over 200 years later at Khyl Norsk, Poland.

The original vodka differed considerably from the vodka of today. It was neither clear nor odorless, and had very low alcohol content due to primitive production techniques. In these early days, the spirits were used primarily for medicine. One widely held claim hailed its use "to increase fertility and awaken lust." This may still be true over 1000 years later!

Around 1400 A.D., vodka became a popular drink in

Poland, and writings over the next 200 years include many mentions of vodka, including a book written in 1693 with recipes for making vodka from rye. Large-scale vodka production began at the end of the 16th century in Kraków and Poznan, a city that had 500 distilleries in 1580 A.D. By the middle of the 17th century it became popular to grant nobility a monopoly on producing and selling vodka in their territories, and, as you might expect, this privilege was a source of substantial profits. One of the most famous distilleries of the aristocracy was established by Princess Lubomirska, and later operated by her grandson Count Potocki. The Vodka Industry Museum is now housed in the Potocki distillery.

By the end of the 18th century, vodka produced by the clergy and the nobility had become a major product known throughout Europe. The beginning of the 19th century inaugurated the production of potato vodka, which immediately revolutionized the market due to its cheap and widespread availability. Also, at this time, new technologies became available which allowed the production of clear vodka.

Today, vodka is commonly defined as a "neutral, colorless, and near flavorless, distilled spirit." Vodkas have been made from potatoes, grains, fruits, even pineapples in Hawaii. Some vodkas are made from molasses, soybeans, grapes, rice, sugar beets, and sometimes even byproducts of oil refining.

The European Union has attempted to establish guidelines requiring vodkas sold in the E.U. to be made from sugar beets, potatoes, or grain. This effort has not been successful; but they do require distillers to specify their ingredients on the bottle.

Vodka is now one of the world's most popular spirits; but up until 1950s, it was rarely consumed outside Europe. By 1975, vodka sales in the U.S. overtook bourbon, which had been in first place for 100 years. Vodka owed its popularity in part to its reputation as an alcoholic beverage that as one advertising campaign put it, "leaves you breathless." Vodka's growth in the U.S. may be linked to a famous story from the New York advertising crowd. Seems the agency president was concerned about the vodka drinking of his account executives. He called a meeting to announce a new agency policy. "From now on," he said, "with clients you will drink only gin martinis and not vodka — because in the afternoon I want them to know you are drunk, not stupid." In addition, its overall neutral flavor (not to be compared with absence of flavor), allows vodka to be mixed with a variety of drinks, often replacing other liquors. The outstanding example of this trend is the vodka martini replacing the traditional use of gin in this drink.

According to The Penguin Book of Spirits and Liquors, "vodka's low level of fusel oils and congeners – impurities that flavor spirits, but contribute to the after-effects of heavy consumption – have led to its being considered among the safer spirits, though not in terms of its powers of intoxication, which depending on strength, may be considerable."

A common property of vodkas produced in Europe and the United States is the extensive use of filtration prior to any additional processing, including the addition of flavorings. Filtration removes impurities known as "foreshots" (heads and tails) that impact the usually desired clean taste of vodka. Heads consist of ethyl acetate and ethyl lactate, and tails include fusel oils. In contrast, the distillery process for whiskey or rum allows portions of the heads and tails to remain, giving them their unique flavors.

Repeated distillation of vodka will increase its alcohol level to a non-acceptable point for drinking purposes. With the right equipment and repeat distillations, the alcohol by volume content could reach 95 to 96% (190 proof), which if drunk straight would burn the esophagus because of rapid evaporation. Therefore, most vodka is diluted with water before bottling, and the source of the water imparts the unique flavor.

In addition to being categorized by alcohol content, vodkas may be classified into two main groups: clear vodkas and flavored vodkas. The range of flavorings used is almost endless, and each country seems to have its own unique favorites. The Poles add the leaves of the local bison grass to produce Zubrowka, and a photo of the native Polish bison is on the label. Poland has two Bison Reserves designed to prevent these large animals from becoming extinct. The vodka has a slightly sweet taste and a light amber color. This vodka has been produced in Poland near the Lithuanian border since the 1500s. Each bottle contains a single blade of bison grass. It also contains coumarin (usually found in fragrances), which is considered a toxin by the U.S. Federal Drug Administration, so it is banned in the U.S. Local lore has it that for the full flavor it is important that the bison urinate on the grass. Another famous Polish vodka is Kaepernick, which contains honey.

(Sweden has over 40 varieties of herb-flavored vodka. The Russians use a combination of honey and pepper as a popular flavor. Everything from flowers, fruits, roots, herb extracts, ginger, watermelon, chocolate and vanilla are currently added to vodka to impart special tastes. In the U.S. citrus flavors are currently the popular fashion.)

Another unique Polish vodka is Starka, made from rye and aged from 5 to 50 years in oak barrels, similar to whiskeys distilled from rye. Even the color is similar to whiskey due to the time it spends in the oak barrel; however, Starka is usually steeped with lime blossoms or apple leaves.

In the olden days, when a child was born, the proud father would make a barrel of Starka, seal it with beeswax, and bury it in the ground. On the day the child got married, the barrel would be exhumed and consumed at the wedding feast.

The major Polish export vodkas are Wyborowa and Luksusowa, both potato vodkas. Goldwasser is 80 proof vodka flavored with roots and herbs. This product is native to the town of Danzig (now Gdansk) and was first produced in 1598. At that time it was widely thought that gold had beneficial medicinal properties. The most notable quality of this brand is the flecks of gold floating in the bottle. Goldwasser became very popular with leaders and nobility as a way to show off their wealth. Today, each bottle contains less than one-tenth of a gram of gold. At current elevated gold prices, this amounts to about five dollars U.S. in each bottle.

When vodka made its entrance on the world stage in the 80s and 90s brands were limited to Russian Smirnov and Swedish Absolut. Both were backed by excellent marketing programs, particularly Absolut, which featured a magazine campaign displaying the unique shape of the bottle in hundreds of creative styles.

The Communists left Poland in 1989, and a fellow by the name of Tad Dorta saw the potential of capitalizing on the product that had been under strict government control. Dorta founded two vodka companies, Chopin and Belvedere, to appeal to the world luxury vodka market. Chopin was the first vodka to be packaged in a frosted bottle with a clear window revealing the magnificent image of composer Frederic Chopin on the back of the bottle. Now every upscale vodka has a frosted bottle. Dorta is a vodka purist and believes true vodka must be made from potatoes or grains. He also believes, contrary to the popular custom, vodkas should be served at room temperature, Dorta believes chilled vodka loses some of the flavor and the subtle taste of the potatoes or grains. Belvedere is distilled from rye grain and Chopin from potatoes, rye, or wheat. It takes 7 pounds of potatoes to make each bottle of Chopin vodka.

Thankfully, some things have not totally changed. I "grew up" in Olean, New York, a town of about 20,000 at the time, with a significant Polish population; there was a Polish church, Church of the Transfiguration, and a Polish grade school, grades kindergarten through eighth. Getting invited to a Polish wedding in Olean, New York in the 50s and 60s was a wonderful opportunity. In addition to the church and the school, there were a couple of private Polish social clubs. One was the Pulaski Club where most of the weddings were held. In those days the wedding was always in the morning. No afternoon Masses in the Catholic Church, and the reception began in the afternoon and lasted until the next morning. This was truly partying all night long. I'm happy to say that this tradition continues, not in Olean, but in Poland, especially in the smaller towns and villages.

Poland is a land of festivals, cultural and religious; every Catholic feast day is celebrated with full-hearted devotion; but for consuming vodka in a major way, weddings are the premier event.

There are a few rules regarding drinking vodka in the

vodka belt countries of Eastern Europe and the Baltic Sea. First, vodka is served neat, no mixers. One reason, orange juice is often more expensive than vodka. Second, never sip; drink what is served in one gulp. Third, when drinking as part of a group, everyone drinks at the same time. It is considered an offense to drink before somebody makes a toast. Last, as in just about every other country, always buy back a round of drinks for everyone that treats you.

Mead is another traditional Polish alcoholic drink. In Polish it is known as miod pitny, which means "drinkable honey." Mead is a beverage similar to wine, with between 14 to 19% alcohol content, and is obtained from the fermentation of a mash of honey diluted with water. Yeast is added to the mash to accelerate the fermentation process. The alcoholic content is evident after 4 to 6 weeks fermentation, and the Mead must then be left to mature for anything between several months or even several years. Mead can be natural without any additives, or more often, spices, herbs, fruits or flowers are added when preparing the mash. Although dating back to biblical times, Mead is not a popular drink around the world these days. Poland and England are two countries where it is still readily available. There are many varieties of Mead available in Poland, depending on the way the mash is prepared. The best is poltorak containing 1 liter of honey for every half liter of water. For optimum quality, poltorak must be aged in oak barrels for 10 years before being drunk. This variety is a dark amber color, very sweet, and has a characteristic aroma due to the added portion of buckwheat honey.

Poland has been producing beer for a very long time. The oldest document mentioning beer in Poland is a chronicle dubbing Polish King Boleslaw the Brave (reign 992-1025) "the beer drinker." Vodka remains the national drink, but as elsewhere in Europe, the popularity of beer is increasing rapidly. Although it is the local brews that are the favorites, Poland has some of the best Pilsner-type lagers worldwide. One well-known brewery is Zywiec, which was founded in 1852, and is now owned by Heineken. Another major brand is Okocim, an old-established brewery founded in 1845, and now owned by Carlsberg. These beers have alcohol content exceeding 5%. There are a large number of small breweries with little market reach, but producing delicious beers. Poland is now the 10th biggest beer market in the world, and ranks number five in Europe. The Poles use beer as a chaser or an appetizer, or as a mixer.

Polish liqueurs, known as nalewkas, are alcoholic extracts from fruits, spices, flowers, or herbs with an alcohol content of 40 to 45%. Contrary to ordinary liqueurs, nalewkas are usually aged. Most nalewkas have their names derived from the main ingredient or the name of the traditional place of manufacture. Traditionally, the recipes for nalewkas were kept secret and passed on to the senior children upon the death of the father. Some of the main ingredients include lily-of-the-valley, black currant, juniper, ginger, cherries, wormwood, anise, apricots, and many more.

Over the centuries, Poland has suffered a great deal at the hands of foreign invaders; but nothing compared to the devastation imposed by the Nazis in World War II. Poland lost over 25% of its total population, and virtually its entire Jewish community. In July 1944, with the advancing Russian army poised on the outskirts of Warsaw, Hitler ordered the entire city to be razed before leaving the ruins to the Russians. This was followed by over 40 years of strict Communist rule. As a result, pubs, cafes and bars with a colorful history do not exist in Warsaw or most of the rest of Poland. There are plenty of bars and Irish pubs, just nothing of historical importance. The entire city of Warsaw had to be rebuilt from scratch.

Kraków, the ancient royal capital, is a popular tourist destination, rivaling the central European elegance of Prague and Vienna. Kraków was the only major city in Poland to come through World War II undamaged. This was a result of the Nazis using the city as their Eastern headquarters during the war. By the end of the 10th century, Kraków had become a major market center, and for centuries it was the home of kings and princes. The Wawel is one of the most striking royal residences in Europe, and like the city center, known as "Old Town," is one of the finest examples of medieval architecture in the world. This area is home to many, many elegant terrace cafés, most famous of which is the Noworolski. This spot was the hub of Kraków's social life in the years before World War I. Lenin was one of the most famous regulars. The Nazis turned the place into an officer's club in World War II; but it resumed its status as the social center of the city after the war. Unfortunately, it is more noted for sipping tea, than downing vodka. Many cafes serve tea and cakes during the daylight hours, and switch to vodka bars at night.

Polish pubs have one distinguishing feature, almost total darkness inside. Sometimes this is born of necessity or convenience in bars buried in deep cellars or hidden in obscure buildings. In other cases, buildings with perfectly good frontage on the street will have windows carefully blacked out.

Something else worth noting about Polish pub culture is the unusual age profile of the customers. In most countries, one of the largest groups of pub-users is the under-30 group; but middle-aged men and women are also well represented. In Poland, it is rare to see anyone over 25 in a pub. The mainstay of public life, the middle-aged male worker having a few beers after his shift, just doesn't exist. One possible reason for this phenomenon is the years of communist rule offered no place to go, so generations of Poles never got into the habit of going out for a few drinks.

The Old Town district of Kraków has a splendid selection of watering holes, both above and below ground level. You may not get very far on a pub crawl since one reliable source claims that Old Town has more bars per square meter than anywhere else in the world.

With a population of 800,000, Krakow has Europe's largest and arguably most gracious medieval square, the Rynek Glowing; Europe's largest Gothic altar, the three-hundred foot-long neo-Byzantine Sukiennice; the Cloth Hall market; kings snug in their heavy stone coffins under Wawel Cathedral on the 15-acre Royal Castle Hill. The main market square can accommodate some 3000 people out of doors at the tables of its chockablock interface. This is simply a delightful atmosphere to enjoy a drink and observe civilization as it passes by. One of the main fruits of Kraków's earlier royal boom is the massive Jagiellonian University, founded by King Kazimierz (Casimir the Great) in 1364. It's Europe's second oldest university – after Charles University in Prague – but the first University to have a chair in mathematics and astronomy. This is where Nicholaus Copernicus, the wealthy Silesian trader's son studied and at a single stroke, revolutionized science with his heliocentric vision of the spheres of the universe. Copernicus studied here between 1491 in 1495 and later became a professor.

Jama Michalika Florianska 45. This atmospheric old café opened in 1895 and has a beautifully preserved Art Nouveau interior.

Noworolski, Rynek Glowny. Another Art Nouveau interior, this historic café opened in 1910, and was once the haunt of the Kraków cultural and political elite.

Re Mikolajska 5. One of the nicest barrel-vaulted bar cellars in Kraków with a great summer outdoor beer garden.

Singer, Estery 22. This is a 19th century café-bar where old tailor's sewing machines serve as tables.

Wierzynek, Rynek Glowny 15. This place makes a claim to be the oldest continuously operated restaurant in all of Europe, dating from 1364. Royalty dined here for centuries, and the place is decorated with antique chandeliers, old battle armor, and a collection of ancient clocks.

A final note: Polish recipe for a delightful hangover cure -- pickle soup. The ingredients are pickles, cream, potatoes (of course), dill and broth. Hot and salty, just what you need after an evening of too many toasts.

The church is near, but the road is icy; the bar is far, but we will walk carefully (Russian Proverb).

Russia needs to be included in this discussion of vodka, since it is an inseparable part of Russian life. According to many sources, the first production of vodka took place in Russia, not Poland, in the late 19th century. Encyclopedia Britannica states the first Russian vodka was made in the 14th century, brewed by the Kroger family, which later evolved into the company now known as Smirnoff.

The taxes on vodka became a key element of government finances in czarist Russia, at times providing up to 40% of state revenue. The government policy of promoting consumption of state-manufactured vodka made it the drink of choice for most Russians by the late 1800s. By 1910, vodka comprised about 90% of all alcohol consumed in Russia; and today, it is still around 70%.

Russia, as a country, has had an alcohol drinking problem for a long time. The Country is definitely one of the world's largest consumers of alcohol per capita. The average Russian drinks more than twice the maximum amount considered healthy by the World Health Organization; this translates into about a pint of vodka a day for the average Russian.

After many years of encouraging drinking, the government has more recently attempted to reign in overconsumption of alcohol. Soviet leader Mikhail Gorbachev introduced a bold campaign to reduce drinking in the mid-1980s. Some of the measures included no alcohol served before 2 PM, closing many vodka distilleries, and eradicating vineyards in Moldova and Armenia. These efforts had limited success, but caused a dramatic surge in moonshining operations.

More recently, in 2010, Russian President Dmitry Medvedev called Russia's rampant alcoholism a "national disaster," and announced a program to reduce consumption by 25% within one year. Good Luck! The first step was to double the price of a bottle of vodka. This continues as an ongoing effort and results are not yet available.

Pub life is not a big item in Russia; but alcohol is available everywhere. One of the primary outlets are kiosks that dispense beer and small bottles of vodka 24 hours a day, seven days a week. As a result, you can see women pushing baby carriages and drinking a can of beer, men having a few swigs of vodka on the way to work, or teenagers drinking a bottle of vodka in a public park. By the way, minimum drinking age is supposed to be 18.

It's pretty difficult not to drink in Russia. A pastor at an Anglican church in downtown Moscow, put it best, "If you surround yourself with people who don't drink, you'll probably be alone most of the time." Moscow's AA chapter is one of the largest in the world.

Russian drinking differs from that of southern Europe, where alcohol is served with food. In Russia, drinking is an occasion of itself; hence much drinking is of the binge variety. As a member of a group, any group, you are expected to drink and "no thanks" is not an acceptable reply.

As in Poland, and so many other places, a few rules apply to social drinking in Russia. Toasts must accompany every drink, along with an appetizer of anything from salty pickles to a spoon of caviar. No sipping allowed, toss the vodka shot down in one gulp. Drinking before a toast is a faux pas of the first order. You'll score points with your host if you propose toasts – doesn't matter if they are in English, and the longer and more eloquent, the better. The vodka must be drunk straight; mixing it with anything else is considered a waste, unless it's beer.

For reasons shrouded in the mists of time, empty bottles are considered bad luck and are immediately discarded or placed on the floor. Keep in mind, frequent toasts will continue throughout the meal. A guest unaccustomed to this routine will definitely find himself under the table.

As in almost every European country, the beverage that has really taken off in the past few years is beer. The number one national beer brand is Baltika, which produces numbered brands from 0 to 9, with zero being the lightest.

There are hundreds of vodka brands in Russia and

some of the best are Flagman, Russky Standart, Beluga and Beloe Zoloto. Two of the major export Russian vodka brands are Stolichnaya and Smirnov (Smirnoff). Both of these brands originated in Russia, but over the years have been acquired by British and U.S. companies. Smirnov was first produced in 1819, and its fame comes from the fact that the House of Smirnov was the purveyor of vodka to the Romanov czars. Smirnov descendents recently won a long court battle and reclaimed ownership of the name. Terms of the agreement allowed a sister brand to be created for the Russian market, Smirnov. Stolichnaya, which has been owned by various large conglomerates, for the export market, is currently produced in Latvia.

SCANDINAVIA

"A drunken man's words are a sober man's thoughts." – Lyric
from "Silent Scream" by Oblique Brown

Access to alcoholic beverages in **Sweden, Norway,** and
Finland is quite restricted and expensive, and the state plays
an active role in limiting exposure to alcohol. Caution is part
of the Swedish culture, and it applies in a major way to the
use of alcohol.

Once again, the difference between Northern and
Southern Europeans' attitude toward alcohol comes into play.
Southern Europeans incorporate drinking with eating and
find outward signs of intoxication embarrassing. The
tradition in Scandinavian countries is to drink less often, but
with the overt intention of getting drunk.

The retail sale of alcohol is monopolized by the non-
profit, government run, liquor store, Systembolaget, or
simply Systemet. Until Sweden joined the European Union,
Systembolaget also monopolized the production and
wholesale distribution of alcohol. European Union rules of
fair competition forced Sweden to give up this monopoly.

Systembolaget, which is known locally as Systemet
(the system) or Bolaget (the company) is the only retail store
allowed to sell alcoholic beverages that contain more than
3.5% alcohol by volume. You must be at least 20 years of age

to purchase alcohol in these outlets. At Swedish bars and restaurants the legal age is 18.

There are no discounts permitted in Systemet stores, such as two for one or 20% off, or buy one, get one for free. No product may be favored, which in effect means that beers are not refrigerated, since <u>all</u> beers would have to be refrigerated, which would be too expensive. Also, Systemet is not allowed to advertise to increase sales; however, the producers of alcoholic products have been allowed to promote their products since 2005.

Serving a market of 9 million Swedes, Systemet is one of the largest buyers of wine and spirits in the world. This naturally gives it significant clout in pricing power. It also, of course, has led to more than one large-scale corruption scandal. In one of the largest trials in Swedish history 77 store managers were charged with accepting bribes from suppliers, 34 were found guilty in 2005. Recently, the Swedish tax agency has been investigating large payments made to a Gibraltar firm by Fondberg, the second largest supplier of wine to Systemet.

Norway has a similar arrangement of state owned alcohol outlets (Vinmonpalet) and Finland follows the same path with government controlled alcohol outlets (Alko). Alcohol with a volume percentage under 4.75% can be sold in regular stores.

Sweden has perhaps the toughest laws in the world regarding drinking and driving. The legal blood alcohol level is .02, compared to .08 in the U.S. This means you just don't get behind the wheel if you've had a drink. In fact, some big drinkers refuse to drive even the next day. There is still a strong temperance movement in Sweden, especially in rural areas, and often connected with the "free churches"

(Protestants outside the Church of Sweden).

A little review of Swedish history may help explain the Swedish attitude toward drinking alcoholic beverages. Since the beginning, beer was the staple beverage in Sweden, drunk in huge quantities to balance the salty food – pickled herring, and salted pork. Distilling was introduced in Sweden in the 15th century.

As Sweden was industrialized and urbanized during the 19th century, industrially produced alcohol became readily available. As in other countries, this period led to alcohol abuse on a major scale. Sweden had 175,000 distillers for a population of 8 million; consumption was estimated at almost 49 quarts of alcohol per adult per year. That compares to about 9½ quarts per year now.

The first temperance organization appeared around 1850, and was fully embraced by the medical profession and the Church of Sweden. Alcohol began to be regulated by the state, and by 1870 all bars and stores were government controlled and profits went to the state.

During the First World War, alcohol was strictly rationed and state bars and stores registered purchases. People were allowed only two liters of liquor every three months, and beer was banned. After the war, the rationing continued and gender, income, wealth and social status decided how much alcohol you were allowed to purchase. Unemployed people and women were not allowed to buy anything at all. This rationing system became very unpopular, surprise, and by 1955, after 40 years, it was abolished and Systembolaget was introduced.

As Sweden entered the European Union in 1995, drinking habits became more continental and regulations were relaxed. The government continues to monopolize the retail sale of alcohol, only beer with an alcohol content of 3.5% (People's beer), or less, can be sold in regular stores with minimum purchase age of 18.

The state also levies high taxes on alcoholic beverages, making drinking an expensive form of entertainment. These high prices have led to a surge in illegal stills in the countryside, and a flourishing black market. Some officials feel one-third of alcohol sold in Sweden is illegal.

Sweden historically has been part of the "vodka belt" of Norway, Sweden, Finland, and Russia. The main Swedish specialty is "brannvin" (literally "burn-wine"), liquor distilled from fermented grain or potatoes. Vodka is the highest grade of brannvin, with Swedish brands like Absolut Vodka and Explorer Vodka.

Aquavit is the special drink most usually associated with Sweden. This is brannvin which has gone through a second distillation with spices added for flavor; caraway, aniseed, coriander, fennel and saffron. Aquavit is served chilled and is consumed in one gulp – great for toasting.

V & S Vin and Spirit AB, owner of Absolut Vodka, owns many Swedish aquavit brands, and is a subsidiary of Pernod Ricard. Absolut — the brand only — was sold by the Swedish government (about 10 years ago) to Pernod Ricard for $1 billion, setting a record as the highest price ever paid for a beverage brand.

Back in the 1970s, the advertising agency in New York City used by the Eastman Kodak company was J. Walter Thompson, located on Lexington Avenue. J. Walter Thompson was a large, world-wide operation and frequently had interns from other countries training for six months to a year at the New York headquarters. One day I was invited to attend a "commencement" luncheon for a young man who was returning to Stockholm. I had never been to this New York City Scandinavian restaurant, Aquavit; but it was certainly first-class. There were probably over a dozen of us at this "going away" party, and the whole event was geared to simulate a typical Swedish, big-time luncheon party. There was a smorgasbord consisting of many, many courses. The meal began with fish, such as marinated herring, smoked eel, crab and breaded plaice fillet, and moved on with slices of roast pork and beef, meatballs, ham and liver pâté. These were all accompanied by onion rings, radish slices, cucumbers, tomatoes, pickles, remoulade, and mayonnaise. Then, of course, there was an assortment of desserts. The part that was my downfall was drinking beer with the food, and then a small glass of chilled aquavit for each toast, following each course – try seven or eight of these! When I stepped out of that front door onto the bright, sunny, crowded sidewalk, the whole world seemed to be rushing at me upside down.

The ritual, "snap vision," is very much alive in Sweden today. It involves singing traditional Swedish drinking songs while making toasts at an event or gathering, which always include a meal. There are over 2000 traditional Swedish drinking songs, many of them passed on by word-of-mouth from generation to generation. These songs are sung to celebrate or promote good health, and to sing the glory of the snap (or small drink) the singer is about to drink.

Beer is legally divided into three classes in Sweden. Class I is called "light beer" with an alcohol content of 2.25% and sold without restrictions. Class II (up to 3.52%) is sold in regular stores, but minimum purchase age is 18; class III, "strong beer" (over 3 1/2%) is sold only in Systembolaget.

"Glogg" is a term for mulled red wine in the Nordic countries, mainly Sweden, Norway, Finland, and Denmark.

The main classic ingredients are usually red wine, sugar and spices (such as cinnamon, ginger, cloves, and bitter orange). Also, as an option, stronger spirits may be used; such as vodka, aquavit or brandy. Glogg is similar in taste to modern wassail or mulled cider.

In Sweden, ready-made Glogg is sold at Systembolaget outlets ready to heat and serve. Glogg is a popular hot drink for the Christmas season, and is served with gingerbread and lussebullar, a type of sweet bun with saffron and raisins. It is served at Julbord, the Christmas buffet. A little Glogg and a few aquavit toasts and a Christmas party could be off to a great start. Other Scandinavian countries have similar rituals.

The typical graduation ceremony in Norway doesn't involve family gatherings or school-hosted all-night parties; it involves binge drinking while wearing specific overalls for 17 straight days. At the end of this "Russ" ceremony the young person has the right to call himself a student and remove the unwashed, 17-day-old overalls. This ritual has been going on since the 1700s.

If you were choosing a country for barhopping, Sweden would probably not be your top choice. However, there are several interesting spots worth a visit. First, you must be careful of the term "bars" in Sweden, many are only self-serve cafeterias, and the strongest drink available may be apple cider.

AHUS – 7 miles southeast of Kristianstad. This small, seaside resort town with a medieval center is the home of Absolut Vodka. Every drop consumed around the globe is distilled here in this little town, and Absolut is the third-largest selling well-known brand of alcohol in the world, after Bacardi and Smirnov. Absolut is sold in 126 countries. Take a 1½ hour tour with tastings.

FALKENBERG –60 miles south of Göteborg. The "Brewery at Falkenberg" brewing Falcon beer since 1867. The tour winds up with dinner and refreshing glasses of the house brew.

STOCKHOLM – **St. Eriksg,** 115 Vasastan.

This wonderful bar boasts having 150 whiskeys and 30 beers.

STOCKHOLM – **Sophie's Bar,** Biblioteksgatan.

Stockholm's celebrity hangout.

STOCKHOLM – **Spy Bar,** Birger Jarlsgatan.

Stockholm's most exclusive club.

SCOTLAND

Lady Astor, speaking at a Temperance Conference, announced, *"I would rather commit adultery than drink a glass of Scotch."* From the audience someone shouted, *"Who wouldn't?"*

Scotland is famed for its beautiful scenery, friendly people, and its quality whisky. That's whiskey without the "e," and in the U.K. that means Scotch whisky.

It is not known when the art of distilling was first practiced in Scotland, but by the 11th century Christian monastic sites were producing the "water of life." Taxes were introduced in 1644, and by 1780, there were eight legal distilleries and 400 illegal ones, producing whisky.

Scotch whisky got a big boost in the late 1800s, when continuous distillation replaced the pot or batch still, and the Phylloxera bug destroyed wine and cognac production in France.

The production of whisky in Scotland has long been closely regulated by the government. The most recent legislation was enacted in 2009. Previous rules only governed the production of whisky: the new act sets regulations regarding labeling, packaging and advertising. The law states the following rules:

1. Scotch whisky must be produced at a distillery in Scotland from water and malt barley with certain other grains

added.

2. Whisky must be aged in oak casks for at least three years.
3. No substances added other than water and caramel coloring.
4. Minimum alcoholic strength of 40%, 80 proof.
5. The age shown on the bottle must reflect the youngest whisky used to produce the product.

The oak casks used to age Scotch whisky for three or more years have all been previously used to store or age wine or bourbon. This imparts an identifiable flavor to the Scotch. Since the U.S. rule specifies the use of new, freshly charred barrels for aging bourbon, the supply of used casks is abundant.

There are two basic types of Scotch whisky from which all blends are made.

Single malt Scotch means product produced from only water and malted barley at a single distillery, by batch distillation in pot stills and aged at least three years.

Single grain Scotch whisky means whisky distilled at a single distillery, but in addition to water and malted barley, other grains may be added. The "single" in the name refers only to the single distillery requirement. The single malt and single grain may be used in blends with whisky from other distilleries. Blended whisky accounts for over 90% of Scotch whisky produced in Scotland. Popular examples of blends include the following: Bells, Dewars, Johnny Walker, Cutty Sark, J and B, Famous Grouse and Chevas Regal.

Single malt brands include Glenlivet, Glenfiddich, Macallan, Glenmorangie and Oban. Since 1876, Glenfiddich distilled in Speyside has used mountain run-off water and is the world's best-selling single malt Scotch. The number one blended Scotch in the world is Johnny Walker. A bottle of

Glenfiddich is not round, but has a triangular shape. The original owner had a habit of bringing a bottle to bed with him at night, and often the bottle would roll onto the floor where he might trip on it in the morning. The triangular shape solved the problem.

Visiting Scotland's distilleries, such as the Dewars operation in Aberfeldy, is a special treat. Enter the august tasting room and you begin to feel the aura of a dark-cathedral. Host employees speak in hushed tones, inquiring thoughtfully about your preference of blends, single malts or special products. Soft music lends a holy note. Pourers offer carefully measured sample shots of precious Scotch. Elegant boards and "interpretive panels" spell out the historic brewing process, pointing out that much must be held as secrets that have been guarded for centuries. Exit and you know this has been a lifetime experience.

To get a real sense of Scottish culture, you must visit its atmospheric pubs and inns. As in other parts of the U.K., pubs in Scotland are much more than just a restaurant or bar. They are gathering places where people go to meet their friends and catch-up on one another's lives.

Two of the most well-known traditional Scottish dishes do not sound very appetizing, haggis (ground-up sheep's organs), and black pudding (made from congealed blood). Beyond these items Scottish pub food is quite good, with a wide variety of fresh seafood available.

Pubs throughout Scotland have been smoke-free since 2007, and the hours of operation are generally from 11 AM to 11 PM. One noteworthy characteristic of Scottish pubs is the absence of table service. You are expected to go to the bar and order a beverage and your meal – this can be a little inconvenient if you happen to be sitting upstairs and the bar is on the first floor. Some pubs have restricted hours for children and the drinking age is 18.

Scotch is certainly the national drink; but the "haggis" is the national dish of Scotland and a pub favorite. This is made by stuffing the sheep's intestines with the animal's minced organs mixed with spices and oatmeal and then boiled. If finely minced and spiced, the taste can approach "acceptable."

Here are some fantastic pubs that you will find interesting and entertaining.

Globe Inn – DUNFRIES Founded in 1610, this was the favorite haunt of the poet Robert Burns (Auld Lang Syne). His favorite chair still survives along with the original fireplace and some lines of poetry he inscribed on the bedroom windows upstairs. Burns liked the place so much he had a child with the barmaid. A small museum is devoted to Burns on the premises.

Old Forge – KNOYDART. The Guinness Book of Records has proclaimed this place the U.K.'s remotest pub. You can only reach this pub if you're prepared to take an 18-mile hike or a 7-mile sea crossing – no roads go to the place. Once here, you can eat, drink and sleep in peace.

The Scotia Bar – GLASGOW. Dating from 1792, this is the oldest bar in Glasgow and is a favorite stop for British celebrities.

Deacon Brodie's Tavern – EDINBURGH. This pub perpetuates the memory of Deacon Brodie; good citizen by day and robber by night; the prototype for Robert Louis Stevenson's "Dr. Jekyll and Mr. Hyde." Founded in 1806.

The Sheep Heid Inn – EDINBURGH. This place, which dates back to 1360, claims to be Scotland's oldest surviving pub. It was a favorite of Mary, Queen of Scots and her son James VI, who would stop off for a game of skittles while touring on Royal business.

The Golf Tavern – EDINBURGH. Located on the edge of the Bruntsfield links and founded in 1456. The Golf Tavern continues to be a popular meeting place for golfers and it houses the largest collection of golf memorabilia in Scotland.

Prince of Whales, ABERDEEN. Furnished with antiques, this place has the city's longest bar and has an authentic Scottish pub atmosphere. Try the special Guinness pie.

Quaich Bar – Craigellachie Speyside Hotel. Just down the road from the Glenfiddich distillery, has the best Scotch selection on earth - over 650 brands. You can sample to your heart's content and stay at the hotel.

Golfers have always debated why the game has 18 holes. At St. Andrews in Scotland, generally considered the original home of golf, legend has it that it's not a coincidence that it takes eighteen swigs to polish off a bottle of whisky - one per hole. It is not a legend, but a fact, that for many, many years the regular caddies at St. Andrews were always drunk by the finish of a round, and sometimes at the beginning.

A Scotsman walking through a field sees a man drinking water from a pool with his hands. The Scotsman shouts, "Don't drink the water, it's full of cow's shit." The man shouts back, "I'm English, speak English, I don't understand you." The Scotsman shouts back, "Use both hands, you'll get more in." By the way, Scotland is holding a referendum in 2013 on the decision to become a separate nation from England.

A Scottish boy came home from school and told his mother he's been given a part in the school play. "Wonderful," says the mother, "what part is it?" The boy says, "I play the part of the Scottish husband." The mother scowls and says, "Go back and tell your teacher you want a speaking part."

Brew Dogs, a Scottish microbrewery, has recently released a beer that set a new record by weighing in at 32% alcohol by volume - more than six times as strong as familiar domestic brands like Budweiser. The beer, dubbed Tactical Nuclear Penguin, is fermented at an ice cream factory at temperatures as low as 21°F for 21 days. Because alcohol freezes at lower temperatures than water, Brew Dog can increase its beer's alcohol concentration by freezing and removing excess water during the brewing process.

Each bottle comes with its own stopper. But if that's not enough to discourage chugging, Brew Dog co-founder James Watt believes that the beer's price tag will be – around $60.

When the Germans introduced a competing brew at 40% alcohol by volume, the Brew Dog boys fired back with a new beer called "Sink the Bismarck" that checks in at 41% alcohol by volume, enough to reclaim the world's strongest beer mantle.

SPAIN

"In wine there is wisdom, in beer there is strength and in water there is bacteria." — Old Proverb

Spain is the playground of Europe. This long-troubled country, from the years of the Spanish Inquisition to the brutal Franco tyranny from the 1930s to the 70s; has emerged with a zest for life. Spaniards love to eat and drink and be merry. Whether it's enjoying tapas with fine wine in Madrid in the south, or the elaborate Basque country equivalent, pintxoc over cider in the north, Spaniards are having a good time. The true Spaniard believes in working only half the year and partying the other half. This culture, of course, may go a long way in explaining Spain's current economic predicament; however, there are quite a few hard-working nations in similar difficult economic conditions.

Spain is especially fascinated with fiestas and festivals. The country's calendar creaks beneath the weight of an endless parade of celebrations, whether religious or pagan, that provide an excuse for eating, drinking and merry-making. What the Irish would call "craic" is of great importance to the Spanish.

There is a live-for-the-moment attitude throughout the country. An extreme effort to enjoy life – today! So it is not surprising that Spain has more drinking places per capita than any other country on earth. And Madrid claims more bars than any other city in the world.

Spain belongs to the wine-drinking countries and wine consumption has been the leading beverage for 1000 years. But just as in France and Italy, beer and distilled spirits are taking over with the younger generation.

Spain usually ranks about third in the world as a wine producing nation. Spanish wine is subject to a complicated system of wine classification with a range of designations marked on the bottle.

Wine accompanies almost every meal in Spain, and people drink often, but rarely to excess. Eighteen is the legal drinking age, but seldom enforced because youth grow up with a responsible attitude toward drinking.

The most common premium red wine is from La Rioja region in the north. It is smooth and fruity, look for the "Do Rioja" on the label. White wines come from Galicia on the northern coast. Cava is a Spanish sparkling wine, similar to champagne. In 1970, the European Union banned the use of the word champagne except when used to describe the sparkling wine produced in the Champagne area of France. Cava is exported by two rival producers, Codorníu and Freixenet. Freixenet is the largest selling sparkling wine in the world.

Cider, the alcoholic variety, is popular in the northern Basque country. There are cider bars that serve it straight from the barrel. Cider production here is a serious business, and handled with the care the French would attach to a fine Bordeaux.

Sherry is Spain's national drink, and is found in every bar and restaurant in the land. Many of the old inns and bars have rows of kegs with spigots for pouring sherry. The production of sherry begins with the pressing of the harvested sherry grapes, which are left to ferment. True sherry only comes from the Jerez region in southern Spain because that is the only place on earth where the unique yeast known as "flora" exists. After a few months, the wine is transferred to cellars in big barrels of American oak. The wines are aged from 3 to 7 years. A small amount of brandy is added before the bottling step. Dry sherry begins as a white wine, but is fortified with grape brandy and also aged. It is the color of straw and is usually drunk as an aperitif. There is sweeter, darker sherry that is good for after dinner (Harvey's Bristol Cream for example). Because sherry is fortified with brandy it has much higher alcohol content than traditional wines – about 15% higher.

There is an extensive list of wineries known as bodegas that welcome visitors. Spaniards consider their wines to be comparable to the best produced in neighboring France.

Ribera del Duero, halfway between Madrid and Santander, is the fastest developing wine district in the country. The Penedés region shipped enormous quantities of wine to the Roman Empire in ancient times, and is now the major source of sparkling wines. Both Codorníu and Freixenet are located here. Codorníu headquarters sits above 19 miles of tunnels used to age their wine.

Patxaran is a sloe berry liqueur from the north of Spain in Basque country. It's typically drunk at the end of a meal as a digestive. This drink originated in the 1820s, and steps have been taken to ensure that production of this sweet cordial stays pure to its origins in Navarre.

The La Rioja region near the Pyrenees, close to the French border, boasts quality-control laws established by a local bishop in the ninth century. Several bodegas here date back over 100 years, and all are open to visitors.

The Galicia region in the northwest corner of Spain

produces white wines praised by connoisseurs as the perfect accompaniment to the wonderful local seafood.

Sangria is another popular Spanish drink made by combining red wine and fruit juice, and is usually consumed during the heat of midday, much like a punch drink. Sangria began as a blend of bar leftovers. After a night of serving, a bartender would mix the dregs of wine bottles into a single beverage—sometimes including some fortified brandy or whiskey. Today's Sangria!

The Muse Provincial del Vino in VALLODOLID is worth a visit. You can learn all about the history of wine-making and visit a castle at the same time.

Ham in Spain deserves special mention since it pairs so well with the Spanish sherry. Spanish ham, Jamón ibérico, comes from black-footed pigs that spend their final months feasting on a continuous diet of acorns. During this period, the pig will double in weight acquiring a layer of fat that permeates the meat in distinct veins. The meat is delicious, succulent and velvety at the same time.

Beer is gaining ground in Spain, and much of it is imported. The two major local brands are San Miguel around Madrid, and Estrella if you are near Barcelona. Order beer in the typical bar and it will usually be on tap.

Gin originated in Holland, and was developed into its most popular style in England; but its most enthusiastic modern-day consumers are to be found in Spain, which has the highest per capita consumption of gin in the world. The U.S. remains the overall top market for gin, which dates back to Prohibition (1920s), and the origin of mixing raw alcohol with juniper berry extract and other flavorings in bathtubs, hence the term "bathtub gin."

In a country that loves to party and prides itself on an endless stream of festivals and fiestas, two stand out in Spain.

Fiesta de San Fermin takes place every July 6-14 in Pamplona. This is a week of non-stop parades, music, dance, fireworks, and the "running of the bulls." Each morning, six bulls are let loose from their corrals and run approximately a half-mile to the bullring, in about 3 minutes. Devotees, known as "mozos," run with, and hopefully ahead of, the bulls. These brave, or foolish, or drunk souls make the news every year as injuries and quite a few fatalities accompany the event. One of those "be a spectator, not a participant" events. The fiesta attracts a half-million people from all over Europe each year.

The other unusual festival, Tomatina, is held the last Wednesday in August in the little town – population 9000 – of Bunol, just west of Valencia. Just before 11:00 AM, truckloads of ripe tomatoes are delivered to the waiting crowd and for the next two hours everyone joins in the frenzied, cheerful tomato battle. At 1 PM an explosion signals the end of the battle, and the local fire brigade hoses everyone down. Time to change clothes and celebrate at one of the local bodegas. It is estimated that the battle consumes over 100,000 pounds of ripe tomatoes.

MADRID has more bars than any city in the world, six for every 100 inhabitants. Quite an accomplishment for a place with less than 4 million people. Madrid's reputation as the "party capital" of Europe was established in the 1980s. Following the long, dark, sad years of Franco's dictatorship, "madrileños" emerged with a zest for life filled with all-night partying, sex, drugs and drinking. The remarkable thing about the movement dubbed "la Morida," is that it was presided over by Enrique Galvan, an aging, former university professor who had been the leading opposition figure under the Franco regime. He became mayor in 1979 with the slogan, in English, "Get stoned and do what's cool." It's no surprise he was Madrid's most popular mayor ever, and when he died in 1986, over 1 million madrileños turned out for the funeral. So, although much calmer, the city remains a place to live life, party and have a good time.

Pub crawling in Dublin or London is lots of fun; but in Madrid it is a major part of the culture. Known as "tapeo," it is the act of strolling from one bar to another to keep yourself amused and fed prior to the fashionable dining hour of 10 PM. Tapas are served just about everywhere, in bars, cafés, tascas -- tascas are bars that serve wine and small plates of food. If you haven't gone out on a tapeo, you haven't experienced Spain.

Tapas, now popular around the world, originated in medieval times as a means of covering a glass of sherry to keep bugs out. Tapas in Spanish means "cover the lid." Later, the government mandated bars to serve "a little something" with each drink to dissipate the effects of alcohol.

A selection of tapas can include everything from almonds and olives to veal rolls, shrimp, crabmeat, salad, and even bull testicles. Each bar in Madrid gains a reputation for its selection of certain favorite foods.

A favorite joke follows: an American was sitting in a Madrid restaurant and noticed an unusual dish served at an adjacent table. The waiter explained they were bull testicles obtained that very afternoon from the nearby bull ring. The American replied that he never heard of such a thing and would like to try it. The waiter explained that they were a delicacy and specialty of the restaurant, he would call when available. A few days later, the restaurant phoned and the American hurried over for his dinner. When the testicles were served he noticed they were considerably smaller than the ones he remembered from a few nights ago. Bringing this to the attention of the waiter, the waiter politely explained. "You see, señor, the matador does not always win; sometimes the bull wins."

Another Madrid custom arrives with the first hint of warmer weather and lasts all summer. Open-air cafés, called "terrazas," are found throughout the city. Locals love to sit, talk, drink, and watch the passers-by from these charming places; the good times can go on until dawn and these places range from high-and glamorous hangouts, to lowly street-corner cafés.

Drinking under the stars is one of Madrid's great pleasures, and some of the best places to start are along Paseo de la Castellana and Paseo de Recoletos, where tables run up and down the sidewalk. Madrid's many plazas make perfect locations for outdoor drinking: Plaza Mayor, Plaza de la Paja, Playa de Oriente, and many, many more.

Another completely Madrid experience involves "la hora del vermut" (vermouth-hour), when families and friends go out for a quick aperitif before Sunday lunch. This custom is deeply ingrained in the Madrid culture and Madrid is loaded with vermouth bars.

There are plenty of drinking spots in Spain that go by the name of "bar" or "restaurant," but there are many variations on the theme:

Bar de Copas: A spot that gets going around midnight and serves hard spirits.

Cerveceria: The focus here is on beer.

Tasca: A tapas bar serving wine and platters of tapas.

Terraza: Open-air bar, a Terraco.

Taverna: Old, rustic barrels for tables, tile décor.

Vinotera: Upscale wine bar.

In Madrid, as you would suspect, it is no problem to find a wonderful spot.

Casa Lucio – This is a venerable old tasca with all the

antique accessories, dozens of cured hams hang from the hand-hewn beams above the bar. The food is Castilian and the clientele well-known public figures. Phone: 913 65 32 52

Cerveceria La Alemana is another Hemingway favorite and a hangout for generations of bullfighters who stayed just across the street in the former Grande H Reina Victoria. With its long bar and extensive tapas menu, it remains a popular meeting place today. 914 29 70 33

Taberna Toscana. This is a favorite spot to begin the nightly tasca crawl. There is a long, tile bar loaded with tasty tidbits and the ambiance resembles a village inn from the 19th century. Phone: 914 29 60 31

Casa Mingo has been known for decades for its cider. The place is very informal and customers share wooden tables. In the summer, tables and chairs extend out onto the sidewalk. Phone: 915 47 79 18

Museo Chicate is a Madrid landmark which claims to have invented over 100 cocktails. The place was a frequent stop for Hemingway, Sophia Loren and Frank Sinatra. It still attracts film stars and socialites, and doesn't get going until after midnight. Phone: 915 32 67 37

Not the oldest bar, but according to the *Guinness Book of Records*, the oldest restaurant in the world, **Sobrino de Botin,** is located in MADRID. Founded in 1725, the restaurant has appeared in many novels, most notably Hemingway's "The Sun Also Rises." Eating in the vaulted cellar is a treat. Goya was once a dishwasher here. Phone: 913 66 42 17

Lhardy. A 19th century gem, with a lot of Spanish history. It is said that the fate of Spain was decided many times in the upstairs dining room. Phone: 915 22 22 07

Casa Alberto opened in 1827. This spot has an Onyx bar, vermouth on tap, and beer too, of course.

BARCELONA

Bar Boadas. This is one of Barcelona's oldest cocktail bars, established in 1933. The place is famous for daiquiris. A rather formal spot, it has catered to the rich and famous for 80 years. Phone: 933 18 88 26.

Bar Marsella. In business since 1820, the Marsella specializes in serving absinthe, a drink often banned for its supposed narcotic qualities. Nothing much has changed here since the 19th century.

Casa Almirall: Operating since 1860, this dark corner bar is unchanged, and attracts a cross-section of the local clientele.

Barcelona is located in the Catalonia province of Spain and even has its own language, Catalan. Although closely related to Castilian, there are significant differences. This leads to many special regional customs, and one of these is the champagne bars, known as "xampanyerias." These are the places to learn about Spanish champagne called cava. Xampanyerias open around 7 PM and close in the wee hours of the morning.

El Xampanyet is an excellent spot to begin tasting these sparkling wines. Run by the same family since 1930, the tavern is decorated with colorful tiles, antiques, marble-top tables, and barrels of wine.

SEVILLE is supposedly where tapas originated, and a great place to try them is **Casa Roman**, where they have been serving them since 1934. Phone: 954 22 84 83.

El Rinconcillo claims to be the oldest bar in Seville, dating from 1630. The decor is 1930s. The bartender will keep your tab in chalk on a well-worn wooden countertop. Phone: 954 22 31 83.

VALENCIA is Spain's third largest city and has a reputation

for the best night life in the country. Two local drinks are special to Valencia. Horchata is a sweet, opaque drink made from pressed tiger nuts. Aqua de Valencia is a mixture of orange juice, Cointreau and sparkling wine, and is famous for "curing all that ails you." **Sant Jaume** is the place to try these drinks since it's a converted pharmacy. Another popular spot is **Café de la Seu** where the Aqua de Valencia is served in pitchers like Sangria.

UNITED STATES

"Beer is proof that God loves us and wants us to be happy" ~
Benjamin Franklin

America was born in a tavern and the tavern's role over the last four centuries has been central to issues ranging from establishing the colonies, waging the war for Independence, settling the West, acting as the home base for machine politics, welcoming immigrants, being the base for the labor movement and fighting for woman's and gay rights. Time and time again during these 400 years, the bar has come under attack as "Satan's headquarters on earth", and during the Prohibition years it was actually legally closed for 12 years (1920 – 1932). This love-hate relationship between the bar and the nation has led to more rules and regulations governing alcohol than in any other country in the world. Currently the legal drinking age is 21, the highest of any developed country. Why this has happened is due to a complex mixture of evangelism, Puritan work ethic, and the bars' own history as a space for exploiting the poor, the disenfranchised, the radical, the revolutionary, and, of course, the "drunk."

The American bar continues under siege in the 21st century as health concerns regarding smoking and drinking,

drinking and driving and higher and higher taxes on alcohol; all threaten its survival. But the biggest threat of all may be the change in social engagement from a form of personal contact, such as sitting and talking to someone next to you in a bar, to an electronic system of messaging (Facebook, Twitter, texting, etc.) now called social media. More and more often we see people in a restaurant, or a Starbucks, or any public space sitting together, but no one is talking, they all have their iPads or cell phones under the table and are viewing or typing messages, young people, and I mean most of them, are retracting into a solitary, on-line world. This behavior is not what gave the bar its character, its purpose, its "reason for being."

This condition is not solely an American one, electronic social connectivity has spread throughout the Western world as well as Asia. There are now more than one billion Facebook subscribers. We are all connected, just not personally, we are friending online, we just don't have any friends. The point has already been reached where older parents have twice as many friends as their middle-aged children. This solitary, isolated behavior by young Americans is evident in voting statistics, which show only a fraction of eligible 18 to 29-year-old voters voted in most recent elections.

Drinking alcoholic beverages in America had an early start, beginning with Sir Walter Raleigh brewing beer at the Roanoke colony in 1587. The Mayflower was blown off-course in 1620, and the pilgrims were forced to land at Plymouth Rock because they were running out of beer. Original plans were made to land farther to the South. November in New England is not the best time to begin building shelters.

When the Spaniards came to the New World, they

were on a religious mission and built churches. The Dutch were worried about security and always built some type of fort, but the English, beginning in the early 1600s, built taverns. As the first villages were established in America, they had only two public buildings, a church or meetinghouse and a drinking place or tavern. The first written record of a tavern in this Country dates to a drinking room in Boston opened by Samuel Cole in 1634.

Copying the English, laws were passed demanding villages have taverns that provided food and lodging for travelers and their horses. The tavern served many more purposes than offering food, drink, and a place to rest. The early tavern was used for town meetings, jury trials, entertainment; in fact, everything of importance took place at the tavern; except religious services. Taverns served as the living room for most neighbors because their houses were too small, poorly heated, crowded with children, and bereft of food and drink. A host would naturally entertain guests at the local tavern.

Drinking in America in the 1600s was limited to cider and beer. At this time, it was pretty well-established in Europe and the New World that water was unsafe to drink, and turning it into beer made it not only safe, but healthful. Each American consumed the equivalent of about a quart of 80 proof whiskey per week, 6 gallons of absolute alcohol per year-- about three times as much alcohol as they do today.

Due to the abundance of apple trees in New England, cider became a popular drink by the mid-to-late 1600s. This drink, known as hard cider, was made by fermenting apples; it had an alcohol content of 5 to 7%, and was stored in barrels and drunk year-round. During the winter, the typical New England family would consume a barrel a week. Everyone drank cider and at every occasion, including breakfast, lunch and dinner. Infants had a glass before going to bed and hard cider offered no religious problem to the Quakers and Puritans, who were pretty much opposed to anything that might hint of enjoyment. Cider remained the most common drink in the colonies for almost 200 years.

While cider was definitely the drink of choice in the 1600s and 1700s, it was not the only alcoholic drink available. Shortly after 1650, trade with Barbados, in the West Indies, began a development that had a profound effect on colonial drinking patterns. Molasses, the waste by-product of sugar refining, provided the raw material for the production of rum. Since molasses was a waste by-product, fermenting and distilling it into rum, made a very cheap alcoholic drink. The major problem with rum was it may have been cheap, but the taste was awful. Almost anything and everything was added to rum to improve the flavor: cinnamon, raisins, cherries, honey, and nuts.

To support the demand for rum in the British colonies of North America, the first rum distillery was set-up on present-day Staten Island near New York City in 1664. Three years later, a second distillery opened in Boston. Within a generation, the production of rum became colonial New England's largest and most prosperous industry. Estimates of rum consumption in the American colonies before the Revolutionary War (1775), had every man, woman and child drinking an average of over three gallons of rum per year. The popularity of rum continued after the war, with George Washington insisting on a barrel of Barbados rum at his 1789 inauguration.

When the British Royal Navy captured the island of Jamaica in 1655, they obtained a cheap source of rum. As a result, the Navy switched the daily ration of liquor given to seamen from French brandy to rum. The Royal Navy continued to give its sailors a daily rum ration for the next 300 years. The practice was abolished after July 1970. The British Navy is credited with spreading the use of rum around the world.

Following the 1805 Battle of Trafalgar in which the British fleet defeated the combined fleets of France and Spain, Admiral Horatio Nelson's body was preserved in a cask of rum to allow transport to England. Upon arrival, the cask was opened and found to be empty of rum. The pickled body was removed and it was discovered that the sailors had drilled a hole in the bottom of the barrel and drunk all the rum. This event is the basis for the famous rum toast, "Tapping the Admiral."

The majority of the world's rum production now occurs in the Caribbean and Latin America. The island of Puerto Rico claims to be "the rum capital of all the world." and the government polices manufacturers to make sure rum is correctly distilled and aged for at least one year. Over 70% of the rum consumed in the US is imported from Puerto Rico. Most of this rum comes from the industry giant – Bacardi Corporation, located in Cantano, Puerto Rico. Don Facunada Barcardi, a Cuban, was the first to develop a soft, light rum back in 1860. The Bacardi operation was moved to Puerto Rico following the Cuban Revolution in the 1950s.

Within the Caribbean, each island or production area has its own unique variation or style of rum. The Spanish-speaking islands and countries produce smooth tasting rum. English-speaking areas are known for darker rums with a fuller taste that retains the underlying molasses flavor. These include rums from Granada, Barbados and Bermuda. French-speaking islands are best-known for rums produced exclusively from sugarcane juice, no molasses. The result is a more expensive, sugarcane-flavored rum. These include products from Haiti, Guadaloupe and Martinique.

The grades and variations used to describe rum depend on the production location; however, the following terms are frequently used to describe various types of rum. Light rum, also known as silver or white rums, generally have very little flavor, and are popular for use in mixed drinks. Golden rums are medium-bodied rums that have been aged in previously used charred oak barrels. They are dark in color and pick up the flavor of the bourbon whiskey previously aged in the barrels. Dark rums can be brown, black or red; and are darker than Gold rums. They have a stronger flavor due to longer aging in the charred oak barrels. There are several other varieties, including spiced rums, flavored rums and premium rums that rival cognac and single-malt Scotches in price.

Many popular drinks use a rum base: daiquiris, piña colada's and the mojito. The arrival of the Tiki fad in the 1940s, and Polynesian restaurants are once again popular, expanded rums' horizons in drinks like the mai tai and the zombie.

Following the end of the Revolutionary War, the rum market began to slowly decline for a variety of reasons. The international market deteriorated because the French and English closed their colonies to American trade. Within the US, sales of rum fell due to erratic supply and higher prices.

In addition, there was a strong feeling of nationalism sweeping the Country, and imported molasses and rum were symbols of old colonialism and reminders that America was not economically self-sufficient. It was not patriotic to depend on foreign nations or their colonies for goods that could be produced here.

The federal government imposed heavy duties on imported rum and molasses; meanwhile, the tax on domestically produced whiskey was repealed. Whiskey was now cheaper than rum and the quality had improved considerably. Whiskey enjoyed a meteoric rise in popularity and replaced rum as the number one spirit drink the first quarter of the 19th century.

As you read this book, you'll notice that most countries have a national drink; Scotch in Scotland, beer in Germany, vodka for Poland and Russia, wine for France -- well, for America, the national drink is bourbon. On May 4, 1964, the US Congress recognized bourbon whiskey as a "distinctive product of the United States."

After the Revolutionary War, pioneers began to push west of the Allegheny Mountains and establish settlements in what is now Kentucky and Tennessee. These settlers were primarily Scottish, Scotch-Irish, English and German; and they brought European distilling skills with them to this Country.

One of the earliest settlements was established in 1785 in eastern Kentucky. The county was named Bourbon, after the French Royal family. Today, this area has been divided into 34 separate counties, one of which is the current Bourbon County of Kentucky.

As these settlers began to farm the area, they developed an excess of grain. The value of grain was such that transporting it to distant markets was not profitable. As had been done before in areas like western Pennsylvania, the next logical step was to produce a value-added product like whiskey that could be shipped to distant markets at a profit.

All the necessary ingredients for whiskey production were readily available; unlimited fresh water, rye and corn grain, white oak for the aging-barrels, and the knowledge of distilling techniques. One unique characteristic of American bourbon is the "sour mash" process by which each new fermentation is conditioned with some amount of spent mash from a previous batch containing live yeast. Using the sour mash controls the growth of bacteria that could taint the whiskey, and creates a proper acidic balance for the yeast to work.

The US government has established federal standards for bourbon produced for US consumption:
1) Made from a grain mixture that is at least 51% corn.
2) Aged in new, charred-oak barrels.
3) Distilled to no more than 80% alcohol by volume.
4) Placed in the barrel for aging at no more than 62 1/2% alcohol by volume, and be bottled (like other whiskeys) at 80 proof or more, 40% alcohol by volume.

Bourbon that meets these requirements and has been aged a minimum of two years and with no added coloring or flavoring may be called "straight bourbon." Bourbon that is labeled "blended bourbon "may contain added coloring, flavoring, and other neutral grain spirits; but at least 51% of the product must be straight bourbon. In practice, almost all bourbons marketed today contain more than two thirds corn, have been aged at least four years and qualify as straight bourbon.

Only new charred-oak barrels may be used for the aging process. Bourbons gain color and flavor from the charred-oak barrels. Although the bourbon gains more flavor and more color the longer they age, maturity is the goal, not age. A bourbon can age too long and become woody and unbalanced in flavor. Each year of the barrel aging process a small amount of the barrel contents is lost to evaporation. This loss can range from 2 to 8% and is known throughout the industry as "the angels' share."

Whiskey sold as "Tennessee Whiskey" is also defined as bourbon under international trade agreements and the

North American Free Trade Agreement. Three out of the four Tennessee producers do not call their finished product bourbon, even though the production method fits the defined characteristics of a bourbon product. These manufacturers claim they use a charcoal-filtering process that draws a distinction between Tennessee whiskey and bourbon. A notable example of one of these brands is Jack Daniels Tennessee Whiskey made in Lynchburg, Tennessee. Jack Daniels, founded in 1866, claims to be the oldest registered distillery in the US, and is America's best-selling brand.

Real Tennessee Whiskey, like Jack Daniels and George Dickel, uses the so-called Lincoln County Process. Milled corn is the primary ingredient, at least 51% in the mash. Yeast is added to ferment the mash, which is cooked in large vats of calcium-rich water. The fermented sour mash is then filtered through Sugar Maple charcoal (The Lincoln County Process). The filtered whiskey goes into oak barrels with a charred interior, where it is aged for several years to gain flavor.

It has been reported that 97% of all bourbon distilled in America is made and aged near Bardstown, Kentucky, which is home to the annual September Bourbon Festival, and calls itself the "Bourbon Capital of the World."

The Kentucky Distillers Association sponsors a program known as the Kentucky Bourbon Trail. There are currently seven distillers offering tours on this trail.

.
. **Four Roses and Wild Turkey** in Lawrenceburg, Kentucky
. **Heaven Hill Visitor Center**, Bardstown, Kentucky
. **Jim Beam,** Claremont, Kentucky.
. **Maker's Mark,** Loretto, Kentucky.
. **Town Branch**, Lexington, Kentucky.
. **Woodford Reserve**, Versailles, Kentucky.

These tours are extremely popular, with over 509,000 visitors to these seven distilleries in 2012.

There is also an American Whiskey Trail, sponsored by the Distilled Spirits Council of the US, and it is designed to promote the history and cultural heritage of distilled beverages in America. The American Whiskey Trail consists of historical sites and operating distilleries open to the public:

The George Washington Distillery and Museum, Mount Vernon, Virginia*.
  Fraunces Tavern, New York City.
. **Gadsby's Tavern Museum**, Alexandria, Virginia
. **Woodville Plantation,** Bridgeville, Pennsylvania
. **Oscar Getz Museum of Whiskey**, Bardstown, Kentucky
. **West Overton Museum**, Scottsdale, Pennsylvania
. **Oliver Miller Homestead, South Park,** Pennsylvania
The whiskey tour also includes the following operating distilleries:
. **Buffalo Trace**, Frankfort, Kentucky
. **Tom Moore,** Bardstown, Kentucky.
. **George Dickel,** Tullahoma, Tennessee.
. **Jack Daniels**, Lynchburg, Tennessee

After serving as the first US president, George Washington retired to his Mount Vernon, Virginia plantation and became the largest whiskey distiller in the nation. The original distillery has been fully restored.

Pappy Van Winkle's Family Reserve Bourbon is produced at the Buffalo Trace Distillery. This is a boutique brand, but it has won numerous awards in spirit rating competition. The 23 year-old aged version has been awarded "Spirit of the Year" by Wine and Spirits magazine, and some consider it the best drink in the world.

In addition to bourbon and Tennessee whiskey, the third major spirit in America is rye whiskey. Rye was early America's favorite whiskey, George Washington had a large distillery at Mount Vernon, and rye was the whiskey of choice in the Eastern US until Prohibition. Following Prohibition, rye almost disappeared; but it is making a strong comeback now, and sales surged 27% last year.

By law in the US, in order to be called rye, the whiskey must be from mash containing at least 51% rye, as opposed to bourbon, which must contain 51% corn. Next to bourbon, rye is spicier, less sweet, and more complex, with unusual peppery and bitter undertones. Wonderful ryes are now being produced by craft distilleries such as Tuthilltown in New York's Hudson Valley, Templeton in Iowa and Catoctin Creek in Virginia. Rye whiskey is a choice for making Manhattans and the new "Frisco" cocktail. The recipe for the Frisco is 2 ounces of rye, quarter ounce of Benedictine, three-quarter ounces of lemon, serve chilled in a cocktail glass with a slice of lemon.

Exports of US spirits grew 16 1/2% to $1.34 billion in 2011, compared to 2010, with American whiskeys accounting for 69% of the growth. Whiskey exports alone were up 13.6% last year, and as a result, new distilleries are popping up around the Country. Several stills have opened in Tennessee and The Tennessee Spirits Company, near Pulaski, is under construction with a proposed capacity of 5 million cases of Tennessee whiskey per year. The brand, already being produced at another site, is named "Jailers Premium Tennessee Whiskey."

The many taverns in colonial America played a significant role in the American Revolutionary War (1775 - 1783). Since the tavern was the absolute center of social life, it naturally became the place to begin plotting the revolt against the rules, laws, and taxes passed by the British Parliament to control the colonies. There was probably not a single tavern that did not play a part, large or small, in the Revolutionary War. Daniel Webster called the tavern "The headquarters of the Revolution", others said it was "the cradle of independence." Both the British and the Americans used taverns as jails, hospitals, barracks, court rooms, headquarters, recruitment stations, and places for secret meetings.

The Green Dragon Tavern, its reproduction located on Boston's Union Street, came to be known as the headquarters of the American Revolution. This is where the group met for a few drinks before dressing as Indians and embarking on the Boston Tea Party.

Fraunces Tavern, a replica of the original 1717 building, is located at 54 Pearl St. in NEW YORK CITY. George Washington chose Fraunces Tavern in 1783 to give his farewell address to his troops and came back in 1789 to celebrate his inauguration as the Country's first president. Next, Washington took the owner, Samuel Fraunces, to the Capitol in Washington as his Executive Steward.

Philadelphia's **Tun Tavern,** built in 1685 and named "Tun" for an old English word for a container of beer. When the Continental Congress enacted a decision to form the US Marine Corps in 1775, the proprietor of Tun Tavern was named "Chief Marine Recruiter." The tavern burned in 1781, but the Marines have erected a replica at the Quantico, Virginia Basic Training Center.

Gadsby's Tavern, 132 Royal St. in Alexandria, Virginia, was built in 1752, and was used frequently as a military headquarters in both the French and Indian War and in the Revolution.

Longfellow's Wayside Inn on Old Boston Post Road

in Sudbury, Massachusetts, claims to be the oldest continuously operated inn in the US, since 1716. The owner, Ezekiel How, led the Sudbury detachment from the tavern to the Battle of Concord Bridge on April 19, 1775, where they fired some of the first shots of the Revolutionary War. This tavern is also the home of Longfellow's "Tales of a Wayside Inn" published in 1863.

The Red Fox Inn in Middleburg, VIRGINIA, just west of Washington, DC, is another tavern claiming to be one of the oldest established inns in the US. A favorite dining spot of Jacqueline Kennedy during the JFK presidency, the building's core dates to 1728, and during the Civil War the bar served as a surgery table.

Historians believe that Thomas Jefferson drafted the original Declaration of Independence at the Raleigh Tavern in Williamsburg, Virginia (fully restored), and wrote the final version at the Indian Queen Tavern in Philadelphia -- probably while having a glass of wine. Jefferson, like most of the Founding Fathers, was a noteworthy drinker and among his many skills (architect, politician, gourmet), he included "wine connoisseur." During his eight years as president, Jefferson managed to run up a wine bill of $10,000, about $200,000 today. In fact, many of the Founding Fathers of this Country were big-time drinkers. John Adams drank a quart of hard cider for breakfast, James Madison drank a pint of whiskey each day, and of course, George Washington had his own distillery. Patrick Henry had his own tavern and tended the bar.

The itemized bill from a farewell party for George Washington held at the City Tavern in Philadelphia three days before the Constitutional Convention ended, September 14, 1787, show the following items:

Food and drink for "55 Gentlemen"
Food
Assorted relishes, olives, meats, etc.
Drink (bottles)
Madeira, 54
Claret, 60
Old Stock (whiskey), 8
> *Porter, 12*
> *Cider, 8*
> *Beer, 12*
> *Bowls of Punch, 7*
> Total Cost 89 pounds

It doesn't take much arithmetic to conclude that these "gentlemen" knew how to party.

The White Horse Tavern, Newport, Rhode Island, dating from 1673, is thought to be the oldest tavern in this Country. In the Revolution, Tories and British troops were quartered here during the Battle of Rhode Island. Today this spot remains a popular drinking and dining tavern and is an outstanding example of 17th century American architecture.

Years later, during the War of 1812 against the British, Francis Scott Key wrote the words to the Star Spangled Banner in a Baltimore tavern. It was September 14, 1814, and Key had just witnessed 50 British warships shell Fort McHenry for 25 hours. When the smoke cleared, after the British had fired over 1800 shells and rockets, the American flag was still aloft over Fort McHenry. Using the tune from an old drinking song, Key sat at a table in the Fountain Inn, one of the newer and fancier public houses of the day, as he composed the words to the Star-Spangled Banner. This song did not become America's national anthem until 1931.

W.J. Rorabaugh published a book in 1979 titled *The Alcoholic Republic*. Rorabaugh examined America's drinking culture during the years it reached its all-time peak. By 1800, the village church and the village tavern continued to stand side-by-side as the two most prominent buildings in town. In the cities men came to their neighborhood taverns daily, and in the countryside the tavern continued to be the home of multiple functions and the center of sociability. Americans drank not only in the tavern, they drank from morning till night, at breakfast, at work, at home, in the fields, at weddings, birthdays, funerals-- or whenever two or three neighbors gathered. Schoolchildren took their morning and afternoon sips of whiskey, clergymen drank between services, (the tavern was next to the church), judges and jury drank in court, physicians drank at the patient's bedside. The notion that alcohol was necessary for good health remained firmly fixed.

There were 2000 distilleries in the US in 1810. Historical evidence estimates that average consumption in 1790 was 5.8 gallons per year of absolute pure alcohol (200 proof) for people aged 15 and over. This rose to 7.1 gallons in 1810, and reached a peak of 9.5 gallons per person in 1830. Over half of this alcohol was in the form of distilled spirits, while the remainder was beer, wine and hard cider. The average American was guzzling about 1.7 bottles of hard liquor per week. The American adult drank about 90 bottles of liquor per year. This is three times today's average. By comparison, average consumption in this Country was 2.5 gallons of pure alcohol per person in 1970. By 2011, Americans were consuming about 21 gallons of beer, 2.3 gallons of wine, and 1.5 gallons of distilled spirits per person per year. This translates to about 2 gallons of pure alcohol per year.

This heaviest drinking in the Country's history eventually spawned the earliest temperance movements. As early as 1784, Dr. Benjamin Rush, signer of the Declaration of Independence, Surgeon General in the Revolutionary War, and the most respected medical authority in America, published a paper titled "An Inquiry into the Effects of Ardent Spirits on the Human Mind." This pamphlet received widespread publication, and many prominent and influential people agreed with Dr. Rush's findings. Rush, at this time, had no quarrel with beer or wine, his purpose was to switch drinkers from rum and whiskey to "healthful beverages", beer and wine. This was the beginning of many temperance movements in America, and eventually Benjamin Rush became known as "The Father of Temperance."

The attitude about alcohol changed slowly, but by 1826, there was enough organized momentum, particularly through Protestant Churches, to establish the American Temperance Society. It's important to realize that the many temperance movements in America were never about temperance, meaning moderation; they were always about total abstinence. Alcohol, which had always been considered not only safer than water, but good for you and necessary for good health; now the "good creature" became known as "Demon rum." By 1829, there were over 1000 temperance societies in America. Two powerful outfits in the crusade were the Methodist Church and the Washington Society, composed of reformed drunks. The effects of the temperance movement were remarkable. By 1840, alcohol consumption had declined by two thirds, to 1.5 gallons per capita. All forms of alcohol were affected, beer, cider, malt liquors and ardent spirits.

By 1855 it looked like the temperance movement had won the battle and America was going "dry." This changed dramatically as the Country battled with the slavery issue, and ultimately the beginning of the Civil War. The movement practically disappeared; but was revived again in 1874, with the founding of the Women's Christian Temperance Union (WCTU).

Meanwhile, an entirely separate force was at work in this Country. A tidal wave of mass immigration from Europe was having a significant impact on American drinking patterns, customs, and attitudes. These ethnic groups, primarily Irish, German and Italian, were strongly opposed to the prohibition of alcohol.

About this time, 1850, the tavern began to be known as the saloon, and its role in society changed significantly. The local tavern took on a flavor based on race, religion or country of origin. Gone was the tavern of colonial days, frequented by everyone on an equal basis. Now the abstinence group, composed mostly of middle and upper class Protestants, looked down upon the saloon, while the drinking group looked back in defiance.

Once again, the saloon provided a variety of services, including back rooms for social clubs, labor unions, and political gatherings, as well as hosting birthday parties, weddings, celebrations and wakes for funerals. If you were a recent immigrant and if the bartender/owner spoke your language, or had emigrated from the same country, the saloon could be a big help in getting you established in this "New World."

The settling of the Western Frontier provided another milestone in developing the character of the American saloon. Thanks to the American movie and television industries, the Western saloon is undoubtedly the most recognizable drinking spot associated with this Country. This is all the more remarkable when you consider that the period involving the settling of the West covered the relatively short span of 50 years between 1850 and 1900. "How solemn and beautiful is the thought that the earliest pioneer of civilization, the van leader of civilization, is never the steamboat, never the railway, never the newspaper, never the Sabbath-school, never the missionary — but always whiskey!" Mark Twain

Once again, similar to the colonial days, the saloon was often the first public building in town, and as a result, it served almost every human need. It was an eatery, a hotel, stable for horses, barbershop, grocery, courtroom, funeral parlor, and the absolute center of social exchange. One key difference between the Western Frontier and colonial times; there was no church standing next to the saloon. On many occasions, in addition to all the functions previously described, the saloon stepped up and served as the town church.

The Western saloon began very modestly, sometimes nothing more than a tent; but as the town grew, and if the mining ore held out, then the bar developed into the fancy places shown in the Western movies and TV shows. The long mahogany bar with the brass rail, the large back-bar gilded mirror, and the fancy, white-shirted, diamond decorated bartender, usually arrived when the train finally came chugging into town.

These were, indeed, wild times with little law and order, and widespread gambling, shooting, prostitution and general lawlessness; including excessive drinking of mainly rot-gut alcohol -- the only thing available. Eventually towns grew, women arrived, marriages took place, families formed, permanent structures were built and the wild frontier began to look like the rest of America.

The interval from around 1870 until the advent of

Prohibition in 1920, is referred to historically as the "Saloon Period." By 1870, the neighborhood saloon was flourishing and was commonly known as "the poor man's club." The number of saloons tripled to 300,000 between 1870 and 1900; and by 1875, a third of all federal revenue came from taxes on whiskey and beer. By 1910, the federal government received 71% of its revenue from taxes paid on the manufacture and sale of alcohol.

A special feature of the American saloon in the late 1800s was the "free lunch." By the early 1880's the "free lunch" had spread from coast-to-coast and was available in the big city bars, neighborhood saloons, and village taverns.
The big brewers and distributors began to buy saloons to provide exclusive outlets for their beer. At this time, America had far too many outlets and the competition was becoming fierce. The national average was one saloon for every 350 persons; this figure included everyone – men, women, and children. By 1916 beer companies owned the furnishings – bar, back bar, décor, virtually everything in 4,000 of Chicago's 7,000 saloons. Two years later, 80% of America's taverns were financially connected to a particular brewery.

At this same time, once again, there was a rising temperance sentiment against the saloon. Temperance advocates began demanding that barrooms provide food to counteract the intoxicating effects of alcohol. The saloons, backed by the big breweries, began offering large amounts of good, cheap food with one bar trying to outdo the other with quality or quantity.

The saloon became the main daytime source of food for much of working-class America. In addition, since anyone could help himself to a decent meal by purchasing a five-cent beer, the saloon became the main food source for the poor and destitute. In 1890, in Chicago, records show that the city's saloons fed more poor people than all the combined city charitable organizations.

This turned out to be a brilliant maneuver by the beer and liquor industry. They were able to simultaneously satisfy the hunger of the working class and the demands of the nutrition-minded temperance reformers, all the while meeting their prime objective of establishing a steady, regular, neighborhood saloon clientele. These lunches ranged from nothing more than potatoes and a Friday fish fry in some Irish saloons, sausage and a variety of pickled items (pig's feet, herring or ham) in a German beer garden, to fancy places like New York's Waldorf Astoria Hotel, where the wait-staff were in white uniforms and the "free lunch" consisted of caviar, Virginia ham, anchovies and canapés. Some saloons had a menu that changed with the day of the week

The "free lunch" lasted for over 30 years; but during this time, the temperance movement continued to apply ever-increasing pressure on the saloon business and drinking in general.

Along came World War I, 1917 in the United States, and the "free lunch" came under attack as a conspiracy between the large German brewers and the saloonkeepers to undermine America's food supply.

The Anti-Saloon League was established at Oberlin College in Ohio in 1893, and by 1895 it was a national organization. The hired manager of the organization, Wayne Wheeler, had no interest in prohibition; but as a political genius he had an insatiable desire for power. As Wheeler put together a coalition of forces, including progressive reformers, white supremacists, socialists, xenophobes, Methodist bishops, Baptist devotees, utopian suffragettes and industrialists like Henry Ford, he eventually controlled six congresses and two presidents.

Meanwhile, the neighborhood saloon continued its decline as too few customers for too many bars took its toll. New forms of amusement had begun to appear to compete with the local bar: movie theaters, nice restaurants, and family oriented parks. In addition, the older immigrant groups had begun an exodus to the dry suburbs. When America entered World War I in April 1917, the time was right for the Anti-Saloon League and the Woman's Christian Temperance Union to accomplish their mission to outlaw alcoholic beverages in the US.

A great wave of anti-German sentiment was sweeping the Country, and the ASL and WCTU exploited this feeling by reminding everyone that American breweries were largely German-owned. In addition, part of the campaign waged by the ASL focused on the conservation of grain as an essential commodity for the war effort. It should not be wasted in the manufacture of booze; and besides, beer and liquor were dangerous in time of war because they corrupted the morals and abilities of our soldiers.

The United States became officially "dry" on January 17, 1920, and remained dry for the next 12 years. Americans as a nation were forbidden to consume or possess alcoholic drink. The law was aimed at the manufacturer, distributor, seller, etc. of alcohol--not at the consumer, and the consumer ignored it from the beginning.

The program was a failure from the start; but it definitely changed the bar scene in America. Instead of eliminating alcohol, Prohibition resulted in establishing organized crime in America. It was also the beginning of women patronizing bars in wholesale numbers; speakeasies became a new word in the English language, and crime and corruption erupted at every level of government.

Once again, the "moral police" in conjunction with organized religious groups, were pretty much able to accomplish the complete opposite of their stated goals. As the most popular wit of the time (Will Rogers) commented, "Prohibition is like communism, it's a great idea, but it simply doesn't work." In 1930, Al Capone's ill-gotten gains from Prohibition amounted to $100 million.

So after 12 years of trying to be a "dry" nation, Americans were fed up with this "noble experiment", (Pres. Herbert M. Hoover's description), and they had more pressing problems of unemployment and the Great Depression following the stock market crash of 1929. Franklin Roosevelt ran against President Hoover in 1932 on a political platform that included the repeal of the 18th Amendment to the U.S. Constitution.

On the first day of legal liquor, April 7, 1933, the newly elected President Roosevelt and his staff celebrated in the White House by drinking his favorite Gordon's Gin martinis. Roosevelt's wife, Eleanor, disappeared and remained "dry" her entire life. It is worth noting that the 18th amendment is the only amendment to the U.S. Constitution ever to be repealed.

Many changes to American drinking customs took place in the years following Prohibition. To prevent the larger brewers from returning to the custom of owning saloons, laws were passed creating the "three tier" system consisting of the producer, the distributor and the retailer. Except for federal taxes, regulation of alcohol was returned to the individual states, which enacted a vast array of rules and regulations, many of these continue in effect today. Seventeen of the fifty states continue to exercise control over liquor, and 11 of the states exercise direct control over the retail sale and price of the liquor; sometimes actually owning the State

Alcoholic Beverage Control stores where liquor is sold.

Idaho and Utah, with heavy Mormon religion populations, offer some bizarre examples of the Alcoholic Beverage Control Board system. These Boards actually decide which brands will be sold in the state stores. Recently, the Idaho State Liquor Department banned the sale of Five Wives Vodka because it might be offensive to the Mormon population in the state. Utah, the headquarters of the Mormon religion, is famous for using its authority to control the sale and use of alcohol. The Mormon Church, which frowns on the use of alcohol, uses its powerful influence to severely limit the number of alcohol licenses in the state. One of the most unusual rules involves requiring bars to have screens (Zion Curtains) to prevent customers from seeing bartenders pour alcohol. This, of course, discourages the very essence of the bar, the conversation between the customer and the bartender. Stiff drinks and doubles are illegal in Utah bars. Bars and restaurants must use meters on their bottles to make sure they do not pour more than 1.5 ounces at a time. It is illegal to stiffen a drink with a second shot. Under the law, a drinker could order a vodka and tonic with a shot of whiskey on the side; but not a vodka and tonic with a shot of vodka on the side. Another law prevents restaurant customers from ordering alcohol unless they also order food, and all public drinking in Utah must end at 1 AM.

Until a few years ago, South Carolina, a beverage control board state, required liquor to be sold in bars in containers of 2 ounces or less, mini-bottles. When the authorities discovered that South Carolina customers were actually getting a larger drink than the standard pour in the rest of the Country, 2 ounces versus 1.25 or 1.5 ounces, they finally repealed the law. Even today, as a vestige of Prohibition, almost 500 counties in the US remain "dry."

In the years leading up to America's entry into World War II in December 1941, a new type of bar became extremely popular in major urban areas. The "nightclub" had come on the scene in the 1930s, but became even more popular during World War II and continued to dominate the upscale drinking landscape into the 1950s. The nightly "happenings" at these places were the subject of gossip columns in every major city morning newspaper. Famous entertainers of the time all performed in equally well-known nightclubs: Frank Sinatra at the Wedgewood Room of the Waldorf Astoria, in New York City; Joe E Lewis and Jimmy Durante at the Copacabana; Perry Como and Dean Martin at the Latin Quarter. Other clubs like New York's Stork Club, Toots Shores, Lindy's and Jack Dempsey's became celebrity hangouts. The Stork Club, which began as a speakeasy during Prohibition and was run by a convicted bootlegger, Sherman Billingsley, welcomed over 2500 customers each night; it was home base for an evening radio broadcast and was made into a movie in 1945, "The Stork Club." Beginning in 1950, a TV show featuring interviews with famous people, was broadcast from the Club.

While nightclubs occupied the upper-end of the drinking spectrum, an abundance of organizations appeared to handle the middle-class. These clubs were located in every city, large or small, and all had clubhouses with prominent bars--the Moose, Elks, Eagles, Knights of Columbus (Catholic), Christopher Columbus Lodge (Italian), Pulaski and St. Stephen's clubs (Polish), Hibernian (Irish), American Legion, Veterans of Foreign Wars (VFW). In addition, there were city clubs, country clubs, hunting and fishing clubs, yacht clubs, University clubs (Yale, Princeton, Harvard had clubs in New York City)--an almost endless supply of private or restricted drinking establishments. Many of these places continue to thrive today, although closings were widespread during the culture change of the 1960s and 70s, and now membership in private clubs is less than one half its peak post World War II level.

The American bar scene changed "big time" for the younger generation during the 1960s and 70s. The long, drawn-out Vietnam War inspired a counter-culture in America, which eventually opposed and attacked all traditions. In addition to opposing the War, these youth movements embraced civil rights, women's lib, and environmental concerns--they were exchanging rights for rules. They also adopted drugs in a big way, beginning with marijuana and spreading to LSD, heroin and cocaine. It was known as the "turn-on, tune-in, drop out" decade. The saying goes, "if you remember the 60s, you weren't there."

In addition to drugs, these tumultuous times also resulted in increased use of alcohol. Between 1960 and 1975, the annual US consumption of alcohol increased by one-third to 2 gallons per capita. The peak for consumption of hard liquor was reached in 1978, 2.82 gallons per person, then a decline set in caused by a national switch to beer and wine.

Women had been excluded from bars, or at least not welcome; well the 60's changed that attitude. "Fern Bars" first appeared in San Francisco in the 70's. These places with an abundance of plants, catered to women, and spawned the chains like TGI Friday's and Bennigans.

Vodka entered the US market in the 1960s, and by 1980, it became the most popular distilled spirit in the Country. The fact that vodka could be mixed with anything and left you "breathless" for alcoholic odor, combined with being cheaper than other liquors, contributed to its popularity.

However, the big alcohol industry news of the 70s and

80s was the increased popularity of wine in the United States. Americans have been producing wine, or trying to produce wine, for over 300 years. In the early colonies of Virginia and the Carolinas, winemaking as an official goal was established in their founding charters. Early efforts were met with failure as native pests and vine disease ravaged the vineyards.

The first commercial winery in the US was established by the Kentucky legislature in November 1799 and two five-gallon oak casks of the first wine produced were delivered to Pres. Thomas Jefferson in Washington, DC in February 1805.

Wine production began to take off in the US during the middle 1800s and vineyards were established from California to Missouri to the Finger Lakes region of New York State. Near the end of the 19th century, the phylloxera epidemic destroyed vineyards in the West, and Pierce's disease ruined the vines in the East. The wine industry was just beginning to recover from these blows when Prohibition was enacted in 1920. A few wineries were able to survive by converting to grape juice production or getting government permission to provide churches with sacramental wine. One loophole in the Prohibition law allowed California wineries to continue to produce "raisin cakes," which were intended for home production of sweet, nonalcoholic grape juice. Demonstrators of the cakes, sales reps of the wine companies, cleverly told customers that "on no account should the jugs of juice be left in a warm place for 21 days because they might ferment and turn into wine; and don't put a stopper in the jug, because that would only aid the fermentation process." Beringer Vineyard in the Napa Valley, still in business today, was a trailblazer in exploiting this loophole in the law, and many other vineyards followed.

Prohibition took its toll on the wine industry, just as it did on the beer breweries. Prior to Prohibition there were over 800 wineries in California, 12 years later, when Prohibition was repealed, there were only 40 still in operation. It took about 30 years for the American wine industry to recover from the blow of Prohibition; but by the middle 1960s, what is known as the "Wine Renaissance" had begun in America.

Today, the US is the fourth-largest wine producing country in the world, after France, Italy, and Spain. Wine production is undertaken in all 50 states, and there are over 3000 commercial vineyards in the US. Eighty nine percent of US wine is produced in California, followed by New York State, with 4% of the total, and Washington State with about 3%. In other words, 96% of US wine production occurs in three states, although all 50 states have some commercial vineyards. The total number of wineries in the U.S. topped 7,000 last year.

If California were a country, it would be the fourth-largest wine producer in the world with over 1200 wineries producing 635,000,000 gallons of wine annually. The first winery in California was established by the Spanish Franciscan monks at San Juan Capistrano in 1779. As each mission was founded, additional vineyards were established. The wine was used for religious sacraments as well as for daily life needs. The original vine cuttings came from Mexico and had been brought to the New World by Hernando Cortez, Spanish explorer, in 1520. These grapes association with the Church caused them to be known as the Mission grapes, and they remained the dominant grape variety in California until the 20th century.

The California Gold Rush, in the mid-1800s, brought a surge in the demand for wine. During this period some of California's oldest wineries were founded in Sonoma County and the Napa Valley--Buena Vista winery, Charles Krug,

Inglenook and Schramsberg.

California is a very geologically diverse region, resulting in a range of climates and "terroirs" favorable for producing a wide variety of wines. Generally, the state is divided into four distinct wine regions: North Coast, north of San Francisco; Central Coast, south and west of San Francisco; South Coast, south of Los Angeles, down to the border with Mexico; Central Valley and Sierra foothills. There are over 100 grape varieties grown in these four regions; but over 75% of all California wine is produced in the Central Valley Region stretching 300 miles from Sacramento to the San Joaquin Valley.

The reliable warm weather allows California wineries to use very ripe grapes, which results in a more "fruit forward" taste, rather than the European earthy or mineralic style of wine. It also creates the opportunity for higher alcohol levels, with many California wines having over 13 1/2% alcohol by volume.

Current US laws allow American wines to be labeled as "American burgundy" or California champagne, even though these names are restricted by the European Union. US laws only require usage to include the qualifying area of origin to go with the generic name. The European Union continues to work through the World Trade Organization to restrict the use of an extensive list of terms, including Claret, Chablis, Chianti, Port, Rhine, Sautern, etc.

The United States has established 187 distinct appellations, known as American Viticulture Areas (AVA). An appellation is a legally defined and protected geographical indication used to identify where the grapes for a particular wine were grown. In order to have an AVA appear on the label, at least 85% of the grapes used to produce the wine must be grown in the AVA. With the larger state and county appellations, laws vary depending upon the area. The US has a few other label requirements. For a particular vintage to appear on the label, 95% of the grapes must be from that year, all labels must list alcohol content by volume, and for the varietal (type of grape) to appear on the label, 75% of the content must be of that varietal.

The US has recently requested permission from the European Union to export "Chateau" and "Clos" labeled wines to Europe, including France. The French are strongly opposed to allowing this practice, claiming use of the terms "Chateau" or "Clos" by other nations will dilute the value of the designation, which has taken hundreds of years to establish. There are big bucks at stake, since last year 34% of US wine exports went to the European Union, accounting for $473 million. In comparison, the EU exports to the US stood at $29 billion, much of it from the top-line Chateau and Clos vintages that have come to define the continent's best wines. The US definition would use less stringent conditions than the French, which specifies the wines be made from grapes belonging to the Chateau and produced on the estate.

The potential for producing quality sparkling wine has attracted French champagne houses to open wineries in California. These include Moet et Chandon, Taittinger and Louis Roederer. Despite being made with mostly the same grapes in similar production techniques, these wines have their own distinct style. The optimal, consistent climate conditions allow most sparkling wine producers to make a vintage dated wine every year, while in Champagne, France this only happens in exceptional years.

In the 60s and 70s, the University of California and the state universities in New York began to concentrate their efforts on improving domestic wine. Extensive research was done in growing grapes and developing wine making techniques and degrees were offered in viticulture. The resulting improved quality of California and New York State wines began to attract worldwide attention.

A watershed moment for the American wine industry occurred in 1976, when a prominent British wine merchant, Steven Spurrier, invited several California wineries to participate in a blind tasting event in Paris. The contest was to compare the best California wines with the best Bordeaux and Burgundy wines of France. In the event, known as the "judgment of Paris", California wines shocked the world by sweeping wine competition in both the red and white wine categories. From then on California slowly emerged to become one of the world's premier wine regions. Robert Mondavi, whose vineyards survive him and prosper, is credited with leading this achievement of winning recognition for California wines.

The tourist industry has hopped on the wine popularity bandwagon with wine tours, wine tastings, and wine trails becoming very popular recreational pursuits in the US. In addition to the most popular Napa Valley region, the Finger Lakes area of central New York State has over 200 wineries and the State recently completed a multi-million dollar Wine Center in Canandaigua, New York. Washington State has over 740 wineries producing nearly every style of wine. Chateau St. Michelle Wine Estates is the largest producer, owning more than one third of all vineyards in the state of Washington.

America's love affair with wine continues. Since the 1990s, there has been an accepted positive medical correlation between consuming moderate quantities of red wine and improved heart health. This information has been a big help in increasing red wine sales in the US and elsewhere. The US is now the largest consumer of wine in the world. Total US wine sales in 2011 from all sources, including foreign imports, climbed to a new record of 347 million cases. By comparison, France consumed about 322 million cases. On a per capita basis, France remains the number one major country, consuming 48 quarts of wine per year per person. Considering all countries, large and small, the Vatican is in first place by a wide margin, consuming 58 quarts per capita annually--they must be saying a lot of daily masses. The US is way down the list, ten quarts per person annually.

Total wine sales by volume in the US have grown for 18 consecutive years. Of the popular table wines, Americans prefer Chardonnay, the most popular at 21% of volume, followed by Cabernet Sauvignon, 12%, and Merlot at 10%.

Currently, the largest wine producers in the US are the following: EJ Gallo winery--accounts for more than a quarter of all US wine sales, and is second in the world. Constellation Brands is the world's largest wine producer and is second in the US, with brands that include Robert Mondavi and Columbia. In third-place, The Wine Group, based in San Francisco, owns Mogen David, Franzia and Concannon Vineyards. Other major producers include the UK based Diageo, Brown-Foreman, Berringer, division of Australian Foster's Group and Kendall-Jackson.

As noted earlier, beer has been an important American drink since the Pilgrims landed at Plymouth Rock in 1620. Over the next 300 years, the beer industry grew to become one of America's premier enterprises. Every city and town, large or small, had competing breweries. Cincinnati, with its large German immigrant population, had 27 German language newspapers and 26 breweries prior to Prohibition. My hometown, Olean, New York; (population in 1920 of 21,000) had three breweries in the 1950s. By 1920, when Prohibition was enacted by approval of the 18th amendment to the U.S. Constitution, there were 3500 breweries operating in America. Following the repeal of Prohibition in 1933, only 400 breweries remained, and 200 of these closed in the 1930s Depression.

It took well into the 1970s for US beer sales to match pre-Prohibition levels. By this time, there were only a few major players dominating the industry; Coors, Anheuser-Busch, Millers, and some regional outfits like Yuengling brewery in Pottsville, Pennsylvania; which had weathered Prohibition by using its refrigeration equipment to produce ice cream. Today, Yuengling is America's oldest brewery, dating from 1829. Yuengling is also America's largest privately owned brewery, and has been owned by the same family for six generations.

In 1977, a new participant appeared on the American beer scene when the New Albion Brewing Company, Sonoma, California offered the first microbrew (so-called because of its small size). The Sierra Nevada Brewing Company opened in 1981 in Chico, California, and microbreweries began to spread throughout the West.

In 2011, there were 1989 total breweries operating in the US. The breakdown of this number includes 1063 brewpubs, 789 microbreweries, 88 regional craft breweries, 21 large breweries, and 28 other non-craft breweries. These numbers change each year because there are many openings and closings in the craft beer business.

"Craft brewer," is a term coined by the American Brewers Association to describe small, independent, and traditional brewers, with annual production of 6 million barrels or less (186 million gallons). A craft brewery cannot be more than 24% owned by another alcoholic company that is not itself a craft brewery. The ABA further groups craft breweries as microbrewery: annual production less than

15,000 barrels (465,000 gallons); brewpub: brews and sells beer on the premises; regional craft brewer produces less than 2 million barrels per year and at least 50% of its volume must be in all-malt beers or in beers which use additives to enhance the flavor.

One other new category, not included in the above types, is the nano brewery. A nano brewery is a very small brewery operation, usually producing less than four barrels per year (124 gallons). These places are fully licensed and regulated by the Alcohol, Tobacco Tax, and Trade Bureau of the federal government. Nano breweries frequently act as a starting point and many have grown into microbreweries or brewpubs. One example is Dogfish Head in Milton, Delaware, which started as an extremely small brewpub in 1995 and produced 75,000 barrels of beer last year. As of September 2011, there were 66 nano breweries operating in the US.

The final segment of beer production is home brewing. Mimicking the wine craze of the 60s and 70s, home-breweries have taken off across the US with over a half million people crafting beer and ales in their kitchens. Kits sell for about $40 and include all the equipment and ingredients to make your home the neighborhood pub. Hammacher Schlemmer, a New York City specialty store, has been selling unusual products through its catalog for 164 years. The current catalog offers a professional microbrewery for home use-- price, $49,000. Recipes are entered on a touch screen computer, and the fully automated system produces 15 gallons of homebrew at a time. Most states permit home brewing by defaulting to federal law, which permits people 21 and older to brew up to 100 gallons per year without a license, and prohibits them from selling it.

Overall US beer sales were flat in 2011, totaling $96

billion from selling 200 million barrels of beer. The average adult over age 21 consumes over 30 gallons of beer annually, or about 320 bottles. There are 31 gallons in a barrel of beer. Just about half the beer sold in the US is produced by Anheuser Busch, and the Miller-Coors group accounts for another 25%.

If the 1960s and 70s were the Renaissance of wine in America, the Renaissance for beer is now. This explosion of breweries and beer-types, the average American now lives within 10 miles of a local brewery, has spawned a business of beer festivals, beer publications, beer tastings, beer classes and beer trails-- just like the wine industry fifty years ago.

America's largest beer celebration is the "Great American Beer Festival" held every October in the Colorado Convention Center in Denver. About 50,000 attendees sample over 3100 beers from 624 brewers over three days. In terms of attendance, of course, this is a small gathering compared to the Munich Oktoberfest with six million visitors over two weeks.

Just as there are wineries in all 50 states, there are breweries everywhere in America; but Vermont is the king on a per capita basis, with over 21 craft breweries. Portland, Oregon   is the leader among cities with over 31 breweries. The state of Oregon is really into the craft beer business, with over 7% of the Country's breweries and only 1% of the population. The craft beer/micro-brewery fad is by no means limited to the US. In fact, the term originated in Great Britain in the 1970s, and now micro brewing has spread to Germany, France, Australia and Japan.

Beer trails are now erupting everywhere, along with beer destinations. One example is the six dozen brewery tour along the Front Range of the Rockies, stretching north of Denver to Ft. Collins. Dubbed the "Napa Valley of beer" this tour is covered in detail by Ed Sealover, author of "Mountain Brew: A Guide to Colorado's Breweries." One brewery, the New Belgium Brewery, was launched twenty years ago in a Fort Collins basement, and is now one of the biggest craft beers in America, shipping its flagship "Fat Tire Ale" to over 30 states. The brewery's one-hour tour is so popular it is booked three months in advance.

The craft beer segment of the US beer market is about 6.3% by volume and 9% by dollars; but business is growing at an annual rate of 13% by volume and 15% in dollars. The largest American craft brewery is the Boston Beer Company, maker of Samuel Adams beer. American beer drinkers are much more knowledgeable than 15 years ago. The beer drinker is discovering hops the way the wine drinker knows grapes. Chefs in major restaurants are cooking with beer and customers are scrutinizing beer menus just like wine lists.

A common custom is to sample three or four beers at dinner. "Girls Pint Out" is a national organization that brings women together for craft local beer tastings. Many major hotels are partnering with local craft breweries and offer their own unique beers. Lobby "happy hours" now consist of beer tastings, presentations on craft beer brewing, or tips on learning to brew beer at home.

There are hundreds of brewpubs that are worth a visit just for the unique beers they create, or for the history of the establishment. The Yorks Brewing Company in Philadelphia uses authentic personal brewing recipes of George Washington, Thomas Jefferson, and Benjamin Franklin. Ben Franklin's recipe is for Poor Richards Tavern Spruce Ale.

Kelly's Caribbean Beer Grill and Brewery is home to the southernmost brewery in the continental United States. Owned by "Top Gun" star Kelly McGillis, the brewery is located in the building that housed the Pan Am ticket office when they began service to Key West in 1927.

The New Glarus Brewing Company in New Glarus, Wisconsin; a reconstructed Swiss-style village; is owned by Deborah Kerry, one of the first women to found and operate a U.S. brewery. This small, hilltop brewery is located in a new 21 million dollar facility. The village, settled in 1845 by Swiss immigrants, really earns its title of Little Switzerland with authentic Swiss bakeries, restaurants, antique stores and two museums.

The popularity of craft beer and small wineries has led to the establishment of small-scale distilleries, and now they are legal, not like the moonshine days. There are more than 250 craft distillers across the USA and they are growing at a rate of about one a month. Many of these distilleries are add-ons to craft beer breweries--a brewery-distillery. These places are spread across the Country. In Portland, Oregon, the New Deal Distillery makes Hot Monkey pepper-flavored vodka. In Indianapolis, Indiana Heartland Distillers makes a full-flavored dry gin called "Prohibition Gin." In Asheville, North Carolina, Troy and Sons distills corn into a moonshine-like whiskey, and in Seneca Falls, New York, Hidden Marsh Distillery makes Bee Vodka, a honey-flavored vodka. As part of the craft beer market, the cider category is "hot" right now. The major beer makers are adding to their selections. Heineken with Strongbow, Stella Artois Cidre, and the debut of Mike's Hard Smashed Apple.

Unlike many other countries, drinking in the USA is a diverse occupation spread over almost every form of drinkable alcohol and consumed in spots ranging from old neighborhood bars to glitzy Las Vegas nightclubs. In between, we have sports bars with pool tables, dartboards, and 50 TV sets, topless bars with naked dancers, biker bars for the motorcycle crowd, wine bars, martini bars, beer gardens, nightclubs, and one of the latest fashions, rooftop bars. Some of these places deserve special discussion.

The "college bar" is a special spot. With the drinking age set at 21, college bars have to be especially careful about serving alcohol to minors, so one of the key ingredients of the college bar, not found in most other drinking spots, is the ritual of gaining entrance by showing your ID (identification), and receiving an appropriate wristband identifying you as over 21. Ironically, and I guess naturally, this requirement has spawned a cottage industry across the country producing fake ID cards. One more time, you make the rules governing behavior and folks will find a way around them.

A good example of a typical college bar is the **"Pot Belly"** located adjacent to the Florida State University campus in TALLAHASSEE, the state capital. This place is situated in two old clapboard houses with a vacant lot (courtyard) between them. Tables are located out front on the sidewalk for checking ID. Inside there is practically nothing, really, except seven separate bars. There may be a few picnic tables and benches, but furniture of any sort is scarce. The drink of choice is overwhelmingly beer, 90% of the customers are drinking beer. This particular evening, the hot item was "loaded Corona"; which consists of a shot of rum poured into the vacant space at the top of a bottle of Corona beer. The entire place, all seven bars, was packed, which apparently is normal; and, keep in mind, this is only one of over 30 bars in town.

Currently, the most popular college bar game is "beer pong." The game typically consists of two to four player teams and multiple cups filled with beer set up at each end of a long table. Rules vary widely, though usually there are six to ten cups at each end of the table arranged in triangle formation, similar to pool or billiards. Each team takes a turn attempting to toss up to four ping-pong balls into the opponents' cups. If a ball lands in a cup, the contents of that cup are drunk by the other team and the cup is set aside. The first side to eliminate all the opponent cups is the winner. The fact that the ball frequently winds up on the floor, and eventually in the cup of beer, does not seem to be a hygiene problem.

Hotel bars deserve special notice in any discussion of drinking establishments because they differ from most bars where people are friendly and know each other; the folks at a hotel bar rarely know anyone else in the room. Hotels are beginning to change this with friendly lobbies, and comfortable lounges. The latest buzz in the business is the "rooftop bar." These were pioneered by boutique hotels; but are now showing up at the bigger hotel chains.

The Conrad New York recently opened **the Loopy Doopy Lounge**, six stories above Battery Park in lower Manhattan. **The Dream Downtown** in New York has covered the rooftop terrace, and with heaters, it plans to stay open year-round with its gorgeous views of uptown New York. **The Ritz Carlton,** in Georgetown, WASHINGTON, DC, shows movies in its rooftop garden bar. The **Saint Hotel** in NEW ORLEANS will soon open "**Halo**," a roof-top lounge serving gourmet food. In Chicago, the **Raffello** recently opened an 18th Floor, rooftop speakeasy-style lounge.

Across America, there is an historical return to the earliest colonial days when the church and the tavern were side-by-side, and often the tavern was the church. Well, once again, in the 21st Century, faith is returning to the bar. Some bars offer live-streaming Sunday services into the bar, while others are actually having the service in the bar. There are people that want to hear the "Word", they just don't want to go to Church to hear it.

Roman Catholics have sponsored "Theology on Tap" for years as a way to reach out to young people. The Catholic diocese of Arlington, Virginia began offering theology on tap meetings aimed at young people in 2001. Beer and Bible sessions are held every second and fourth Tuesday at the Irish Club in Raleigh, North Carolina; coincidentally, it is also "pint night." The idea is that the bar is serving its original purpose by promoting conversation and discussion.

Another recent American drinking trend involves fast food restaurants beginning to serve alcohol with your burger and fries. Burger King has begun opening "Whopper Bars" that serve beer, and Starbucks is experimenting with beer and wine sales at several locations in its home base, Seattle, and will open a **Starbucks Bar** in NEW YORK CITY in 2014. **Sonic,** the drive-in chain, is offering 25 kinds of bottled beer, three drafts, and 10 wine varieties to customers that eat on its patios--alcoholic beverages are not available to folks who are eating in their cars. These are tough economic times, and everyone is looking for a niche. Soon you will flash your ID when you enter a McDonalds.

One of the most recent cultural trends, capitalizing on last years' especially hot summer, is spiked, frosty treats. Alcohol is increasingly showing up in everything from milkshakes to ice cream sandwiches and snow cones. The **Cheesecake Factory** restaurant chain has a selection of eight "Spiked Shakes" on the menu. In addition to wine shakes and spiked ice cream sandwiches, frozen popsicles made from craft beer are becoming quite popular. Hotels in Houston, Texas, have a promotion featuring snow cones with a shot of booze.

There is no end to the ever-changing American bar scene. On a recent Tuesday evening at **Brown's Town Lounge** in SALEM, OREGON, over 100 people packed the place, not for a band or for happy hour; but for a lecture on "behavioral endocrinology"--in a bar. Known as "science pubs" or "science cafes", the trend started in Britain in the late 1990s, and today the Cafe Scientific Organization promotes and tracks science cafes worldwide. The Denver, Colorado Cafe Scientific, founded in November 2003, claims to be the oldest in the US. Last year there were a total of 150 science pubs in America, and the number is growing with 27 new ones in 2013.

It's an enjoyable experience for a lot of people to have a couple of beers, slice of pizza and hear a presentation by a local university professor, museum director or some other expert. There is no shortage of speakers, since most organizations and individuals are delighted to have the opportunity to reach out to these audiences. Once again, the bar provides a unique space for people to gather informally and exchange information. Another advantage, people attending these events are not in a hurry, as they usually are at the typical breakfast or luncheon presentation.

Americans have some special occasions where drinking is a major ingredient in the celebration. One of these is the nationwide tradition of "tailgating" at college and professional football games. This custom has developed into an elaborate event, and no longer consists of just opening the trunk of the car, or rear door of the station wagon, and having a few beers and a hot dog. Now it means setting up tables with tablecloths, preparing charcoal grills, cooking gourmet dishes, using special utensils, toting mega coolers of beer and wine. Some of these tailgate setups resemble a small restaurant. The event begins in the parking lot early in the morning of the game, and extends until the lot closes hours after the game ends. As you might expect, there are "drinking problems" that can result from these extended parties.

Football stadiums first attempted to curtail alcohol consumption by limiting the size of drinks, especially beer, and the hours they were available. For example, behavior became such a problem at Rich Stadium in Buffalo, New York, home of the Buffalo Bills that no alcohol was sold after the end of the first half. Now, the authorities are not opening the parking lot for tailgate parties until two hours prior to the kickoff time.

A few other days of the year call for extra special drinking efforts in the US. The Fourth of July accounts for more beer sales than any other day of the year, just as pizza sales peak on Super Bowl Sunday.

Halloween has always been a wonderful, scary, and mischief-filled night for children. Now it has become another major adult celebration, and bars have capitalized on the opportunity. Special drinks, elaborate decorations, and most importantly, prizes for best costumes, make the whole package a joyous event.

America also celebrates two other ethnic holidays in a big way. St. Patrick's Day, March 17, is observed from one end of the Country to the other by everyone, whether your name begins with an "O" (O'Malley), or ends with an "O" (Caruso), you are living-it-up on St. Patrick's Day. At many Irish bars, and there are many these days, St. Pat's Day is observed for a full week, and the parties are packed and rambunctious. Major celebrations take place in New York City, Boston, Chicago, Cleveland and Savannah, a city of 140,000 that attracts about a million for St. Pat's Day.

The Germans are not left out of these American celebrations, and Oktoberfest's are spread throughout the land each October. Not rivaling Munich's famous beer fest, which is the world's largest, but some of these American parties are pretty good. The largest **American Oktoberfest** is held in CINCINNATI each year, and attended by over a half million people. Sponsored by Samuel Adams beer, one of the premier attractions is the annual "Running of the Wieners", where dachshunds race in complete hot dog regalia.

Americans consumption of alcohol reached a twenty-five year high in 2010, when 65% reported drinking alcoholic beverages, according to a Gallup polls. Despite the current economic recession, this is a level unseen since the late 1970s, when 71% of Americans said they drank. Breaking the number down further, 51% of the population reported drinking regularly, 14% drink sometimes, 14% don't drink anymore, and 21% are lifetime abstainers.

Wine consumption reached an all-time peak in 2010 at 2.3 gallons per person. That is an increase of more than one third since 1994. Sales of spirits climbed 18% to 1.5 gallons per person, while beer intake dropped 7% to 20.7 gallons. It is interesting that wine and spirits sales are strong in California, the Southwest, and the East Coast, while beer sales dominate the center of the Country.

Beer sales, although slipping, still count for almost half of the beverage alcohol market. Even a small change in market share can be a big deal in the $60 billion beverage industry, where each point is worth $600 million at wholesale. The current recession has been a bigger blow to the beer brewers than to the wine industry, since beer drinkers, who have lower incomes, took more of the brunt of the downturn.

On the plus side, the legal drinking age population continues to grow in this country, providing an ever larger total market for alcohol.

Following the end of Prohibition, the United States returned the control of alcohol to the individual 50 states, and as a result, America has an overabundance of rules, regulations, and laws governing the production, sale and consumption of alcohol. The minimum drinking age is a consistent 21 in all 50 states only because the federal government threatened to withhold highway funds from any state that did not raise the age to 21.

By the way, no other developed country has a drinking age as high as 21; and there is no doubt the law has created a large under-age drinking problem and a cottage industry producing fake ID. This is another example of a highly organized minority imposing its will on the unorganized majority. It happened with the Anti-Saloon League bringing about Prohibition, the National Rifle Association (NRA) opposing gun control; and in this case, MADD (the Mothers Against Drunk Driving) successfully getting lawmakers to increase the drinking age to 21. Eighteen year-olds are able to drive, vote, and be drafted into the military for wartime duties; but they are resolutely not allowed to consume alcohol.

Many factors have had a profound effect on alcohol consumption in the US over the past 25 years, including "no smoking" in bars, health warnings concerning alcohol use, and increased emphasis on eliminating drunk driving as a major cause of auto accidents. It has been found that most alcohol-impaired drivers are "binge drinkers," meaning for men, drinking five or more drinks within a short period of time, or for women, four or more drinks. Surveys have shown that one in six adults in the USA is a "binge drinker", and does so about four times a month. This dangerous habit is twice as likely among men as among women and is most prevalent for those between 18 and 34 years old. The fad is especially popular on college campuses today. This problem is not limited to the US, and is practiced widely in European countries. It is interesting that most of these "binge drinkers" are not classified as "alcoholics."

Mothers Against Drunk Driving (MADD) was founded in 1980 by Candy Lightner and a small group of mothers in California, following the death of her teenage daughter by a repeat-offender drunk driver. MADD, which was the major force behind the 1984 law raising the drinking age to 21, has been an extremely successful organization over the past 30 years. It claims not to be a crusade against alcohol consumption. Its mission is to stop drunk driving, support the victims of drunk driving, and prevent underage drinking. MADD's efforts have made driving under the influence (DWI), a very serious offense, and the minimum bloodstream alcohol level is now at .08%.

Many believe the ultimate goal of MADD is to lower the alcohol limit to zero--no drinking and driving. Keep in mind, most countries have more liberal laws than the US regarding consuming alcohol; but they are all extremely strict regarding drinking and driving. The battle against drunk driving in the U.S. has been very successful, reducing the deaths from 20,000 to less than 10,000 per year over the past three decades. Now the National Transportation Board is encouraging the use of ignition interlocks, alcohol detection devices that drivers must blow into to start their cars. Eighteen states have made these mandatory for convicted drunken drivers.

We Americans are still a little "hung up" on bars and drinking. To lots of people, bars remain "Satan's headquarters on Earth"; home of drunks, politicians, rabble-rousers and revolutionaries. A place that cannot be trusted to deal with children. Meanwhile in the rest of the world, children are welcome and accepted in the pubs of Ireland, cafes of Italy or Spain, and the beer gardens of Germany. In fact, in many European countries the local pub, tavern, cafe, or bistro is a cherished treasure.

As it has for over three centuries, the American bar struggles on with the creation of brewpubs, sports bars, wine bars and even science bars. Surely people will continue to have a drink or two to celebrate a newborn baby, a team win, a wedding; and, of course to soothe a loss or a disappointment.

The fabled neighborhood bar is fading away in America, just as the local pub is disappearing in England. English pubs are closing at the rate of one a day, and Irish pubs are disappearing at a rate of one every other day. Chicago is a typical example of the trend. In 1990, about 3300 Chicago establishments had tavern licenses allowing them to serve alcoholic beverages. Places that also offer live entertainment, or serve food as their primary business, require different or additional licenses. The number has fallen to about 1200, where it has held steady for the past few years. Neighborhood bars are being squeezed out by many factors, including the economy, changing tastes, city regulations, and old, ethnic neighborhoods being gentrified for the well-to-do. Getting a tavern license in a residential neighborhood is virtually impossible.

As mentioned earlier, the social isolation resulting from the electronics generation is also having a major negative effect on the local bar. An example, Simons Tavern, located in the old Swedish section of Chicago, Andersonville, is now the only bar on the street that used to have 15 drinking spots.

The following is a short list and a brief description of some of the historical bars still operating today. The latest "in places," "Hotspots", or current fashion hangouts, are not included due to their often brief period in the spotlight.

BOSTON

Bull and Finch Pub. The original source for the hit TV show of the 90s, "Cheers," this bar was dismantled in England and shipped to the US. It does not resemble the bar scene on "Cheers"; an exact replica of the "Cheers" bar has been re-created at another Boston location.

Doyle's Café. A wonderful Irish pub dating from 1882 in a city noted for its Irish politicians; this is a political landmark.

Bell-in-Hand. This has been around since 1795, and claims to be the oldest continuously operating bar in the US. The first owner was Jimmie Wilson, who was the "town crier" for 50 years. He refused to serve the "hard stuff," no whiskey, rum or gin, only ale. The ale was so thick it was served in two mugs, one for the ale, and one for the froth. The bar has a long list of famous patrons: Daniel Webster, Paul Revere, and William McKinley, to name a few.

Green Dragon. Opened in 1654, and came to be known as "the Headquarters of the Revolution," the original location on Union Street was demolished in 1854, and a reproduction is now open at 11 Marshall St.

BUFFALO

Frank and Teresa's Anchor Bar is where spicy-hot chicken wings were invented in 1964. The wings idea took place when friends came in late one evening, after the kitchen had closed. Teresa Ballissimo, wife of the owner, took some chicken wings she had intended for soup stock, fried them, and tossed them with some hot sauce she stirred up on the spot, and the "chicken wing" fad was born. This place serves and ships over 2000 pounds of chicken wings each day. Located on Main Street, the place has a photo gallery of all the famous visitors.

The Buffalo Chicken Wing Festival is held each summer at the local baseball stadium and attracts over 40,000 people. The chicken wing eating contest record, so far, is 173 wings in 12 minutes.

CHICAGO

The John Barleycorn dates from 1890, and was a Chinese laundry during Prohibition, and served as a front for bootleggers who rolled laundry carts of booze to the basement. John Dillinger was a frequent customer, often treating the house with his stolen money. The bar is filled with hand-made replicas of ships collected by the former Dutch proprietor on his many travels to the Far East. Location: 658 W. Belden St.

The Pump Room opened in 1938, inspired by the 18th century original still operating in Bath, England. For the next 50 years, this place became a magnet for celebrities. Booth One has hosted everyone from Humphrey Bogart and Lauren Bacall on their honeymoon, to Salvador Dali, who drew on the tablecloths. Harry Carey, the beloved Chicago baseball announcer, stopped in every evening before the game "To get ready." Location: Ambassador East Hotel.

The Green Mill opened in 1907, and was a mecca for Chicago's movie industry before it moved to Hollywood. Al Capone's right-hand man, Jack "Machine Gun" McGurn ran the place during Prohibition. McGurn is infamous for orchestrating the St. Valentine's Day Massacre. Al Capone was a frequent visitor. **The Green Mill** is now a favorite jazz spot, and the place has appeared in many movies and the 1980s TV show," Crime Story." Location: 4800 N. Broadway

The Billy Goat Tavern is a celebrated little dive located one flight below street level on N. Michigan Ave. Made famous by all the newspaper and TV types that hang out there, and by a "Saturday Night Live" TV sketch in the 70s, even a few presidents have dropped by for a beer. Location: 430 Michigan Avenue

Resi's Bierstube is a great example of Chicago's German beer heritage. The building has housed a bar since 1913, and like so many Chicago bars, operated without a problem during Prohibition. Resi's is home to Chicago's oldest beer garden. Many of Chicago's German bars originally featured beer gardens; but they were banned during World War II to prevent Germans from congregating outside. The ban lasted until Resi's opened their beer garden in 1965. Location: 2034 W. Irving Park Rd.

Schaller's Pump is noteworthy as Chicago's oldest, continuously operating tavern, opening in 1881. Schaller's Pump refers to the mechanism that once pumped beer directly to the bar from the Ambrosia Brewery next door. Schaller's represents two American traditions: politics and baseball. Close to the stadium, Schaller is a haven for White Sox fans. The district's Democratic headquarters is across the street, and Schaller's has served as a second office for no less than five of Chicago's Democratic mayors, all hailing from the Bridgeport neighborhood, including both Richard Daley and his son. It is a perfect example of the classic Chicago neighborhood bar. Location: 3714 S. Halstead Street.

Two other spots worth a visit on any trip to Chicago are the **Signature Lounge** on the 96th floor of the John Hancock building; you can see four states on a clear day; and the **Coq d'Or** (Golden cockerel rooster) in the Drake Hotel. Past visitors have included Winston Churchill, Emperor Hirohito, Queen Elizabeth II, Princess Diana, and Ronald Reagan. Noted for its decor, live piano jazz and the 16- ounce Executive Martini.

CLEVELAND

This is home to the renowned Great Lakes Brewing Company and the **Garage Bar.** This has been a local attraction for over a century; but now, with the craft beer craze, it's filled with visitors from everywhere. The Dortmunder Gold crisp lager, a major award-winner, is the main attraction.

Nearby is the **Brew Kettle Taproom**, noted by <u>ratebeer</u> as the number one brewpub in America. Visitors can brew their own beer in the fermentation room, or select from the impressive variety of craft beers on tap.

FORT WORTH, TEXAS, is home of "**Billy Bob's.**" This place is big, even by Texas standards; 40 bars, indoor rodeo arena, two dance halls, live music every night, and room for over 6000 people.

INDIANAPOLIS, INDIANA. This interesting old bar, **The Slippery Noodle Inn**, has been serving drinks since 1850. John Dillinger's gang hung around the bar, and they've had a couple murders inside, the last one in 1953. The authorities shut down the brothel the same year. The place is open for business each and every day at seven AM, bullet holes in the wall and all.

KEY WEST, FLORIDA When you mention drinking spots in the USA., this place has to be included; famous for bars, fishing, Harry Truman and Ernest Hemingway. President Truman had his own bar constructed in the "Little White House," along with a pair of poker tables. The bar was usually staffed with two Navy corpsman as bartenders.

Duval Street is lined with bars, and most of them are filled with entertainment and worth a visit. **The Hog's Breath Saloon,** whose motto is "Hog's breath is better than no breath at all", is a must stop. **The Schooner Wharf Pub** is an open-air bar with a dirt floor, umbrellas over the tables and a makeshift roof over the bar--real Key West.

Sloppy Joe's was a favorite of Hemingway. Interestingly, Hemingway, who lived for 12 years right in the center of town, wrote his novels in the studio over the carriage house each morning; and then, generally drank in one of these bars most of the evening. Some of his finest work was done in this studio: "A Farewell to Arms" and "Snows of Kilimanjaro." When Sloppy Joe's was remodeled in the mid-1930s, Hemingway had one of the urinals installed in the yard of his residence as a water fountain, where it remains today. Hemingway's house is a private, for-profit, landmark and tourist attraction.

LAS VEGAS -This is certainly not the home of some of America's oldest and historical bars, but it is the place with an abundance of "over-the-top" drinking opportunities. The state of Nevada legalized gambling and prostitution in 1931, hoping the combination would attract capital and people in the midst of the Great Depression. It definitely worked, although much of the capital came from organized crime-- another result of the Prohibition years. Las Vegas has recently opened a museum dedicated to the role of organized crime families in developing the now famous resort. Among the show-stopping exhibits is the entire bullet-ridden wall from the 1939 Valentine's Day Massacre in a Chicago garage.

A few spots are worth a visit; all are located on the famous 3.8 mile long "Strip."

The **Bellagio Hotel**, has a wine cellar 5000 bottles deep and more master sommeliers than anywhere else in the world. In the past 40 years, only about 175 people have achieved the Master Sommelier Status.

Mandalay Bay Casino. The Aureole Restaurant has a 40 foot, four-story tower in the center of the room that houses almost 10,000 bottles of wine.

Las Vegas, or Vegas, as it is commonly known, is home to the annual "World Series of Beer Pong," the popular college game described earlier. Over 1000 contestants, who pay an entry fee, similar to the Texas Hold 'Em tournament, compete for a $50,000 prize.

Rio Las Vegas Hotel, the **Voodoo Lounge** on the 51st floor is a bar that offers a prime example of "Flair Bartending." This is a mix between a drink and a show, with bartenders that can juggle, throw and flip bottles, as well as pour them. Bartenders in this end of the business enter contests all across the country. The signature drink here is the "Witch Doctor" made with four rum varieties, various fruits, dry ice cubes, and served with straws in a fishbowl. Speaking of "over-the-top," the **Sporting House Bar and Grill** inside New York-New York Hotel, has over 130 TV sets, showing almost every possible sports competition around the world.

LOS ANGELES. **The Montage Beverly Hills Hotel** deserves mention only because of the secluded, exclusive **Macallan Scotch bar** located above the posh **Scarpetta** restaurant, called the **"Pound 10."** Sink into a plush leather armchair, and let the barman wheel up a mahogany cart filled with Lalique crystal, chilled soapstone rocks (no ice to dilute the scotch), or ice spheres made from pure Scottish Springwater, house-made bitters, and an array of rare single malts. Try a goblet of the 64-year-old, Macallan, that will set you back most of your winnings, plus the tip. Location 225 N. Canyon Dr., Beverly Hills.

NEW ORLEANS. In addition to having some of America's oldest and best-known bars, New Orleans has two unique drinks for which it is world-famous. The Ramos Gin Fizz combines gin, heavy cream, fresh lemon juice, lime juice, a few drops of orange flower water, club soda, cracked ice; shaken and served in a tall glass. The Sazerac is one of history's classic drinks. Combine 2 ounces of bourbon or rye whiskey with two dashes of peychaud's bitters, two dashes of absinthe, or other anise-flavored spirit, half ounce of sugar and a twist of lemon.

New Orleans is filled with wonderful bars that stay

open all night. A town where you can spend the night in a bar and greet a whole new crowd at 7 a.m... A town where you can stroll around carrying a drink. The following is only a brief sampling of the delightful places available; all are located in the French Quarter.

Antoine's, a New Orleans landmark since 1840.

Arnaud's Restaurant. This place is "real New Orleans" — tile floor, wrought iron porches, and Dixieland jazz.

Armand's French 75 is a historic French-Creole restaurant. Don't miss Armand's Mardi Gras Museum, a revered New Orleans institution.

Brennan's Restaurant is famous for "Breakfast at Brennan's."

The **Carousel Bar,** located in the historic Monteleone Hotel, operates like a merry-go-round; your barstool moves and the bar stays put. This place is a lot of fun, and affords ample opportunity for meeting strangers.

Lafitte's Blacksmith Shop dates from 1770, and may be the oldest building in New Orleans. The pirates, Pierre and Sean Lafitte, used it as a "front" for disposing of their "ill-gotten" gains.

Napoleon House dates from around 1797 and is a "must" visit as one of America's best bars.

Tujaque's was established in 1856, making this the city's second oldest restaurant.

O'Briens is famous, ironically after hurricane Katrina practically destroyed the city in 2005, for its "Hurricane" drink, served in a 29 ounce hurricane lamp, souvenir glass. This place claims to sell more alcohol than anywhere else in the world.

The Old Absinthe House, dating from about 1807, has entertained guests that include Franklin Roosevelt, Mark

Twain, Frank Sinatra and Oscar Wilde.

NEW YORK CITY

The largest, most important, and one of the oldest cities in the USA is filled with wonderful old bars. The following is only a brief listing of the highlights.

McSorley's opened in 1854 and is the City's oldest continuously operated saloon, including during the Prohibition period. Everyone from Abe Lincoln to John Lennon has passed through McSorley's swinging doors, though no women were allowed until 1970. The walls are covered with memorabilia, including newspapers announcing the British victory at Waterloo. Don't expect anything fancy, and they only serve two types of beer, light and dark, and you have to order two at a time. Bring cash and exact change if you are able, because McSorley's has never had a cash register and never plans to have one. Location 15 7th St., near Cooper Square.

PJ Clark's began operating in 1854, and despite momentous changes all around over the past 150 years, the bar remains unchanged. This is the place where Johnny Mercer penned "One For My Baby" on a napkin while sitting at the bar; and where "Lost Weekend." with Ray Milland was filmed in 1945. This is the legendary haunt of Frank Sinatra, Elizabeth Taylor, Jackie Kennedy, and countless others. Now there are about a dozen franchises located around the US. Location Third Avenue at 55th St.

Algonquin Hotel is home to the **Oak Room** noted for the "Writers Round Table" where Dorothy Parker and other famous writers of the day gathered for lunch. Dorothy Parker is famous for many sarcastic remarks, but one of my favorites is the following: "I like to have a martini. Two at the very most. After three, I'm under the table. After four I'm under the host." Location: 44th St. near Sixth Avenue

A replica of the original **Fraunces Tavern** building houses a museum and restaurant. The role of this tavern in the Revolutionary War was described earlier. Location: 54 Pearl St. near Broad Street.

The Stonewall Bar was the scene of the famous confrontation between New York police and gays in 1969. The original was next door at 51 Christopher St. Location: 53 Christopher St.

The 21 Club was a famous speakeasy during Prohibition and continues to draw big crowds for lunch and dinner. This place has hosted just about every U.S. President since it opened in the Depression. In addition, over a dozen movies have been filmed here, including "All About Eve", "One Fine Day", "Sex and the City" and "Written on the Wind." Location 51st St.

The King Cole Room, named after the famous mural by Maxfield Parrish behind the bar, is located in the posh, old (1907) St. Regis Hotel. This bar is simply awash with history and celebrity stories. The mural has its own mystique and legend, which you can try to guess after staring at it for a while. The bartender will give you the answer. Birthplace of the Bloody Mary. Location 2 E. 55th St.

OAKLAND, CALIFORNIA

The **Last Chance Saloon** is the bar mentioned frequently in Jack London's novels. London had a favorite table where he would often write. The place dates from 1893 and is packed with memorabilia hanging from the walls and ceiling. Many of the furnishings are original, including the bar, gas lights and pot-bellied stove. Location: 56 Jack London Sq.

PHILADELPHIA, PENNSYLVANIA

McGillin's Old Ale House is Philadelphia's oldest tavern, and the wall behind the bar is decorated with licenses dating from 1860. Long wooden tables fill the tavern, and a large stone fireplace dominates the back wall. When Philadelphia's theater district was more popular, this was a popular spot for actors who could slip in and out the backdoor. Will Rogers, John Barrymore, Tennessee Williams, Ethel Merman, Billy Daniels and many more drank here.

City Tavern, founded in 1773, served many a "Founding Father." The current version is a faithful re-creation of the original and captures the colonial spirit. Location: Second and Walnut streets.

PORTLAND, OREGON

This city claims to have more breweries than any other city on the planet, 31, according to the Brewers Association. As a result, beer fanatics flock here and beer is taken very seriously. Two places to begin your pub-crawl are the **Lucky Labrador Brew Pub** and the famous **Deschutes Brewery Portland Public House.** The latter is a classic beer-going spot that serves craft brew icons and small-batch experimentals.

SAN FRANCISCO

The Top of the Mark was the famous gathering spot for servicemen going to, and returning from, the Pacific during World War II. Has views to die for! Location Mark Hopkins Hotel.

Pied Piper Bar is located in the Palace Hotel and is another spot famous for the Maxfield Parrish mural behind the bar "The Pied Piper of Hamelin." Noted for "two olive martinis", the bar has been open since 1875.

The Buena Vista Bar has been a mecca for Irish coffee connoisseur's since 1952. Location: Fisherman's Wharf.

The Saloon is recognized as the oldest bar in the Bay Area. Dating from 1861, the spot is noted for "blues" music and many famous artists have performed here. The place has withstood several fires and the earthquake of 1906. Many consider its good fortune a result of the close proximity of the fire brigade and their eagerness to protect the bar and the brothel upstairs.

SAVANNAH, GEORGIA

The Pirates House, located in downtown Savannah, was established in 1753, and is the oldest standing building in the state of Georgia. In the cellar, there is a tunnel that leads to the Savannah River where unsuspecting or unconscious drunken sailors were often smuggled to pirate ships to spend a life of bondage among the pirates. The term "Shanghaied" originated here because the sailors were thought to have been taken off to China, or some other faraway place, never to be seen or heard from again. Once a haven for the underbelly of society, the Pirates House is a major tourist attraction today.

WASHINGTON, DC

Here is an abundance of famous and historical bars.

Off the Record is not a bad name for a Washington bar, usually packed with politicians. The walls are covered with caricatures of politicos past, and this place has seen a lot of history. Location: Hay Adams Hotel

The Old Ebbitt Grill has four bars and has been here for 155 years. The walrus head on the wall was snagged by Teddy Roosevelt on one of his many hunting excursions. Location: 675 15th St. NW.

The Round Robin circular bar is located in the Willard Hotel, where lobbying began during the Grant administration. Grant did not like being cooped-up in the White House and retired every evening to the lobby of the

Willard Hotel, across the street. There, in the lobby, he smoked cigars, drank whiskey and entertained and interviewed an endless line of petitioners--hence the term "lobbyist."

A few other places deserve a mention. **Tune Inn** is a legendary Capitol Hill bar on Pennsylvania Avenue. **The 1789 Restaurant** and the **Tomb Bar** located in the basement, 36th Street NW, in Georgetown, near the University. The walls of the **Occidental Restaurant** and **Bar** display over 3000 black-and-white photographs of the "movers and shakers" that have dined and drunk here over the years. It is located adjacent to the Willard Hotel. **Martin's Tavern** where John Kennedy proposed to Jackie when he was a dashing young senator from Massachusetts.

ROSLYN / SEATTLE, WASHINGTON,

About 90 miles east of Seattle is the home of the **"Brick Bar."** The Brick is the oldest bar in the state of Washington, over 100 years old. The important point is that The Brick was the main attraction in the TV series "Northern Exposure." (1990-1995). The popular weekly television show was about life in a small Alaskan town; but it was actually filmed at The Brick in Roslyn, Washington

Brouwer's Cafe located in the Fremont Hotel in Seattle is a beer lovers' heaven with 64 beers on tap, more than 300 more in bottles, hailing from 18 countries. There are also 60 different whiskeys and countless varieties of liquor.

WILLIAMSBURG, VIRGINIA

A completely restored colonial village offering wonderful examples of some of the finest drinking and dining places of the Colonial Period.

The **Raleigh Tavern** on Duke of Gloucester Street, was erected in 1717, and became the center of social and political life in colonial Virginia. George Washington, Thomas

Jefferson, and Patrick Henry are just a few of the Patriots who helped make history in this tavern. Students from the nearby College of William and Mary founded Phi Beta Kappa in the Apollo Room in 1776. The building was reconstructed after a fire in 1859.

There are several other taverns among the restored buildings in Williamsburg. All these places, including The Raleigh Tavern, are fully staffed and serve drinks and authentic colonial dining fare.

Weatherspoon's Tavern has been operating for over 200 years

Chowning's Tavern in its colonial days attracted the "ordinary sort," while the Raleigh Tavern catered to the upper-class.

Christiana Campbell's Tavern was a favorite of George Washington, where he often enjoyed the oysters.

The Kings Arms Tavern opened in 1772, while **Shields Tavern** was one of the earliest and catered to a middle-class clientele. All of these taverns afford a wonderful opportunity to sample the food and drinking customs of colonial America.

LAST CALL

"Without good wine, there is no good living." ~ Benjamin Franklin

Benjamin Franklin was indeed a wise man, the quotation shown above, dated 1784, is one of many famous Franklin quotes. He was correct, of course, around this world of ours, wine, or some type of alcoholic beverage, is consumed whenever and wherever people are enjoying "good living." It may be as important as a birth or a wedding, or as minor as finishing mowing the lawn, or completing a game of tennis. The important fact is that every single civilized country on this planet, (omitting the Arab nations where alcohol is banned, but consumed), enjoys some form of alcoholic beverage. The reality is that every culture has its own customs, festivals, drinks and practices associated with drinking. Some are funny, some are sacred, still others are little odd; but each country brings to the table a different culture steeped in its own history. These drinking practices have been developing and evolving for at least 12,000 years.

Drinking alcohol has been an important ingredient in "good living" throughout history. As discussed earlier, the Egyptians provided daily beer rations to the thousands of workers building the pyramids thousands of years ago. Later, the British provided rum rations to its seamen when Britannia ruled the waves. A Chinese imperial edict, around 1100 BC, declared the use of alcohol in moderation as prescribed by heaven. Hammurabi had many references to the use of alcohol in ancient Babylon (1795 - 1750 BC), and the great Greek philosophers from Socrates to Plato frequently quoted the many benefits of drinking. Socrates wrote, "Wine does in truth moisten the soul and will all our griefs to sleep."

The Romans enjoyed the "good life" to the extreme while the empire began to crumble around 100 A.D. When Christianity arrived on the scene, the Jewish people were already using wine in their sacred rituals. We are familiar with the gospel describing Jesus, turning water into wine at the "Wedding Feast at Cana", and the role of wine in the Catholic and Episcopalian services. Quoting Ecclesiastes from the Bible, "Go thy way, eat thy bread with joy, and drink thy wine with a merry heart, for God now accepted thy works."

An old proverb states, "Beer, the wonderful drink, has been helping ugly people enjoy sex for 4000 years."

Military and political leaders have had a close association with alcohol throughout history. The records of Alexander the Great, apparently an alcoholic, Marco Polo, and Napoleon are filled with details of parties and drinking. Ulysses S Grant, Civil War general and US President, noted for heavy drinking and once considered a drunk, is now being regarded by historians as one of America's premier leaders. As noted earlier, the Allied leaders during the Second World War: Franklin Roosevelt, Joseph Stalin and Winston Churchill, were all noted for liberal drinking habits. Churchill, pretty much drank all day beginning at breakfast and ending around 2 AM when he wrote most of his famous works. Churchill once remarked, "Don't worry, I have taken more out of alcohol than alcohol has taken out of me." Churchill died at 90 and is considered the greatest statesman of the 20th century.

Harry Truman, who replaced Roosevelt as President in 1945, started every day with a bourbon and orange juice, "to get the juices flowing." Truman also had a bar and two poker tables installed in the winter White House in Key West,

Florida. Two Navy corpsmen acted as bartenders. Later, Lyndon Johnson often toured his Texas ranch in a Lincoln convertible. Whenever Johnson held his empty glass out the window, a trailing secret service auto came alongside and exchanged it for a fresh bourbon.

Meanwhile, the Axis leaders: Hitler, Tojo, and Benito Mussolini were all teetotalers. Tojo drank 20 to 40 cups of tea each day. These are three of the worst people to ever inhabit the earth. You might wonder if a good drinking session at a cozy tavern, with everyone present, could have averted the worst disaster in history (63 million people killed).

It must be noted that Joseph Stalin, although part of the Allies in World War II, is regarded as the most murderous individual in history, responsible for over 20 million deaths, including millions of his own Russian people. Stalin's problem was he did not drink to enjoy the experience; he drank (vodka) to get drunk. A habit that continues in Russia today.

Reviewing the role of alcohol in the arts field indicates that drinking has almost been a pre-requisite for critical success in the literary world. Beginning with the poet Homer who wrote extensively of the benefits of wine, a string of scholarly individuals attest to the creative powers of alcohol. Geoffrey Chaucer (d. 1400) whose Canterbury Tales commence in the Tabard Inn at Southwark, wrote extensively of drinking and its effects. We know Chaucer drank regularly for in 1374 King Edward III granted the poet a pitcher (8 pints) of wine per day for life. This was later supplemented with another royal grant of a ton of wine per year.

Shakespeare, who is noted for "living it up" at the Mermaid tavern, and was a member of its Friday Street Club, along with Sir Walter Raleigh and Benjamin Johnson,often wrote of drinking in his many works. Charles Dickens visited his many London pubs on a daily basis. Writing and drinking seem to go together like pen and paper.

American songwriter Cole Porter in 1924 wrote in the Greenwich Follies, " they've learned the foundation of youth is a mixture of gin and vermouth." The list of American authors who had a close association with alcohol is lengthy: Jack London, Scott Fitzgerald, Sinclair Lewis, John O'Hara, Hemingway, Faulkner, Capote and many more. They didn't just drink alcohol; they bragged about it and wrote about it.

The list of famous painters linked with drinking is impressive: Manet, Picasso, Degas and most notably Toulouse Lautrec relied on absinthe for much of their inspiration. America's Abstract Impressionists — Rothko, Pollock, and DeKooning were all alcoholics. There had to be something wrong!

So alcohol has been a major part of history on this Earth and has been used by poets, authors, artists, statesman, kings, queens, generals, slaves, farmers, sailors, soldiers, and laborers to enhance the pursuit of "good living."

In examining the culture and customs associated with consuming alcohol in over 20 countries, some interesting facts become evident. Among the 20 countries included in this book, over half have a type of alcoholic drink peculiar to their country, Sake in Japan, Cachaca in Brazil, Ouzo in Greece, etc. Each country has its own set of drinking rules, and of the 20 different nationalities, no two are exactly alike. Drinking regulations in the United States have multiple layers of laws, including national or federal law and 50 states with their own rules, all of which are supplemented by a maze of county, town and city statutes. Meanwhile, Denmark has no minimum drinking age and tradition allows teens to begin drinking alcohol after Confirmation - around 13 years old, and beer and alcohol are available everywhere, including from vending machines.

Every country has enacted laws governing drinking and driving; however, the level of enforcement and the blood alcohol levels permitted vary considerably. The following is a list in descending order of the top 10 alcohol consuming countries:

Portugal 2.98*
Luxembourg 2.95
France 2.87
Hungary 2.66
Spain 2.66
Czech Republic, 2.64
Denmark 2.61
Germany 2.50
Austria 2.50
Switzerland 2.43
The United States ranks far down the list at 32nd.
*Gallons of pure alcohol per capita per year.

Reviewing the list it is interesting to note that all the top ten consuming countries have extremely liberal attitudes regarding alcohol; but they also have the fewest problems relating to drinking. None of these nations has ever even remotely considered prohibiting alcohol.

The nations with the most rules, and the most problems, and the most attempts at temperance or prohibition of alcohol, are located across the top of the northern hemisphere - - United States, Britain, Scandinavia and Russia. These are also the countries where public drinking is usually confined to bars or pubs or saloons with darkened or frosted windows. Even the interiors are subdivided into small rooms or compartments. These nations all seem to have a love-hate relationship with alcohol.

In France, Spain and Italy, drinking occurs outdoors in

cafes or plazas; Germany has huge beer gardens, and in Denmark, the "good life" is everywhere. Some of this difference, of course, may be explained by the weather; but much is due to the people's attitude toward alcohol. The French, Spanish and Italians grow up with alcohol, wine is part of living, a key ingredient of a meal, and essential for relaxing, celebrating or mourning. It is a major component of what the French term *joie de vivre* and the Irish call *craic*.

These people have never drunk just to get "drunk", they drink to enhance the enjoyment of life. It does not occur to them that children need to be shielded from cafes, the terrazzos or beer gardens; hence the population matures with an understanding and acceptance of the role of alcohol in life's routines. The Puritan work ethic combined with certain religious affiliations that continue to have a negative view of alcohol use never established a position on the European continent.

A review of Denmark and its relationship toward drinking is a useful exercise. As discussed earlier, the Danes are noted for their open-minded drinking culture.

The role of Carlsberg Beer in this small country is remarkable. Carlsberg Breweries is owned by the Carlsberg Foundation, which has become the major supporter of arts and sciences in Denmark. Carlsberg was founded in 1847 by J.C. Jacobsen, who had a deep interest in science and an abiding love for his native Country. In 1922, Niels Bohr, a Dane and contemporary of Albert Einstein, was awarded the Nobel Prize for physics. The Carlsberg Foundation presented Bohr with a house and laboratory next to the brewery with a direct beer pipeline from the brewery to the house. Niels Bohr went on to become one of the greatest scientists in history, and is credited with major discoveries relating to quantum mechanics. It's fun to speculate that alcohol not only helped all those statesmen, poets, generals and artists; it also played a key role in advancing scientific discovery.

Meanwhile, at approximately the same time, 1920s, Henry Ford actually hired spies to observe employees who might be drinking, and if they were, termination was immediate. He also had a host of other undesirable traits.

Today, the Carlsberg Foundation continues to fund the Niels Bohr Institute, (known as the Carlsberg Laboratory), and an extensive list of cultural projects, including Tivoli Gardens in Copenhagen, and the Museum of Natural History at the Fredericksburg Palace.

Lastly, keep in mind in survey after survey, the Danes are in first place as the "happiest people on earth." This, despite having the highest tax rate on the planet. An example of it's not just taxes, it's how they are used that matters. A special note: these Danish taxes are not unfairly levied on alcohol.

Finally, a look at what's happening now. The two oldest beverages still dominate drinking around the world - - beer and wine. As discussed, individual countries may have a favorite type of alcohol or a special drink: Sake in Japan, Grappa in Italy or Cachaca in Brazil; but beer and wine are consumed everywhere, and always have been. Today, beer consumption is really "on a roll", primarily due to the emergence of microbrews and craft beers worldwide. Countries that have always been closely associated with wine: France, Italy,and Spain, are noticing a trend where the younger generation prefers beer. Now, similar to 100 years ago, even the smaller towns and villages have their own locally brewed slate of beers. In 2012, the Brewers Association reported that of the 2,126 breweries in the US, 2,075 or 97% were considered craft breweries. This included 1,195 brewpubs, 790 microbreweries and 90 regional craft breweries. These craft beers are available in an endless number of varieties, depending upon strength, flavor, aroma and carbonation. The opportunity to sample all these varieties and match them with food, together with new brews available every day, has turned "Just gimme a Bud" into a field for connoisseurs.

Now, beer has joined wine, and unsophisticated, old-fashioned drinking beer from the can is considered unwholesome and unhealthy. These new beer drinkers aren't drinkers at all; they're connoisseurs - sniffers and tasters, discerning, knowledgeable critics. Now we have beer tastings, competitions, and even beer advisors. All this in spite of the fact that in test after test not one in ten consumers can select a top-rated wine versus the cheapest or lowest rated in any sampling. Similar results prevail for beer and vodka.

In addition to craft beers and microbreweries, changes in laws and improvements in equipment have resulted in a surge of interest in home brewing. Now, your best friend cannot wait to invite you over for an evening of tasting his most recent creations.

Global beer sales now exceed $500 billion, led by Belgian AB InBev that owns Anheuser Busch, SABMiller, Heinekin and Carlsberg. Leading worldwide brands are Bud Lite in first place by a wide margin, Budweiser, Coor's Light and Miller Light. Ranked on a per capita consumption basis, the Czechs are in first place, followed by the Irish, Germans and Austrians.

Worldwide wine sales fell slightly for a few years (2009 - 2011); but thanks to Asia and the US, sales are now stable. The leading countries for wine sales remain France and the US; France leads by a wide margin in wine consumption per capita. Americans drank more wine than ever in 2012, 2.3

gallons a piece. That's up 35% since 1994.

One of the major changes effecting the global drinking culture is the closing of the bistros, pubs, bars, and neighborhood saloons from England and Ireland to France and the US. There are many reasons for the closings, of course; smoking bans, drunk driving enforcement, the lousy economy, higher taxes on alcohol; but the primary force behind these closings is the cultural change beginning in the 1960s and accelerating recently with the electronic revolution.

The decline in "community engagement" began with the move from the neighborhood in the city to the suburbs, and continued with the advent of television in the home. But the introduction of the personal computer, with all its nuances: Facebook, Twitter, iPad, iPhone, e-mail, etc, has changed behavior big time.

The social web really began to unravel in the 90s. A recent survey found that while 25% of Americans had nobody to talk to, they have plenty of people to connect with online - - millions if they wish, but no one on a personal basis. No longer do we stroll down to the local pub, bar, bistro or cafe to soothe our wounded spirit or broken heart; nor do we rush there to celebrate our good news, or just to listen to someone else. Now we use Facebook or Twitter to share our tidings with the whole world at once. Human companionship has dropped far down in our priorities, and other people only interrupt our more exciting electronic options.

Health and alcohol has been a controversial subject since Dr. Benjamin Rush, the US Surgeon General, published 'The Effect of Ardent Spirits on the Human Mind' in 1784. Now we have aspirin for headaches, Prozac for comfort, Valium for courage, Sleep Aid for a good night's sleep and professional counseling for everything from dealing with death and divorce to understanding our children's behavior at school. Who needs a bar, a drink, an understanding bartender and a sympathetic listener on the next stool?

Sales of wine have been aided in recent years by several medical studies indicating a glass or two of red wine each day improves cardiovascular health. However, alcohol is a known carcinogen and other studies attribute various types of cancer to overuse of alcohol in any form.

After reviewing the drinking customs and cultures around the world more than a few interesting and surprising facts stand out. Australia is a country widely recognized for enjoying life, especially outdoors. It is a beer drinking nation that has assumed a major role in wine production and consumption.

Belgium, largely due to the six beer-producing Tappist Monasteries scattered around this small country, is well regarded as the place to go to enjoy beer. Also, it's home to the largest beer company in the world - - AB InBev.

Brazil, where Cachaca is the number one distilled beverage, a drink that is rarely available anywhere else in the world, is also home to the pre-Lenten celebration known as Carnival, the Rio de Janeiro version is considered to be the world's biggest party.

Britain is, of course, famous for its pubs. A wonderful place to go and visit drinking history. You could sit in the same pubs that welcomed Sir Walter Raleigh, Shakespeare and Charles Dickens, to name just a few famous guests.

China is apparently where drinking began about 12,000 years ago. One peculiar aspect of Chinese drinking is the Chinese fascination with Cognac, based, apparently, primarily on a need to "show off" newly acquired wealth.

The Czech Republic is in a tie with Belgium as the best place in the world to drink beer. Three unique facts: first, the Czechs drink more beer than water; second, almost all the

303

beer is produced within the Czech Republic, less than 1% is imported; third, there are no drinking problems in the Czech Republic, and drunkenness is rare and the ABV limit for drunk driving is zero.

France, of course, is synonymous with wine and drinking, ranking first in the world in per capita wine consumption and third in per capita alcohol consumed. Paris is home to **Harry's New York Bar,** arguably the world's most famous bar.

Greece has been celebrating the many virtues of wine for over 2000 years. No other country has a drink so closely linked to its culture as Ouzo and Greece.

Sandwiched between two of the largest beer-drinking nations, Germany and Belgium, the Netherlands is the gin capital of the world. Famous for its "brown cafes" and liberal approach to just about everything from sex to drugs; it is not surprising there are very few rules, and, once again, very few problems.

Ireland and the Irish, and drinking - - they seem to go together like bread and butter or fun and laughter. The land of Guinness, Irish Whiskey, wonderful pubs with wonderful stories, and wonderful times known as "craic." In Ireland drinking may be the "culture." One last Irish story: a new arrival in Cork visits the pub every day and orders three beers, drinks and leaves. Some of the curious regulars ask him, "Why exactly 3 beers every day?" He replies, "That when my two brothers left Ireland, we all agreed to have a drink for each other every day of the year." One day in March he came into the pub and ordered only two beers. This went on for a couple of weeks, and finally the bartender let him know how sad everyone was, assuming one of his brothers had died. "Oh, no one has died." he replied. "You see, it's just that I have given up beer for Lent."

Unlike many other countries, including Japan, the Italians have a "sipping culture" rather than a "drinking culture." Drinking is not an activity by itself in Italy; it is almost always accompanied by food. Wine has been served with dinner for centuries and children grow up from an early age accustomed to drinking alcohol. As a result, drunkenness is rare in Italy and not an accepted form of behavior.

Who would believe that Japan is considered the best place in the world to drink, widely acclaimed as a "drinker's paradise." Just like everything else, the Japanese take alcohol seriously and both consumption and production are big businesses. Japan is the home of sake, which comes in thousands of variations, and is pretty much ignored everywhere else on the planet. This is a country where people plan to get drunk and drunken behavior is widely accepted.

Mexico is another country with its own popular drink, tequila, made from the blue agave cactus-like plant, that doesn't grow anywhere else on earth. The Margarita drink, made with tequila, extremely popular worldwide; is not a popular beverage in Mexico. Mexicans drink tequila straight.

Two unusual characteristics of the Polish pub-drinking culture relate to the profile of the customers and the pub itself. Polish bars or pubs are dark. Sometimes this dark atmosphere is a result of being located in cellars or tucked away in obscure places; but even when ample light is available, windows will be blackened, artificial light minimized. The other distinct feature involves the customers, and an almost total absence of the middle-aged group. In Poland it is rare to see folks over 25 enjoying a drink in a bar.

The absolute tragedy of life in Poland over the past century is largely the cause of this phenomenon. First, the Germans, followed by the Russians (and communism) destroyed Poland, physically and culturally. Older Poles never had the opportunity to develop the habit of visiting a bar or pub.

Scandinavia, including Finland, Norway, and Sweden, demonstrates graphically the cultural differences regarding the use of alcohol in Northern European countries versus the south of Europe. Access to alcohol is restricted and alcohol and beverages containing over 3.5% alcohol are only sold in government outlets. The government also controls the brands available, and the price (expensive). As we've seen in other countries, the more rules and regulations, the more problems; including corruption, bootlegging and intoxication. Scandinavian drinking may be limited; but when Scandinavians drink, unlike Italians, they tend to drink a great deal.

It is difficult to explain why Spain is now considered the "playground of Europe", and why Madrid has more drinking spots than any other city on earth. Spaniards make a real effort at enjoying life, and they grow up with a responsible attitude toward alcohol. The drinking age is 18; but rarely enforced, and problems are few. These people love to celebrate, and as a result, the country is loaded with fairs, festivals, holidays, fiestas and holy days - - all occasions for drinking and having a good time.

The next time you are looking for enjoyment, no matter the occasion or where you are, seek out a local watering hole or a Skytop lounge, sit at the bar, leave your "electronics" at home, and if you're lucky, strike up a conversation with the bartender, or the person next to you. You can listen, brag or inform, advise or inquire, laugh or cry, and enjoy a drink at the same time - - and remember, people on this earth have been doing this for at least 12,000 years.

"What though youth gave love and roses, age still leaves us friends and wine." ~St. Thomas Moore

BIBLIOGRAPHY

Ade, George. *The Old-Time Saloon*. Old Town, 1993.

Allen, Greg. Poland - *Culture Smart!: the essential guide to customs & culture*.

Aird, Alisdair. *The Good Pub Guide*. Ebury Press, 2006.

Atkinson, Lee. Frommer's *Australia*. Frommers, 2012.

Baker, Mark. *Lonely Planet Prague & the Czech Republic*. Lonely Planet, 2012.

Barr, Andrew. *Drink: A Social History*. London: Pimlico, 1998.

Battenberry, Michael. *On the Town in New York*. Charles Scribner, 1973.

Behr, Edward. *Prohibition: Thirteen Years That Changed America*. Arcade Publishing, 1996.

Blumenthal, Ralph. *Stork Club: America's Most Famous Nightspot and the Lost World of Cafe Society*. Little, Brown and Co., 2000.

Brown, John Hull. *Early American Beverages*. C.E. Tuttle Co., 1966.

Bruno, Nick. *Eating Out in Scotland*. Fodor's Travel Guide, 2012.

Bunting, Chris. *Drinking Japan: A Guide to Japan's Best Drinks and Drinking Establishments*. Tuttle Publishing, 2011.

Colonial Williamsburg Foundation, Michael Olmert, and Suzanne E. Coffman. *Official Guide to Colonial Williamsburg*. Colonial Williamsburg Foundation, 1998.

Daugherty, Christi. *Frommer's Ireland*. Frommers, 2011.

Dillon-Malone, Audrey. *Historic Pubs of Dublin*. Prion Books Ltd., 2001.

Dornbusch, Horst D. *Prost!: The Story of German Beer*. Brewers Publications, 1998.

Duis, Perry R. *The Saloon: Public Drinking in Chicago and Boston, 1880-1920*. University of Illinois Press, 1998.

Earle, Alice. *Stagecoach and Tavern Days*. MacMillan, 1900.

Emmons, Bob. *The Book of Tequila*. Open Court Publishing, 2003.

Engs, Ruth C. *Western European Drinking Practices*. Indiana University, 1991.

Erdoes, Richard. *Saloons of the Old West*. Gramercy Books, 1979.

Erenberg, Lewis A. *Steppin' Out: New York Nightlife and the Transformation of American Culture, 1890-1930*. University of Chicago Press, 1981.

Field, Edward. *The Colonial Tavern*. Providence, 1897.

Friedrich, Jacqueline. *The Wines of France*. Ten Speed Press, Berkeley, CA, 2006.

Garrett, Oliver. *The Oxford Companion to Beer*. Oxford University Press, NY, NY, 2012.

Gately, Iain. *Drink: A Cultural History of Alcohol*. Penguin Group Publishers, 2008.

Goodman, Jack. *While You Were Gone*. Simon and Schuster, 1946.

Hanson, David J. *Alcohol, Culture and Control*. Praeger, 1995.

Herlihy, Patricia. *Vodka, A Global History*. Reaktion Books, London, 2012.

Holland, Barbara. *The Joy of Drinking*. Bloomsburg USA, 2007.

Holt, Mack P. *Alcohol: A Social and Cultural History*. Bloomsbury Academic, 2006.

Hops Magazine, May 2012.

H. Lucinda Hutson. *Tequila!: The Spirit of Mexico*. Ten Speed Press, 1995.

Kallen, Stuart A. *History Firsthand: The Roaring Twenties*. Greenhaven Press, 2001.

Klein, Jef. *The History and Stories of the Best Bars of New York*. Turner Publishing Co., 2006.

Lamprey, Zane. *Three Sheets*. Villard Books, 2010.

Larkin, Jack. *The Reshaping of Everyday Life, 1790-1840*. Harper and Rowe, 1988.

Lathrop, Elise. *Early American Inns and Taverns*. New York: Tudor Publishing Co., 1937.

Lendler, Ian. *Alcoholica Esoterica*. New York, Penguin Books, 2005.

London, Jack. *John Barleycorn*. Random House, 1913.

Martin, Brian. *Tales from the Country Pub*. David & Charles Publishing, 1998.

Martin, Cy. *Whiskey and Wild Women*. Hart Publishing Co., 1974.

Martin, James and Lender, Mark. *Drinking in America*. New York: Free Press, 1982.

McDonald, George. *Frommer's Belgium, Holland and Luxembourg*. Frommers, 2011.

Mitchell, Joseph. *McSorley's Wonderful Saloon*. Pantheon Books, 1992.

Moehringer, J.R. *The Tender Bar: A Memoir*. Hyperion, Inc., 2005.

Modern Marvels: Saloons DVD. The History Channel. 2004.

Myline, Lee. *Great Australian Pubs*, 2012.

Okrent, Daniel. *Last Call: The Rise and Fall of Prohibition*. Scribner, 2010.

Popham, Robert. *The Social History of the Tavern. Research Advances in Alcohol and Drugs*. Springer Us, 1978.

Powers, Madelon. *Faces Along the Bar*. University of Chicago Press, 1998.

Rice, Kym S. *Early American Taverns for the Entertainment of Friends and Strangers*. Chicago: Regnery Gateway, 1983.

Rorabaugh, William. The *Alcoholic Republic: An American Tradition*. New York: Oxford University Press, 1979.

Rose, Lesley Anne. *Best Pubs of Scotland*. Frommers, 2011.

Salinger, Sharon. *Taverns and Drinking in Early America*. Johns Hopkins University Press, 2002.

Simmons, James. *Star Spangled Eden: 19th Century America Through the Eyes of Dickens, Wilde, Frances Trollope, Frank Harris and Other British Travelers*. Carrol & Graf Publishers, 2000.

Sismondo, Christine. *America Walks into a Bar*. Oxford Press, 2011.

Social Issues Research Center. *Social and Cultural Aspects of Drinking*. Oxford, England, 2011.

Steves, Rick. *Rick Steves' Ireland 2012*. Avalon Travel Publishing, 2012.

Steves, Rick. *Rick Steves' Prague and the Czech Republic*. Avalon Travel Publishing, 2010.

Sylvester, Robert. *No Cover Charge: A Backward Look at the Night Clubs*. Dial Press, 1956.

The American Brew: History of Beer in America. Washington, D.C.: Here's to Beer, Inc., 2007.

Thompson, Peter. *Rum Punch and Revolution: Taverngoing and Public Life in Eighteenth-Century Philadelphia*. Philadelphia: University of Pennsylvania Press, 1999.

Tucker, Abigail. *Dig, Drink, and Be Merry*. Smithsonian, August, 2011.

Tyrell, Ian. *Sobering Up: From Temperance to Prohibition in Antebellum America, 1800-1860*. Greenwood Press, 1979.

Walton, Stuart. *Out of It: A Cultural History of Intoxication*. Harmony Books, 2002.

Webb, Tim. *Good Beer Guide to Belgium*, CAMRA Books, 2009.

Weiser, Kathy. *The Great American Bars and Saloons*. Chartwell Books, 2006.

West, Elliott. *The Saloon on the Rocky Mountain Mining Frontier*. University of Nebraska Press, 1979.

Wilson, Thomas M. *Drinking Cultures*. Berg Publishers, 2005.

Xin, Wang Kai Qi. *History of Chinese Civilization*. Encyclopedia of China Publishing House, 2009.

La Maison Publishing, Inc.
www.lamaisonpublishing.com
ISBN: 978-0-9885902-8-1

CPSIA information can be obtained at www.ICGtesting.com
Printed in the USA
LVOW05s0736300314

379383LV00003B/597/P